THE REVE⁝

Former general editors
Clifford Leech
F. David Hoeniger
E. A. J. Honigmann
Eugene M. Waith

General editors
David Bevington, Richard Dutton, Alison Findlay,
J. R. Mulryne and Helen Ostovich

AN HUMOROUS DAY'S MIRTH

Manchester University Press

THE REVELS PLAYS

ANON *Thomas of Woodstock or King Richard the Second, Part One*

BEAUMONT *The Knight of the Burning Pestle*

BEAUMONT AND FLETCHER *A King and No King   Philaster, or Loves Lies a-Bleeding   The Maid's Tragedy*

CHAPMAN *Bussy d'Ambois*

An Humorous Day's Mirth

CHAPMAN, JONSON, MARSTON *Eastward Ho*

DEKKER *The Shoemaker's Holiday*

FORD *Love's Sacrifice*

HEYWOOD *The First and Second Parts of King Edward IV*

JONSON *The Alchemist   The Devil Is an Ass
Epicene, or The Silent Woman   Every Man In His Humour
Every Man Out of His Humour   The Magnetic LadyPoetaster
Sejanus: His Fall   The Staple of News   Volpone*

LYLY *Campaspe* and *Sappho and Phao   Endymion
Galatea* and *Midas   Love's Metamorphosis*

Mother Bombie

The Woman in the Moon

MARLOWE *Doctor Faustus   Edward the Second
The Jew of Malta   Tamburlaine the Great*

MARSTON *Antonio and Mellida   Antonio's Revenge
The Malcontent*

MASSINGER *The Roman Actor*

MIDDLETON *A Game at Chess   Michaelmas Term*

MIDDLETON AND DEKKER *The Roaring Girl*

MUNDAY AND OTHERS *Sir Thomas More*

WEBSTER *The Duchess of Malfi*

THE REVELS PLAYS

AN HUMOROUS DAY'S MIRTH

GEORGE CHAPMAN

edited by Charles Edelman

MANCHESTER
UNIVERSITY PRESS

This edition published by Manchester University Press
Altrincham Street, Manchester M1 7JA, UK
www.manchesteruniversitypress.co.uk

British Library Cataloguing-in-Publication Data
A catalogue record for this book is available from the
British Library

ISBN 978 1 5261 1692 5 paperback

First published by Manchester University Press in hardback 2010

Typeset
by Toppan Best-set Premedia Limited
Printed in Great Britain
by CPI Group (UK) Ltd, Croydon, CR0 4YY

for R. A. Foakes

Contents

General Editors' Preface

Clifford Leech conceived of the Revels Plays as a series in the mid-1950s, modelling the project on the New Arden Shakespeare. The aim, as he wrote in 1958, was 'to apply to Shakespeare's predecessors, contemporaries and successors the methods that are now used in Shakespeare's editing'. The plays chosen were to include well-known works from the early Tudor period to about 1700, as well as others less familiar but of literary and theatrical merit: 'the plays included', Leech wrote, 'should be such as to deserve and indeed demand performance'. We owe it to Clifford Leech that the idea became reality. He set the high standards of the series, ensuring that editors of individual volumes produced work of lasting merit, equally useful for teachers and students, theatre directors and actors. Clifford Leech remained General Editor until 1971, and was succeeded by F. David Hoeniger, who retired in 1985.

From 1985 the Revels Plays were under the direction of four General Editors: initially David Bevington, E. A. J. Honigmann, J. R. Mulryne and E. M. Waith. E. A. J. Honigmann retired in 2000 and was succeeded by Richard Dutton. E. M. Waith retired in 2003 and was succeeded by Alison Findlay and Helen Ostovich. Published originally by Methuen, the series is now published by Manchester University Press, embodying essentially the same format, scholarly character and high editorial standards of the series as first conceived. The series concentrates on plays from the period 1558–1642, and includes a small number of non-dramatic works of interest to students of drama. Some slight changes have been made: for example, in editions from 1978 onward, notes to the introduction are placed together at the end, not at the foot of the page. Collation and commentary notes continue, however, to appear on the relevant pages.

The text of each Revels play, in accordance with established practice in the series, is edited afresh from the original text of best authority (in a few instances, texts), but spelling and punctuation are modernised and speech headings are silently made consistent. Elisions in the original are also silently regularised, except where metre would be affected by the change; since 1968 the '-ed' form is used for non-syllabic terminations in past tenses and past participles

('-'d' earlier), and '-èd' for syllabic ('-ed' earlier). The editor emends, as distinct from modernises, the original only in instances where error is patent, or at least very probable, and correction persuasive. Act divisions are given only if they appear in the original or if the structure of the play clearly points to them. Those act and scene divisions not in the original are provided in small type. Square brackets are also used for any other additions to or changes in the stage directions of the original.

Revels Plays do not provide a variorum collation, but only those variants which require the critical attention of serious textual students. All departures of substance from 'copy-text' are listed, including any relineation and those changes in punctuation which involve to any degree a decision between alternative interpretations; but not such accidentals as turned letters, nor necessary additions to stage directions whose editorial nature is already made clear by the use of brackets. Press corrections in the 'copy-text' are likewise collated. Of later emendations of the text, only those are given which as alternative readings still deserve attention.

One of the hallmarks of the Revels Plays is the thoroughness of their annotations. Besides explaining the meaning of difficult words and passages, the editor provides comments on customs or usage, text or stage-business – indeed, on anything judged pertinent and helpful. Each volume contains an Index to the Commentary, in which particular attention is drawn to meanings for words not listed in *OED*, and (starting in 1996) an indexing of proper names and topics in the Introduction and Commentary.

The introduction to a Revels play assesses the authority of the 'copy-text' on which it is based, and discusses the editorial methods employed in dealing with it; the editor also considers the play's date and (where relevant) sources, together with its place in the work of the author and in the theatre of its time. Stage history is offered, and in the case of a play by an author not previously represented in the series a brief biography is given.

It is our hope that plays edited in this fashion will promote further scholarly and theatrical investigation of one of the richest periods in theatrical history.

DAVID BEVINGTON
RICHARD DUTTON
ALISON FINDLAY
J. R. MULRYNE
HELEN OSTOVICH

Acknowledgements

I am particularly grateful to David Bevington, for his very generous willingness to share both his knowledge and his expertise. Many other friends and colleagues provided advice and encouragement, and special thanks go to Alan Brissenden, Toby Burrows, David Elder, Andrew Gurr, Peter Holland, Judith Moreland-Mitchell, Ruperto Nunez, Richard Proudfoot, Carol Chillington Rutter, R. S. White, Andrew Wilson and H. R. Woudhuysen. As usual, Lesley Edelman provided support in innumerable ways. The title page of the 1599 Quarto is reproduced by permission of the Folger Shakespeare Library.

References

PREVIOUS EDITIONS

This edition relies on W. W. Greg's Malone Society reprint of the 1599 quarto, prepared with the assistance of David Smith (Oxford, 1938). As I will note in the Introduction (p. 39), Greg saw only four of the fifteen extant copies, but Akihiro Yamada has shown that, while the variants are many, almost all are trivial and do not affect meaning; the very few substantive variants are recorded in the collation.

R. H. Shepherd's first edition of 1873 is a diplomatic reprint of the quarto, without notes or textual apparatus; not differing from *Q* in any substantive way, it is not cited in the collation.

Shepherd's second edition (1874) is the first to use modern spelling; speech headings remain abbreviated but are regularised, and some errors in *Q* are emended, although Shepherd introduces new errors of his own. As with his first edition, no commentary or textual apparatus is included.

T. M. Parrott's edition of 1914 is a major advance in Chapman scholarship. Inconsistencies in the quarto are carefully considered, and many of his emendations are persuasive. Only a few commentary notes per scene are offered, but textual notes are more extensive.

Allan Holaday's 1970 edition, the most recent to have been published, is a strange mix. Holaday goes back to the quarto spelling, but incorporates many of Shepherd's and Parrott's emendations. He also provides a historical collation and an extensive collation of variants – unfortunately the excessive use of symbols makes for very hard work, and Yamada's article (see Introduction, p. 39) is much more approachable.

The quarto has no act or scene divisions. Holaday imposes a five-act structure that cannot be justified on either historical or critical grounds; Parrott and Greg, more appropriately, divide the play into numbered scenes, Parrott fourteen and Greg fifteen. This edition has thirteen scenes; what constitutes a new scene in early modern plays is, of course, a subject of debate. I adopt the convention of marking a scene break whenever the stage is clear of actors. This is also a matter of opinion in this text, however, owing to the quarto's frequently missing exit directions.

I do not include the differences in prose or verse lineation between this edition and its three predecessors in the collation (see Introduction, pp. 37–8). To do so would make the collation impossibly complicated.

EDITIONS AND TEXTUAL STUDIES COLLATED, IN CHRONOLOGICAL ORDER

Q *A pleasant Comedy entituled: An humerous dayes Myrth. As it hath beene sundrie times publikely acted by the right honourable the Earle of Nottingham Lord high Admirall his servants. By G. C. At London. Printed by Valentine Syms: 1599.*

Shepherd R. H. Shepherd, ed., *The Works of George Chapman*, 2nd ed., vol. 1, London, 1874.

Deighton K. Deighton, *The Old Dramatists: Conjectural Readings on the Texts of Marston, Beaumont and Fletcher, Peele, Marlowe, Chapman, Heywood, Greene, Middleton, Dekker, Webster*, Westminster, 1896.

Brereton Le Gay Brereton, 'Notes on the Text of Chapman's Plays', *Modern Language Review* 3 (1907): 56–68.

Parrott Thomas Marc Parrott, ed., *The Plays of George Chapman: The Comedies*, London, 1914, reprint ed. 2 vols [sequentially paginated], New York, 1961.

Greg Conjectural readings and marginal notations in W. W. Greg, ed., *An Humorous Day's Mirth*, Malone Society Reprints, Oxford, 1938.

Yamada Akihiro Yamada, 'Bibliographical Studies of George Chapman's *An Humorous Day's Mirth*', *Shakespeare Studies* (Japan) 5 (1967): 119–49.

Holaday Allan Holaday, ed., assisted by Michael Kiernan, *The Plays of George Chapman: The Comedies, a Critical Edition*, Urbana, 1970.

EDITIONS OF EARLY MODERN DRAMATIC WORKS CITED IN COMMENTARY

The spelling of all early modern texts quoted in the commentary is silently modernised when no modern spelling edition is available.

Capt. Thomas Stukeley	*The Life and Death of Captain Thomas Stuke-ley*, ed. Charles Edelman, in *The Stukeley Plays*, Manchester, 2005.
Chapman	T. M. Parrott, ed., *The Plays of George Chapman: The Comedies,* and *George Chapman: The Tragedies,* London, 1907–14, reprint ed. 2 vols each [sequentially paginated], New York, 1961.
Cooke	*Greene's Tu Quoque, or The Cittie Gallant,* ed. Alan J. Berman, New York, 1984.
Dekker	*Shoemaker's Holiday,* ed. R. L. Smallwood and Stanley Wells, Manchester, 1979. All other plays from *The Dramatic Works of Thomas Dekker,* ed. Fredson Bowers, 4 vols, Cambridge, 1953–61.
Eastward Ho	George Chapman, Ben Jonson, John Marston, *Eastward Ho,* ed. R. W. Van Fossen, Manchester, 1999.
Fair Maid	*The Fair Maid of the Exchange,* ed. Barron Field, London, 1846.
Fletcher	*A Wife for a Month,* ed. David Rush Miller, Amsterdam, 1983.
Greene	*Friar Bacon and Friar Bungay,* ed. Daniel Seltzer, Lincoln, 1963.
Heywood	*The Dramatic Works of Thomas Heywood,* vol. 3, New York, 1964.
Jonson	*Every Man in His Humour* [quarto version], ed. Robert S. Miola, Manchester, 2000. *Every Man Out of His Humour,* ed. Helen Ostovich, Manchester, 2001. *The Masque of Augurs,* in *The Complete Masques,* ed. Stephen Orgel, New Haven, 1969. All other plays from *The Complete Plays of Ben Jonson,* ed. G. A. Wilkes, 4 vols, Oxford, 1981–82.
Kyd	*The Spanish Tragedy,* ed. Philip Edwards, London, 1959.
Leir	*The History of King Leir,* ed. W. W. Greg and R. Warwick Bond, London, 1907.

Lodge	*Wounds of Civil War*, ed. Joseph W. Houppert, London, 1969.
Lyly	*Midas*, ed. David Bevington, Manchester, 2000.
Marlowe	*Edward II*, ed. Charles R. Forker, Manchester, 1994.
Marston	*Antonio and Mellida*, ed. W. Reavley Gair, Manchester, 2004.
	The Malcontent, ed. George K. Hunter, Manchester, 1999.
	What You Will, ed. M. R. Woodhead, Nottingham, 1980.
Middleton	*A Chaste Maid in Cheapside*, ed. Alan Brissenden, London, 1968.
	The Family of Love, ed. Simon Shepherd, Nottingham, 1979.
	Your Five Gallants, ed. C. Lee Colgrove, New York, 1979.
Peele	*The Battle of Alcazar*, ed. Charles Edelman, in *The Stukeley Plays*, Manchester, 2005.
Philaster	Beaumont and Fletcher, *Philaster*, ed. Andrew Gurr, Manchester, 2003.
Preston	*A Lamentable Tragedy Mixed Full of Pleasant Mirth containing the life of Cambyses, King of Persia*, London, c. 1570.
Rowley	*A Shoemaker, A Gentleman*, ed. Trudy L. Darby, London, 2002.
Shakespeare	*The First Quarto of Hamlet*, ed. Kathleen O. Irace, Cambridge, 1998.
	All other works from *The Riverside Shakespeare*, 2nd ed., Boston, 1997.
Sir John Oldcastle	*The Oldcastle Controversy: Sir John Oldcastle, Part I and The Famous Victories of Henry V*, ed. Peter Corbin and Douglas Sedge, Manchester, 1991.
Travels	John Day, William Rowley, George Wilkins, *The Travels of the Three English Brothers*, in *Three Renaissance Travel Plays*, ed. Anthony Parr, Manchester, 1995.
Troublesome Reign	*The Troublesome Raigne of John, King of England*, London, 1591.

Webster   *The Devil's Law-Case*, ed. Frances A.
                   Shirley, London, 1972.
                   Northward Ho, Westward Ho [see Dekker].
Whetstone   *Promos and Cassandra*, London, 1578.

OTHER PRIMARY WORKS CITED IN COMMENTARY

Andrewes   Lancelot Andrewes, *Works*, vol. 1, New York,
                   1967.
Anstey   Christopher Anstey, *The Monopolist; or The
                   Installation of Sir John Barleycorn, Knight*, Bath,
                   1795.
Arber   Edward Arber, *An English Garner: Ingatherings
                   from Our History and Literature*, vol. 8, London,
                   1896.
Bacon   *Of the Advancement of Learning*, ed. Arthur
                   Johnston, Oxford, 1974.
Becon   Thomas Becon, *The Catechism of Thomas
                   Becon*, ed. John Ayre, Cambridge, 1844.
Bible   *The Bishops' Bible*, 1568 (unless otherwise
                   noted).
Bk Common Prayer John E. Booty, ed., *The Book of Common Prayer
                   1559: An Elizabethan Prayer Book*, Charlottes-
                   ville, 1976.
Bright   Timothy Bright, *A Treatise of Melancholy*,
                   London, 1586.
Brooke   Arthur Brooke, *Romeus and Juliet*, in G. Blake-
                   more Evans, ed., *Romeo and Juliet*, Cambridge,
                   1984.
Chapman   *Chapman's Homer: The Iliad, the Odyssey and
                   the Lesser Homerica*, ed. Allardyce Nicoll,
                   London, 1957.
                   The Georgicks of Hesiod, London, 1618.
                   The Poems of George Chapman, ed. Phyllis
                   Brooks Bartlett, New York, 1962.
Chaucer   *The Riverside Chaucer*, 3rd ed., Oxford, 1987.
Cicero   M. Tulli Ciceronis, *De Officiis*, ed. Hubert
                   Ashton Holden, Cambridge, 1899.
                   Marcus Tullius Cicero, *Tusculan Disputations*,
                   ed. and tr. J. E. King, London, 1927.

Davies   The Poems of Sir John Davies, ed. Robert
                      Krueger, Oxford, 1975.

Day   The Works of John Day, ed. A. H. Bullen,
                      London, 1963.

Diogenes Laertius   Lives of Eminent Philosophers, ed. and tr. R. D.
                      Hicks, London, 1925.

Dekker   The Gull's Hornbook, ed. P. D. Hendry,
                      London, 1967.
                      News from Hell, in Non-Dramatic Works, vol. 2,
                      ed. A. B. Grosart, New York, 1963.

Dolman   John Dolman, Those fyve Questions, which
                      Marke Tullye Cicero, disputed in his manor of
                      Tusculanum, London, 1561.

Donne   Paradoxes and Problems, ed. Helen Peters,
                      Oxford, Clarendon, 1980.

Eliot   John Eliot, Ortho-Epia Gallica: Eliots Fruits for
                      the French, London, 1593.

Epictetus   The manuell of Epictetus, translated out of Greeke
                      into French, and now into English, London,
                      1567.

Erasmus   Adages, in Collected Works, vols 31–6, ed. R. J.
                      Schoeck et al., Toronto, 1982–2006.

Florio   Florios second frutes to be gathered of twelve trees,
                      of divers but delightsome tastes to the tongues of
                      Italians and Englishmen, London, 1591.
                      A worlde of wordes, or, most copious and exact
                      dictionarie in Italian and English, London, 1598.

Franklin   Benjamin Franklin, Autobiography, Poor
                      Richard, and Later Writings, New York, 1997.

Golding   Arthur Golding, Shakespeare's Ovid: Being
                      Arthur Golding's translation of the Metamorpho-
                      ses, ed. W. H. D. Rouse, Carbondale, 1961.

Greene   The Life and Complete Works in Prose and Verse
                      of Robert Greene, 15 vols, New York, 1964.

Henslowe   Henslowe's Diary, ed. R. H. Foakes, Cam-
                      bridge, 2002.

Jonson   Discoveries and Conversations with William
                      Drummond of Hawthornden, ed. G. B. Harrison,
                      London, 1923.

La Primaudaye   Pierre de La Primaudaye, The French Academie,
                      London, 1618.

Lodge   *The Complete Works of Thomas Lodge*, 4 vols,
                      London, 1883.
Marlowe   *Ovid's Elegies*, in *Poems*, ed. Millar MacLure,
                      London, 1968.
Marston   *Entertainment of the Dowager-Countess of Derby*,
                      in *The Poems of John Marston*, ed. Arnold
                      Davenport, Liverpool, 1961.
Overbury   Thomas Overbury, *Miscellaneous Works in
                      Prose and Verse*, ed. Edward F. Rimbault,
                      London, 1856.
Ovid [English]   *Metamorphoses*, tr. A. D. Melville, Oxford,
                      1986.
Ovid [Latin]   *Metamorphoses*, ed. Frank Justus Miller, revised
                      by G. P. Goold, London, 1977.
Plautus   *Works*, tr. Paul Nixon, vol. 5, London, 1917.
Pliny   *Natural History*, tr. H. Rackham, vol. 2,
                      London, 1947.
Plutarch   *Moralia*, tr. W. C. Helmbold, vol. 6, London,
                      1957.
                      *Selected Lives from the Lives of the Noble Grecians
                      and Romans*, tr. Thomas North, ed. Paul
                      Turner, vol. 2, Fontwell, 1963.
Proclamations   *Tudor Royal Proclamations*, ed. Paul L. Hughes
                      and James F. Larkin, 3 vols, New Haven,
                      1964–69.
Purchas   Samuel Purchas, *Hakluytus Posthumus, or,
                      Purchas his Pilgrimes*, vol. 8, Glasgow, 1905.
Spenser   *Amoretti*, in *The Yale Edition of the Shorter
                      Poems of Edmund Spenser*, ed. William A. Oram,
                      Einar Bjorvand, and Ronald Bond, New
                      Haven, 1989.
                      The Faerie Queene, ed. J. C. S. Smith, 2 vols,
                      Oxford 1961.
Stubbes   Philip Stubbes, *The Anatomy of Abuses*, ed.
                      Margaret Jane Kidnie, Tempe, 2002.
Taverner   *Proverbes or adagies with newe addicions gathered
                      out of the Chiliades of Erasmus*, London, 1539.
Terence   *Works*, ed. and tr. John Barsby, vol. 2, Cam-
                      bridge, 2001.
Topsell   Edward Topsell, *The Historie of Serpents*,
                      London, 1608.

SECONDARY WORKS CITED IN COMMENTARY

Arikha   Nogo Arikha, *Passions and Tempers: A History of the Humours*, New York, 2007.

Abbott   E. A. Abbott, *A Shakespearian Grammar*, London, 1883.

Ashton   John Ashton, *A History of English Lotteries*, London, 1893.

Baldwin   T. W. Baldwin, *William Shakspere's Small Latine and Lesse Greeke*, 2 vols, Urbana, 1944.

Bennett   Fordyce Judson Bennett, *The Use of the Bible in the Dramatic Works of George Chapman, Thomas Dekker, John Marston, Cyril Tourneur and John Webster*, PhD thesis, University of Illinois, 1964.

Bundy   Murray W. Bundy, 'Shakespeare and Elizabethan Psychology', *Journal of English and Germanic Philology* 22 (1924): 516–49.

Burford   E. J. Burford, *Bawds and Lodgings: A History of the London Bankside Brothels c.* 100–1675, London, 1976.

Chalfant   Fran C. Chalfant, *Ben Jonson's London: A Jacobean Placename Dictionary*, Athens, 1978.

Clark   Andrew Clark, ed., *The Shirburn Ballads: 1585–1616*, Oxford, 1907.

Dent   R. W. Dent, *Proverbial Language in English Drama Exclusive of Shakespeare, 1495–1616*, Berkeley, 1984.

Edelman   Charles Edelman, *Shakespeare's Military Language: A Dictionary*, London, 2000.

Gurr   Andrew Gurr, *The Shakespearean Stage 1574–1642*, 3rd ed., Cambridge, 1992.

Hope   Jonathan Hope, *Shakespeare's Grammar*, London, 2003.

Hoy   Cyrus Hoy, *Introductions, Notes, and Commentaries to Texts in The Dramatic Works of Thomas Dekker, edited by Fredson Bowers*, 4 vols, Cambridge, 1980.

Jorgensen   Paul A. Jorgensen, 'Redeeming Time in Shakespeare's *Henry IV*', in *Shakespeare*:

Henry IV Parts 1 & 2: *A Casebook*, ed.
G. K. Hunter, London, 1970.

Lyons   Bridget Gellert Lyons, *Voices of Melancholy:*
                        Studies in Literary Treatments of Melancholy
                        in Renaissance England, New York, 1971.

MacLure   Millar MacLure, *George Chapman: A Criti-*
                        cal Study, Toronto, 1966.

Newton   Alfred Newton, *A Dictionary of Birds*,
                        London, 1896.

Noel and Clark   E. B. Noel and J. O. M. Clark, *A History of*
                        Tennis, London, 1924.

Paster   Gail Kern Paster, *Humoring the Body: Emo-*
                        tions and the Shakespearean Stage, Chicago,
                        2004.

Powell   William C. Powell, *Christopher Anstey: Bath*
                        Laureate, PhD thesis, University of Pennsyl-
                        vania, 1944.

Rollins   Hyder E. Rollins, 'The Black-Letter Broad-
                        side Ballad', *PMLA* 34 (1919): 258–339.

Schoell   F. L. Schoell, 'G. Chapman's Common-
                        place Book', *Modern Philology* 17 (1919):
                        23–42.

Shakespeare's England *Shakespeare's England: An Account of the Life*
                        and Manners of his Age, 2 vols, Oxford,
                        1916.

Sherman   William H. Sherman, *Used Books: Marking*
                        Readers in Renaissance England, Philadel-
                        phia, 2008.

Sugden   Edward H. Sugden, *A Topographical Dic-*
                        tionary to the Works of Shakespeare and His
                        Fellow Dramatists, Manchester, 1925.

Swinburne   'Essay on the Poetical and Dramatic Works
                        of George Chapman', in *The Works of George*
                        Chapman: Poems and Minor Translations,
                        London, 1904.

Tilley   Morris Palmer Tilley, *A Dictionary of the*
                        Proverbs in England in the Sixteenth and
                        Seventeenth Centuries, Ann Arbor, 1950.

Williams   Gordon Williams, *A Dictionary of Sexual*
                        Language and Imagery in Shakespearean and
                        Stuart Literature, London, 1994.

| Wilson | Daniel Wilson, *The Right Hand: Left-handedness*, London, 1891. |
| Zwager | Nicolaas Zwager, *Glimpses of Ben Jonson's London*, Amsterdam, 1926. |

ABBREVIATIONS: NOTES AND COLLATION

cf.	compare with, see also
conj.	conjectural reading
DNB	*Oxford Dictionary of National Biography* (2004)
ed.	edition, edited by
et al.	and others
F	First Folio of Jonson's Plays (1616)
fol.	folio number, identifying page in early texts
intro.	introduction
l., ll.	line, lines
n.	note
OED	*Oxford English Dictionary*
Q	quarto
SD	stage direction
SH	speech heading
sig.	signature, identifying page in early texts
subst.	substantially
This ed.	a reading adopted for the first time in this edition
tr.	translator, translated by
vol.	volume

Introduction

On 3 March 1597, after the customary break for Lent,[1] the Lord Admiral's Men opened their spring season at the Rose with *What Will Be Shall Be*. Henslowe's *Diary* shows that takings for this (lost) play were meagre at only 9 s; perhaps audiences were not expecting the theatre to be back in business so soon after Ash Wednesday. Things improved slightly over the next few days as performances of *Alexander and Lodowick*, *A Woman Hard to Please* (both also lost) and the old favourite *The Spanish Tragedy* each took in over £1.[2] Nevertheless, anything less than £2 was not a particularly good day, and over the next two months only six performances reached that total. Four of them were premieres, as indicated by Henslowe's 'ne' in his *Diary*, and premieres almost always drew larger audiences: the lost plays *Guido* (19 March), *Five Plays in One* (7 April), *A French Comedy* (18 April) and *Uther Pendragon* (29 April) did well, as did repeat performances of *Alexander and Lodowick* and *Guido* on Easter Monday and Tuesday 29–30 March. Still, the Admiral's Men were clearly in need of a hit, and on Wednesday 11 May they found what R. A. Foakes describes as a 'phenomenal' one,[3] when George Chapman's new comedy *An Humorous Day's Mirth* opened (as he so often did, Henslowe decided on his own title, but there is no doubt whatsoever that this is the *Comedy of Humours*, as we find it under various spellings in the *Diary*).

That the Admiral's Men turned to Chapman is hardly surprising. As Andrew Gurr notes,

> one noteworthy feature of the Admiral's repertory in these years that has been rather underrated is the evident readiness in the company not just to renew old favourites but to admit innovations, new kinds of play. Shakespeare's company's repertoire in some respects seems conservative by comparison with the kind of novelty that the Admiral's were prepared to undertake.[4]

One such play was Chapman's first extant work for the theatre, *The Blind Beggar of Alexandria*, Henslowe's most profitable offering for all of 1596.[5]

I

In some respects, *The Blind Beggar* is a comedy of humours. The eponymous hero, English drama's first quick-change artist, assumes three other identities, and often refers to his disguises as 'humours': the banished Duke Cleanthes, the 'wild and frantic' (1.335) Count Hermes, and Leon the rich usurer. As Hermes and Leon he marries two different women and cuckolds himself with the 'other''s' wife; then the banished Duke Cleanthes 'returns' as a conqueror. If the Admiral's star, Edward Alleyn, played the Blind Beggar, he would have enjoyed doing so, since he got to parody two of his greatest roles: Barabas in the 'bottle-nosed' Leon (7.84), and Tamburlaine in Cleanthes, who enters leading four vanquished kings, demanding, 'Come, yield your crowns and homages to me' (10.3), although there is no mention of a chariot.

Running in parallel with this plot is a romantic one, in which Cleanthes presumably wins the hand of Princess Aspasia of Egypt – 'presumably' because most of these scenes are missing from the short and obviously corrupt text. T. M. Parrott argues persuasively that in its original state, the romance story of *The Blind Beggar* would have had greater emphasis; Martin Wiggins, in his very valuable *Shakespeare and the Drama of His Time*, views the play as

> a romance with comic interludes, set in a landscape of near-eastern potentates and exotic geographical references. In this it is one of the last plays to exploit *Tamburlaine*'s success before fashion and taste turned elsewhere.[6]

Wiggins's mention of *Tamburlaine* points to another reason the Admiral's Men would be seeking a different type of play in 1597: they were rapidly becoming a different type of company. Edward Alleyn, although only thirty and at the height of his fame, was soon to retire, albeit temporarily, from the stage. Henslowe's *Diary* shows that Alleyn had 'left [p]laying' by the autumn of 1597, and, as S. P. Ceresano notes, 'Alleyn's leaving was not only planned... it was well coordinated'.[7] While the exact time of Alleyn's decision to pursue other interests cannot be known, it is more than likely that, by May, he and his father-in-law Henslowe knew that there would be no point in commissioning an imitation of *Tamburlaine* or *The Battle of Alcazar*, in which Alleyn's absence would be all the more glaring. Also, *The Blind Beggar* had run its course: two recent performances earned only 18s and 5s respectively, but, given its overall success, hopes for another Chapman effort must have been high.

In the event, *An Humorous Day's Mirth* proved to be something of a 'sleeper'. Gurr writes,

> the takings for the first six performances are striking, because the 'ne' performance, which might usually be expected to produce good receipts, brought only £2. 3s, while the next five went on a rising curve, to £2. 15s., £2. 18s., £3. 4s., £3. 6s., and £3. 10s. This was evidently a play whose reputation grew in the course of the month, attracting larger and larger crowds as it went on.[8]

Five more performances in July drew an average of £2 7s until all London's theatres were closed after the Privy Council objected to the 'very seditious and scandalous matter' of the play *The Isle of Dogs*. When the Rose reopened in October, *The Spanish Tragedy* and *An Humorous Day's Mirth* were the first plays offered.[9]

One person brought to the Rose by word of mouth was John Chamberlain. With an independent income and little to do, Chamberlain wrote regularly to his friend Dudley Carleton, the English ambassador to Paris, informing him of all the goings on back in London. The very first of his letters, dated 11 June 1597, reads, 'We have here a new play of humours in very great request, and I was drawn along to it by the common applause, but my opinion of it is (as the fellow said of the shearing of hogs) that there was great cry for so little wool.' Obviously, Chamberlain found the day less than mirthful; indeed, it looks as if the experience made him swear off the theatre for life. In twenty-nine more years of letters to Carleton, he never again mentioned going to a public playhouse, his reaction to the rebuilding of the Globe in 1614 being, 'I hear much speech about this new playhouse which is said to be the fairest that ever was in England, so that if I live but seven years longer I may chance to make a journey to see it.'[10]

However unimpressed Chamberlain was with this 'new play of humours', his references to 'great request' and 'common applause' show him to be in a minority. Of all the poets Francis Meres names in *Palladis Tamia, Wits Treasury*, entered in the Stationers' Register on 7 September 1598, only two rate a mention as being both 'our best for tragedy' and 'the best poets for comedy': Shakespeare and Chapman.[11] No wonder that, by then, the Lord Chamberlain's Men had moved with the times and were performing Ben Jonson's *Every Man in His Humour* at the Curtain.[12]

A TYPICAL LONDON DAY

Of the many experimental and innovative aspects of *An Humorous
Day's Mirth*, the most striking is that it is the first English comedy
to be set in contemporary London, wherein the manners, habits,
and social pretensions of English men and women – the same men
and women sitting or standing at the Rose – are satirised. This
may seem an odd thing to say about a play ostensibly placed in
Paris, but this is Paris in name only (here, too, Jonson was to
follow Chapman, placing the original version of *Every Man in His
Humour* in a very English Florence). Most of the names are recognisably French, and the men are consistently addressed as *Monsieur*, but otherwise there is little to indicate a Parisian locale – the
word 'France' is not heard until Scene 4, and spoken only three
more times, while 'Paris' is also heard only four times, once in
Scene 5 and thrice in Scene 8, set in an ordinary, where both staff
and customers partake of an afternoon at a typical London eating
house.

An Humorous Day's Mirth is a day in the life of four families. First,
we meet Count Labervele, old, impotent, and hence unable to give
his young (second) wife, Florilla, a child. She, in turn, acts and
dresses like a puritan,* although Labervele fears that her self-denial
and constancy will crumble should she meet a young man to her
liking. Labervele's troubles do not end with his wife: his son (by a
first marriage), the young Dowsecer, is in the throes of melancholy,
determined to lead a stoical, contemplative life and avoid all social
contact, especially with women. Second is Monsieur Foyes, a gentleman and father of the 'beauteous Martia' (6.119) whom he is trying
to marry off to the 'vain gull' (2.76) Labesha, as stupid as he is rich.
She, of course, has other ideas. Third, we have Count Moren, who
seems not to mind being married to the much older Countess,
except that she is insanely jealous and goes into a rage if he so much
as looks at another woman.

---

*There are good arguments for both the lower- and upper-case 'p' in
'puritan'. In choosing the former, I follow Patrick Collinson, a leading
historian of Elizabethan puritanism. In the 1590s puritanism was neither a
separate religion nor a clearly defined political group; 'puritan' was a
derogatory term in general circulation, applied very loosely to those who
were over-precise in their religious attitudes or who made a point of
showing their piety in whatever they did (see Collinson, *The Elizabethan
Puritan Movement*, London, 1967; also pp. 30–2 below).

One of Chapman's stranger decisions was to include our fourth couple, the King and Queen – strange because a royal couple seems totally incongruous with an urban atmosphere, be it Paris or London. This King and Queen go about the city unguarded, no one is the slightest bit deferential to either, and no affair of state is ever mentioned. There are other affairs a-plenty, though, as the King is always on the lookout for a new mistress, and has decided on Martia as his next conquest. If Chapman lived in a later age, perhaps with King and Queen translated into Duke and Duchess, or Prince and Princess of Wales, this would all seem quite realistic, but even in 1597 it is a disbelief willingly and easily suspended. True, no king of that time could possibly, even if he wanted to, walk over to the local ordinary, unguarded and unaccompanied, for a meal and a quick assignation. But Queen Elizabeth, disguised or not, would never travel to the South Bank to attend a play at the Globe – yet her doing so in the delightful *Shakespeare in Love* does not detract from the film.

The real 'king' of the play, as he says himself, is the young gallant Lemot, who in his first appearance promises to preside over the day 'like an old king in an old fashion play' (2.12–13). Purely for the fun of driving Labervele mad, he convinces the 'old doter' (9.22) that Lemot should be allowed to 'prove' Florilla's constancy by making amorous advances to her (the only sequence that might be said to have a 'source', as it is somewhat like a story in *The Decameron*).[13] Florilla drops her puritan demeanour, falls in love with Lemot, and agrees to meet him later at the ordinary run by the sprightly innkeeper, Verone. Lemot also finds a way of getting Martia away from Foyes and Labesha, so that she can meet the King, and then convinces Countess Moren that her husband should be allowed an afternoon's enjoyment at Verone's, assuring her, 'No ladies use to come to ordinaries, madam' (7.235).

Lemot has no sexual interest at all in Florilla, nor does he care whether the King and Moren manage to escape from their jealous wives for a day. He sends word to Labervele and Foyes, informing them where Florilla and Martia are, runs over to Count Moren's house himself to tell the Countess what her husband is up to, and then frightens the Queen with a wild story that Dowsecer, having heard that the King had abducted Martia,

> with a friend
> Of his and two or three black ruffians more,
> Brake desperately upon the person of the King,

Swearing to take from him, in traitorous fashion,
The instrument of procreation.
(11.80–4)

Mission accomplished, Lemot returns to Verone's to enjoy the show.

Our last group of characters comprises Lemot's friends: Colinet, Catalian, Blanuel, Rowley, and Berger. They assist him in his schemes, serve as the butt of his jokes, and often, with Lemot's encouragement, display the most ridiculously fashionable attitudes and utter the most ridiculously fashionable sayings. There are some very good moments in this, but unfortunately little consistency – as discussed in more detail below, the play has a number of false starts, when a characterisation established in one scene completely changes in the next. Still, just the sight of young men, arriving at an ordinary all hot and sweaty from a game of tennis or a visit to a brothel, then demanding a pipe of tobacco before sitting down to a game of cards, would have delighted the original audience for its novelty alone.

THE PHILOSOPHY OF MIRTH

> The truth to us philosophers is always an interim judgement. (Tom Stoppard, *Jumpers*)

From the very brief description I have given, it might seem that Chapman's comedy of humours is only, to quote Parrott, 'an exhibition of fantastic and amusing characters',[14] an early version of *Monty Python's Flying Circus* and its Ministry of Silly Walks. Even if this were true, the play would still be worthwhile, but there is more to it than that: *An Humorous Day's Mirth* is also, as Mark Thornton Burnett observes in his *Dictionary of National Biography* article on Chapman, an exploration of 'genuine and false learning'.

T. S. Eliot rates Chapman as 'the most erudite of Elizabethan dramatists…a particularly interesting example of English Renaissance learning united with English Renaissance poetic genius'.[15] To Douglas Bush, his entire literary career was 'a crusade for the humanistic tradition, its aristocratic learning and ethical wisdom, the control of the rebellious passions by the reason and the will, the ideal of stoic strength and completeness'.[16] Bush names Ficino, Erasmus, Plutarch, and Epictetus as providers of 'philosophical nourishment' to Chapman – as will be discussed below, Ficino rightly comes first – and an extended list would include Plato,

Cicero, and any number of others. One might say he knew the field from A to Z: Aristotle to Zeno. The extent to which Chapman studied the ancient philosophers and poets, even Homer, in the original rather than in 'modern' translations is a topic of debate amongst commentators, but by whatever route they may have taken, their presence in *An Humorous Day's Mirth* is palpable.

Chapman does not distance his play from everyday English life by making the search for self-knowledge, to any Renaissance humanist the foundation of all other knowledge, central to it. English grammar school education was, by definition, 'humanist', since the great Greek and Latin poets and philosophers (the Greeks often in Latin 'cribs') were required reading. Nor was this knowledge restricted to those who learned Latin at school; we must also account for the popularity and influence of such works as Pierre de La Primaudaye's *The French Academy*, translated in four parts between 1586 and 1618, and sometimes considered to have inspired the idea for *Love's Labour's Lost*. As in Shakespeare, with the King of Navarre's 'little academe / Still and contemplative in living art' (1.1.13–14), we have four French noblemen who retire from the world of affairs and start an academy in order to study 'all things necessary for the institution of manners and happy life in all estates and callings'. Their conversations, running to more than a thousand pages in the collected four volumes, form a humanist compendium that includes, as Frances Yates writes, 'public as well as private conduct, politics as well as ethics'.[17] That London printers put out nine editions argues for a wide readership.

With his love of philosophical speculation, Chapman can be, as Jonathan Bate notes, a 'self-consciously learned' poet, and both the poems and tragedies can be heavy going.[18] In addition to the learned allusions and references, we must also consider Chapman's notorious penchant for arcane vocabulary and what Frank Kermode calls his 'irresponsible' and 'discourteous syntax, with its disregard for the normal amenities of exposition'.[19] *An Humorous Day's Mirth* does have its share of Chapman's esoteric words, but they do not present a major problem in understanding – one 'gets the gist'. Any actor, however, would find communicating the sense of some speeches difficult. To some extent, what F. S. Boas writes in the introduction to his 1905 edition of *Bussy D'Ambois* applies here: 'there are some passages ... where the thread of meaning seems to disappear amidst his fertile imagery – one feels not that sense is lacking, but that one has failed to find the clue to the zigzag movements of

Chapman's brain'.[20] Fortunately, there are not too many of these; unfortunately one of the worst is Labervele's soliloquy that starts the play, a welter of strange expressions buried in subordinate clauses. Things get much better after that; one senses that Chapman was working out what style he wanted the play to be in as he went.

The word always associated with this side of Chapman is 'obscurity', a self-inflicted wound. In his dedicatory preface to *Ovid's Banquet of Sense*, addressed to the poet Matthew Roydon, Chapman scorns 'the wilful poverty of judgements' given 'in contempt of the divine discipline of poesy', and boasts, 'the profane multitude I hate, and only consecrate my strange poems to these searching spirits, whom learning hath made noble, and nobilities sacred'. Poetry should be work:

> that which being with a little endeavour searched, adds a kind of majesty to poesy…Obscurity in affection of words and indigested conceits, is pedantical and childish; but where it shroudeth itself in the heart of his subject, uttered with fitness of figures and expressive epithets; with that darkness will I still labour to be shadowed.

To compound the offence, he denies that poetry 'should be as pervial as oratory', 'pervial' being a word never seen before nor used by anyone since.[21]

We need to be wary of taking Chapman too literally, though, since praising readers for their supreme intelligence and good taste (Roydon has the 'actual means to sound the philosophical conceits')[22] was conventional. The readership for 'obscure' poetry would not have been completely identical to the audience for comedy, and, however much Chapman may have hated the 'profane multitude', he must have known that the profane multitude are the people who buy theatre tickets. Overall, Chapman wears his learning proudly but lightly in *An Humorous Day's Mirth*, which has the effect of increasing our interest in it. Anyone who has enjoyed a play by Tom Stoppard knows that the 'entire library of moral philosophy'[23] is very much at home in comedy.

THE FOUR HUMOURS

> I can no longer sit back and allow communist infiltration, communist indoctrination, communist subversion, and the international communist conspiracy to sap and impurify all of our precious bodily fluids. (General Jack D. Ripper in Stanley Kubrick's *Dr Strangelove*)

So far, except for quotations, I have not used 'humour' or 'humorous' in this Introduction, although most readers would be aware that the melancholy of Dowsecer is a 'humour', as is the jealousy of Count Labervele or Countess Moren. However, even these examples rely on two different uses of the word; *OED* gives six distinct definitions for 'humour' that were current up to 1600, and all six are appropriated in our play. Therefore, to fully appreciate what the comedy of humours is, something more than a brief examination is required.

The Elizabethans would have laughed as loudly at a good joke as anyone else, but they did not understand what it meant to have a sense of humour, as we think of it. Ask anyone today except an English professor what 'humour' means, and the answer would inevitably be associated with comedy, jokes, or laughter; but that is *OED*'s seventh definition, the earliest citation dated 1682, and the first use of 'humorous' as 'jocular, comical, funny' did not appear until 1705. Before then, there was nothing necessarily funny about the subject, unless we want to think of *Titus Andronicus* and *Othello* as comedies, since Titus's madness and Othello's jealousy are frequently described as 'humours'. Obviously, shifts in usage do not happen instantly, nor was it a purely literary phenomenon – developments in medicine were gradually removing 'humour' from the scientific vocabulary. Even so, Chapman deserves at least some of the credit for establishing today's most common meaning.

By the time Chapman wrote *An Humorous Day's Mirth*, 'humour' had become something of an all-purpose word in the theatre. Lyly, Kyd, and Marlowe make constant reference to their characters' humours, and Shakespeare uses 'humour' so often in his early plays that in *The Merry Wives of Windsor*, where everything, according to Nym, is a humour, he could be poking fun at himself as well as Chapman or Jonson.

In the Induction to *Every Man Out of His Humour*, first performed in 1599, Jonson has Asper express his disgust at the daily 'abuse of this word humour', and Cordatus asks him to explain 'how this poor innocent word / Is racked and tortured' (Ind. 78, 82–3). Asper readily assents, and begins by taking us nicely through the history of the humours; that this oft-quoted speech exists at all is in itself evidence that the word was both ubiquitous and open to a number of interpretations. He begins:

Why, *humour* (as 'tis, *ens*) we thus define it
To be a quality of air or water,
And in itself holds these two properties:
Moisture, and fluxure. As, for demonstration,
Pour water on this floor, 'twill wet and run;
Likewise, the air, forced through a horn or trumpet,
Flows instantly away, and leaves behind
A kind of dew; and hence we do conclude
That whatsoe'er hath fluxure and humidity,
As wanting power to contain itself,
Is *humour*. So, in every human body,
The choler, melancholy, phlegm, and blood,
By reason that they flow continually
In some one part, and are not continent,
Receive the name of humours.
                              (Ind. 86–100)[24]

OED agrees, giving its first definition of humour as 'moisture, damp exhalation, vapour', the second being 'in ancient and medieval physiology, one of the four chief fluids...of the body'. This ancient physiological theory derives from the even more ancient theory that all matter consists of a combination of elements, a concept not attributable to any one person, but most often associated with the Greek philosopher, Empedocles (c. 490–430 BC). As F. David Hoeniger notes in *Medicine and Shakespeare in the English Renaissance*, the idea

> came to be widely accepted in the ancient and medieval world. All material things were thought to be composed, in different proportion, of four essences or basic elements: earth, water, air, and fire. Each element was characterized by two primary and opposite qualities, its relative warmth or coolness, moisture or dryness.[25]

It was not long before others applied Empedoclean theory to the human body, giving each of the four elements its counterpart in one of the four bodily humours. They are described and discussed in the many texts collected under the name of Hippocrates (460–377 BC), generally spoken of as the father of medical science, although little is actually known of him (much, if not all, of the Hippocratic corpus, gathered at the Alexandrian library in about 250 BC, was written by others).[26] In *On the Nature of Man*, attributed by Aristotle to Hippocrates's son-in-law, Polybus, we read,

The human body contains blood, phlegm, yellow bile and black bile. These are the things that make up its constitution and cause its pains and health. Health is primarily that state in which these constituent substances are in correct proportion to each other, both in strength and quantity, and are well mixed.[27]

The list is the same as Asper's, although in a different order, yellow bile being another name for choler, and black bile being the same as melancholy. Not everyone agreed about the number of humours, or about the places in the body they were generated and stored, but as Nogo Arikha writes in *Passions and Tempers: A History of the Humours*,

> the useful symmetry inherent in the fourfold division of the universe into seasons, qualities, and elements was applied to the bodily humours as well. Air corresponded to blood (which was perhaps categorized as a humour to preserve the fourfold division); water corresponded to phlegm, fire corresponded to choler, the yellow bile; and earth corresponded to melancholy, the black bile. To each humour corresponded two of the basic qualities associated with its element: blood was hot and moist, phlegm was cold and moist, choler or yellow bile was hot and dry, and melancholy or black bile was cold and dry.[28]

In about the ninth century, Arab writers tied astrology to the humours, assigning each to a planet: sanguinity to Jupiter, phlegm to the moon or Venus, choler to Mars, and melancholy to Saturn, hence a 'saturnine' complexion.[29]

Amongst the many early modern texts describing the functions of the humours, one of the most delightful is Sir John Harington's *The Englishman's Doctor or The Schoole of Salerne*, a translation of the health manual in Latin verse collected by doctors at the medical school of Salerno in about the thirteenth century.[30] Harington sets out the humoral system with his customary wit and precision:

> Four humours reign within our bodies wholly,
> And these compared to four elements,
> The sanguine, choler, phlegm and melancholy,
> The latter two are heavy, dull of sense,
> Th' other two are more jovial, quick, and jolly,
> And may be likened thus without offence,
> Like air both warm and moist, is sanguine clear,
> Like fire doth choler hot and dry appear.
> Like water cold and moist is phlegmatic,
> The melancholy cold, dry earth is like.[31]

As most diseases were caused by an imbalance of the humours, treatment was designed to correct it. The physician could reduce an excess humour through phlebotomy (bleeding), purging, or administering an enema, but the overwhelming majority of therapies used diet as the means of replacing a deficient humour; that 'you are what you eat' was fundamental to Hippocratic medicine. Treatment was preventative as well as curative; the Hippocratic text *Regimen for Health* is a complete guide to diet, exercise and sex, offering specific advice depending on age, physique, or the season of the year.[32]

Not many plays deal specifically with the diagnosis and treatment of physical pathologies, and humoral theory would not have had much literary impact if the idea that good health depended on the humours being well proportioned related only to one's physical condition. The humours also correlated with one's 'temperament', or 'complexion', described in terms that are still part of our everyday vocabulary: blood promotes a 'sanguine' complexion, cheerfully optimistic and sensuous; 'phlegmatic' people are calm and imperturbable, although an excess of phlegm makes one sluggish and apathetic. Too much choler made one 'choleric', angry and ill-tempered, and lastly we have melancholy: cold, dry, and generally thought to be stored in the spleen, therefore causing a 'splenetic' complexion – morose, peevish, unsociable.

We now return to the Induction of *Every Man Out*. Having given a primary definition of 'humour', Asper adds,

> It may by metaphor apply itself
> Unto the general disposition;
> As when some one peculiar quality
> Doth so possess a man that it doth draw
> All his affects, his spirits, and his powers
> In their confluxions all to run one way:
> This may be truly said to be a *humour*.
>   (Ind. 101–7)

This statement is taken by many to be a 'definitive' account of the humours in Jonson's (and by implication Chapman's) comedies, what Robert S. Miola describes as a character's 'dominant affectation or folly; one's humour becomes an *idée fixe* and a defining trait, each character has his or her own pathology'.[33] It is precisely correct, but also somewhat misleading: by relegating humours to the status of 'metaphor' in their application 'unto the general disposition', Jonson implies that there is another, literal, terminology available to describe the workings of a man's 'affects, his spirits, and his powers'. But no such terminology existed, neither in general use nor in what we would today call the scientific community. Indeed, if Asper has no other means of saying how 'one peculiar quality' can possess a man other than by having his 'confluxions run one way', he might just as well have said, 'humour can be taken as a metaphor for humour'.[34]

Jonson writes of *affects*, *spirits*, and *powers*. The title page of *The Touchstone of Complexions* (1576), the English translation of a work by the Dutch physician Levinus Lemnius, promises that, by reading this book, one will know the 'exact state, habit, disposition, and constitution, of his own body outwardly', and 'also the *inclinations*, *affections*, *motions*, and *desires* of his mind inwardly' (italics added). To these words we might add *imagination*, *sense*, *appetite*, and *passion* to form a (still partial) list of terms used to indicate a person's thoughts, feelings, and emotions – that is, his or her psychology.

In her 1954 study, *Endeavors of Art*, Madeleine Doran offers a prescient comment on how Elizabethan dramatists – she names Marlowe, Shakespeare, Chapman, and Jonson – found 'a way to intensify tragedy': they took the ethical scheme of the morality play, 'with its contest between the virtues and the vices for the soul of every man', and turned it into a psychological contest, 'the conflict between reason and passion'. Doran goes on to say,

> In the highly developed psychological theories of the passions in which there was at the time such great interest, dramatists found the means of deepening motivation and intensifying internal conflict. This making of the conflict personal gave, in turn, new immediacy, poignancy, and subtlety to the moral problem.[35]

The only addition I would make to this analysis is that it applies equally to comedy in every respect. I am far from the first critic to observe that Othello's desperate struggle for command of his passions contains echoes of Thorello's (*F*: Kitely's) torment in *Every Man In*.[36] Indeed, it would not take much rewriting to transfer some complete speeches from one play to the other.

Another comedy benefiting greatly from a 'deepening motivation and intensifying internal conflict' is one which preceded *An Humorous Day's Mirth* by perhaps two years, *Love's Labour's Lost*. Little credence is now attached to the once popular theory that 'the school of night' (4.3.251) is a pointed reference to Chapman's supposed membership in 'a secret atheistical, philosophical and scientific academy' of that name, whose other members included Sir Walter

Raleigh, Matthew Roydon, the mathematician Sir Thomas Harriott, and Henry Percy, the Earl of Northumberland.[37] Without a School of Night there is no need for Chapman to reply to Shakespeare, although the number of verbal correspondences between the two plays argues for some measure of parody on Chapman's part.[38] More importantly, as H. R. Woudhuysen notes, the similarities rest on a shared 'social, political, philosophical and literary culture'; the hopeless attempt by Shakespeare's French lords to 'make war against [their] own affections / And the huge army of the world's desires' (1.1.9–10) is informed with the same philosophical conceits we find in *An Humorous Day's Mirth*.[39]

This reorienting of drama to the internal, psychological lives of its characters is especially prominent in Chapman. To Hardin Craig, 'one could almost reconstruct the subject of Elizabethan psychology from his plays alone'.[40] Chapman is

> the psychological dramatist *par excellence*. He not only delights in depicting the psychological states of his characters in and for themselves, but he makes poetry of them. With him psychological states are fact, figures of speech, and the things suggested by figurative language. There are almost no minor doctrines and distinctions that he does not know familiarly... [they] are both a poetic subject and a poetic instrument in his hands as a poet.[41]

Craig is commenting on Chapman's most celebrated tragedy, *Bussy D'Ambois*, but again, if we substitute the words 'comedy' and 'comic' for 'poetry' and 'poetic' in the passage just quoted, it could apply also to *An Humorous Day's Mirth*.

Doran's and Craig's use of 'psychology' in reference to Elizabethan drama is only slightly anachronistic – while much older than many people might think, the word postdates the period by only some half a century. In early modern terms, we are dealing with the study of the soul, the splendidly comprehensive word that stands for the mind in all its many functions. It is the seat of our thoughts, actions and desires.

THE HUMOURS AND THE SOUL

> I was thrown out of college for cheating on the metaphysics exam. I looked into the soul of the boy sitting next to me. (Woody Allen)

As we learn from Sir Toby Belch's urging his drinking companions to 'rouse the night-owl in a catch that will draw three souls out of one weaver' (2.3.58–9), we have three souls, not one. The most familiar account of this division is found in the fourth book of Plato's *Republic*, an extended analogy of the three levels of the state – workers, guardians, philosopher kings – to the three levels of the human soul, which he calls appetite, spirit, and reason. Just as the ideal state is one in which the three groups function harmoniously with one another, the wise and just individual

> harmonizes the three parts of himself like three limiting notes in a musical scale – high, low, and middle. He binds together those parts and any others there may be in between, and from having been many things he becomes entirely one, moderate and harmonious.[42]

Plato then extends the analogy to physical health, in purely Hippocratic terms:

> To produce health is to establish the components of the body in a natural relation of control and being controlled, one by another, while to produce disease is to establish a relation of ruling and being ruled contrary to nature.[43]

While it would be impossible to overestimate the cultural significance of these ideas, their purpose in *The Republic* is to provide illustrations and examples in discussion of a wider subject; the same might be said of Plato's well-known comments on the soul in *Phaedo* and *Timaeus*. It was left to Plato's student, Aristotle, to provide a detailed and systematic study of the soul in his *De anima* (*On the Soul*), the first, and in many ways the most important, psychological textbook ever written.

In broad terms, Aristotle's three souls are similar to Plato's: the first, commonly called the 'nutritive', accounts for nourishment and growth in all living things, including plants and lower animals. The second, given various names such as 'sensible', 'sensitive', or just 'the sense', is responsible for our desires, appetites, and passions. Third is the 'rational' soul, the seat of our higher cognitive functions, what John Donne and Sir Francis Bacon would later call the soul of 'reason' and 'understanding'.[44]

Plato insisted that the soul had no physical substance; Aristotle's great breakthrough was to ground his psychology in a detailed physiology: 'there seems to be no case in which the soul can act or be acted upon without involving the body, e.g. anger, courage, appetite and sensation generally...passions, gentleness, fear, pity, courage, joy, loving, and hating; in all these there is a concurrent affection of the body'. He places great emphasis on the workings of our five external senses: 'sensation depends…on a process of movement or affection from without'.[45]

Balance, right reason, and controlling one's passions, prized by both Plato and Aristotle, were also central to the philosophy of the stoics, for it contributed to their ideal of constancy, a life lived 'harmoniously' or 'consistently'.[46] The stoics also advanced the concept of *pneuma*, Greek for 'breath' or 'wind', an invisible, dynamic substance underlying the four elements and permeating the world. In early modern English, the most common equivalent is 'spirit', from the Latin *spiritus*.[47]

At this point, another major player enters the game. So far I have referred to humoral theory as Hippocratic, but no one in medieval or Renaissance Europe would have done so: Hippocrates must make way for the Roman physician Galen (AD 129–c. 200), whose medical texts were the standard reference for the next 1500 years.[48] Not only was Galen completely familiar with the Hippocratic corpus, he studied philosophy as well, reading widely in Plato, Aristotle, and the stoics – indeed one of his important works is *On the Doctrines of Hippocrates and Plato*.

If the five external senses and three internal souls are all going to cohabit within one body, some means of their communicating with one another would be a very nice thing to have. Galen took the stoics' universal pneuma and combined it with ideas from Plato and Aristotle to devise an early version of the central nervous system, with the 'psychic pneuma', or 'spirit', travelling about the body along with the humours.[49] This spirit, as we read in Timothy Bright's *Treatise of Melancholy* (1586), serves as 'the chief instrument, and immediate, whereby the soul bestoweth the exercises of her faculty in her body, that passeth to and fro in a moment'.[50] It is

> the most universal instrument of the soul, and embraceth at full, so far as bodily uses require, all the universal faculty, wherewith the soul is endued, and directeth it, and guideth it, unto more particular instruments, for more special and private uses, as to the eye to see with, to the ear to hear, to the nose to smell, to the bowels, stomach, and liver to nourish, to the heart to maintain life, and to other parts, to the end of propagation: this is all performed by the self same, one, and single spirit.[51]

In *An Humorous Day's Mirth*, Lemot puts this 'scientific' knowledge to good use in his 'proof' of Florilla's constancy, suggesting that it should begin 'with a kiss'. When she asks 'how kissing is the best proof of chaste ladies', he replies, 'To give you a reason for that, you must give me leave to be obscure and philosophical' (4.186–8). He then launches into an explanation of how 'imagination and appetite' alter, and potentially control, our sensory impressions: 'Then thus, madam: every kiss is made as the voice is, by imagination and appetite, and as both those are presented to the ear in the voice, so are they to the silent spirits in our kisses' (4.190–3).

Once a kiss is tasted (an object viewed, a word heard), the psychic spirit starts its journey. In the model presented by Aristotle in *De anima* and further developed by Thomas Aquinas, all such sensory perceptions go through the 'common sense' – not our modern idiom of clear, straightforward thinking, but the part of the soul held 'in common' by the senses, a clearing house, as it were, where information is collected and processed. As La Primaudaye writes in *The French Academy*, the common sense

> receiveth all the images and shapes that are offered and brought unto it…the external senses have no judgement of that which they outwardly receive but by means of the common sense, unto which they make relation…In this manner therefore is the common sense of all the internal senses the next unto the external, so is it the means whereby they communicate one with an other.[52]

Things get complicated at this point, for, as Lemot says, the sensitive soul enters the fray in the guise of 'imagination', which can turn good spirits into bad. In *Of Wisdom* (c. 1608), Peter Charron writes, 'the imagination is very strong and powerful, it is it that makes all the stir, all the clatter, yea the perturbation of the world proceeds from it…it is either the only, or at least the most active and stirring faculty of the soul'.[53] La Primaudaye sometimes uses the word 'fantasy', but adds that both words 'are taken by many for one and the same faculty and virtue of the soul'.[54] He agrees with Charron that it is fundamentally opposed to reason,[55] and is

> a very dangerous thing…for it be not guided and bridled by reason, it troubleth and moveth all the sense and understanding, as a tempest doth the sea. For it is easily stirred up not only by external senses, but also by the complexion and disposition of the body. Hereof it proceedeth that even the spirits both good and bad have great access unto it, to stir it up to either good or evil, and that by means unknown to us.[56]

The same process is described in *Nosce Teipsum* (*Know Thyself*), the long and very witty poem on the nature of the soul by Chapman's

friend Sir John Davies, probably written about 1594, though not
published until 1599:[57]

> These spirits of sense, in fantasy's high court,
> Judge of the forms of objects, ill or well;
> And so they send a good or ill report.
> Down to the heart, where all affections dwell.
>
> (1125–8)

Since absolutely none of this is based on empirical evidence, every
writer on the subject has his own version of the workings of body
and soul, although they all agree that the humours do not always
act on their own, but are stimulated by contact with the outside
world, through the external senses. This is especially true when
dealing with love, the strongest of all appetites, and the most likely
to be victorious in its battle with reason. Although diet or lack of
exercise could promote a humoral imbalance leading to sensual
desire, and attraction might arise from a couple having the same
complexion or the right star sign,[58] for most people the main cause
is finding someone suitably qualified to be an object of desire, then
letting the senses go to work.

How each of the external senses contributes to this process is a
topic with a long intellectual history and is a favourite theme of
Chapman's. It is particularly noticeable in his last major poem
before writing *An Humorous Day's Mirth*, the brilliant but notori-
ously difficult *Ovid's Banquet of Sense* (1595), wherein he both analy-
ses and celebrates the delights and dangers of the five senses. The
historical framework of the poem is a tradition (later dramatised in
Jonson's *Poetaster*) that 'Corynna', to whom Ovid's erotic *Amores*
are addressed, was Emperor Augustus's daughter Julia, and that a
romantic involvement led to Ovid's banishment from Rome. In the
Argument preceding the narrative of *Ovid's Banquet*, we learn,

> Ovid, newly enamoured of Julia, (daughter to Octavius Augustus Caesar,
> after by him called Corynna,) secretly conveyed himself into a garden of
> the Emperor's court: in an arbour whereof, Corynna was bathing; playing
> upon her lute, and singing: which Ovid overhearing, was exceedingly
> pleased with the sweetness of her voice, and to himself uttered the comfort
> he conceived in his sense of hearing.

Ovid's senses proceed to 'the odours she used in her bath', and,
after much hesitation, 'he ventures to see her in the pride of her
nakedness'. He then 'entreats a kiss to serve for satisfaction of his
taste, which he obtains', but alas, after several verses of blissful

anticipation of what his hands are about to experience, he is 'inter-rupted' by the arrival of Corynna's maids and the sense of touch goes (for now) ungratified.[59]

Chapman allows each of the courses in Ovid's banquet its proper due, but sight, coming third, is given more than twice as many stanzas as any of the other four. To privilege sight is typical of Renaissance writers: Berowne in *Love's Labour's Lost* knows that love is 'first learned in a lady's eyes' (4.3.324), while in Lodge's *Margarite of America* (1596), Princess Margarite tells Arsadachus that love is discovered 'by the eyes...which are the keys of desire, which both open the way for love to enter and lock him up when he is let in'.[60]

The way this happens in terms of humoral physiology is quite interesting, and is alluded to in *An Humorous Day's Mirth*, when Lemot tells Florilla,

> Madam, in proving you I find no proof
> Against your piercing glancings,
> But swear I am shot thorough with your love
>
> (6.71–3)

and later, when he informs the Queen of the King's mad love for Martia:

> But when he viewed her radiant eyes again,
> Blind was he strucken with her fervent beams.
>
> (11.50–1)

Florilla's 'piercing glancings' and Martia's 'fervent beams' are the 'eye-spirits' or 'eye-beams' that Galen believed to be the media of sight, taking the idea, as he so often did, from Plato. In the *Timaeus*, Plato puts Empedocles' element of fire to use as an internal spirit that does not burn, but gives off beams of light that exit the body via the eyes, strike the eternal object, then transfer images back to the eye and from there via the spirits to the soul.[61] Pierre Boaistuau (1517–66), an eclectic author, editor, translator, and compiler of stories, describes the physiological process in *Theatrum Mundi*:

> Philosophers have said, that when we cast our sight upon that which we desire, suddenly certain spirits that are engendered of the most perfectest part of blood, proceedeth from the heart of the party which we do love, and promptly ascendeth even up to the eyes, and afterward converteth into vapours invisible, and entereth into our eyes which are bent to receive them, even so as in looking in a glass there remaineth therein some spot

of breathing, and so from the eyes it penetrateth to the heart, even so by little and little it spreadeth all about and therefore the miserable lover being drawn to, by the new spirits, the which desire always to join and draw near, with their principal and natural habitation, is constrained to mourn and lament his lost liberty.[62]

Boaistuau follows convention is assuming that love is a painful experience; in fact *Theatrum Mundi* might be subtitled *1001 Ways to be Totally Miserable*. In *An Humorous Day's Mirth*, however, 'the fire of love' enables the melancholy Dowsecer to end his misery and recover his 'lost wits' (13.56, 59). For love to cure the humour of melancholy seems like a contradiction in terms; to see if this is so, we proceed to a closer look at what the Abbess of *The Comedy of Errors* calls 'moody and dull melancholy / Kinsman to grim and comfortless despair' (5.1.79–80).

MELANCHOLY

I have of late, but wherefore I know not, lost all my mirth. (*Hamlet*)

He surveyed the fence, and all gladness left him and a deep melancholy settled down upon his spirit. Thirty yards of board fence nine feet high. Life to him seemed hollow, and existence but a burden. (*Tom Sawyer*)

Few Shakespearean scholars have attributed Hamlet's melancholy to being told to paint the Elsinore fences, but all Elizabethans would know that Hamlet and Tom suffer from precisely the same condition, one that they studied, talked about and frequently aspired to, for at that time melancholy was, in Charles Rosen's apt phrase, 'not so much a disease as a basic component of civilization'.[63] Lengthy treatises were written describing its causes and recommending all sorts of cures, including eating more vegetables, rubbing your body all over with butter after a hot bath, and something that will appeal to many a student reading this edition: finding an easier subject to study.[64] Fascination with the subject reached its zenith in 1621, with the publication of the English clergyman and perpetual student Robert Burton's massive compendium, *The Anatomy of Melancholy*, which grew progressively more massive in five subsequent editions, the last published posthumously in 1651.[65] (Since Burton came at the end of what might be called the age of melancholy, I have avoided quoting him, preferring to rely on some of the same earlier texts that he did.)

As one of humanity's four basic complexions and a common synonym for 'sad', 'melancholy' was everywhere in English drama well before Chapman wrote *An Humorous Day's Mirth*; its being a four-syllable word that fits beautifully into a blank verse line certainly would have helped. However, our visit to Labervele's house to 'see the humour of the young lord Dowsecer' (5.200–1) represents the first known opportunity to meet a character who is actually defined by what Arikha considers 'the most ineffable and illustrious of all humours'.[66]

Dowsecer is a melancholy scholar, not necessarily a student but one well versed in classical literature, whose reading in philosophy brings him nothing but discontent. Such unhappy fellows are nicely described in Harington's *The Englishman's Doctor*:

> The melancholy from the rest do vary,
> Both sport and ease, and company refusing,
> Exceeding studious, ever solitary,
> Inclining pensive still to be, and musing.[67]

I refer to Dowsecer as 'the first known opportunity' because there is every reason to believe that the 'ur-Hamlet' was, like Shakespeare's character, a well-read young man who would like nothing more than to return to his studies; as we shall see, several passages in *An Humorous Day's Mirth* could well be Chapman's parody of this most famous of lost plays.[68]

Within its strict Galenic sense, melancholy is a debilitating condition with a seemingly limitless number of symptoms, none of them good. Andreas Du Laurens (c. 1558–1609), Professor of Medicine at the University of Montpellier, writes:

> The melancholic man properly so called...is ordinarily out of heart, always fearful and trembling, in such sort as that he is afraid of every thing, yea and maketh himself a terror unto himself, as the beast which looketh himself in a glass; he would run away and cannot go, he goeth oftentimes sighing, troubled with the hicket [hiccups] and with an unseparable sadness, which oftentimes turneth into despair; he is always disquieted both in body and spirit, he is subject to watchfulness, which doth consume him on the one side: for if he think to make truce with his passions by taking some rest, behold so soon as he would shut his eyelids, he is assailed with a thousand vain visions, and hideous buggards [goblins, bogies], with fantastical inventions, and dreadful dreams, if he would call any to help him, his speech is cut off before it be half ended, and what he speaketh cometh out in fasting and stammering sort, he cannot live with company.[69]

If these symptoms are not enough, Levinus Lemnius supplies some others: melancholy men are 'lean, dry, lank, pilled-skinned and without hair, crook-nailed...the face becometh pale, yellowish and swarty...touching the notes and marks of their minds, they are churlish, whining...obstinate, greedy of worldly goods and covetous of money, pinching and sparing when they have got it'. He notes the astrological connection with Saturn and lists some aspects of the melancholic's social behaviour:

> A man may also know them by their kind of gait, for they use a certain slow pace and soft nice gait, holding down their heads, with countenance and look so grim and frowning...the grim and surly planet of Saturn, together with melancholy so disposeth them that (as though they were bound by silence and taciturnity) a man shall scarcely get a word out of their mouths.[70]

Social paradigms are much more interesting to satirists and dramatists than are physical symptoms, and so the character of the 'malcontent', akin to the melancholy scholar, took shape. He considered himself too superior to ordinary men to have anything to do with them, although he was not necessarily a bitter railer like Malevole, the hero of Marston's *The Malcontent*.[71] The character Pansa in Everard Guilpin's verse satire *Skialetheia* (1598) is typical:

> Fine spruce young Pansa's grown a malcontent,
> A mighty malcontent though young and spruce,
> As heresy he shuns all merriment,
> And turned good husband, puts forth sighs to use,
> Like hate-man Timon in his cell, he sits
> Misted with darkness like a smoky room,
> And if he be so mad to walk the streets,
> To his sights life, his hat becomes a tomb.[72]

Pansa's large hat, with its brim pulled down so far he cannot see, is the malcontent's most recognisable sartorial affectation: 'Meditations of a Gull', one of the *Epigrams* by Sir John Davies, begins

> See, yonder melancholy gentleman,
> Which, hood-winked with his hat, alone doth sit!
> Think what he thinks, and tell me if you can,
> What great affairs troubles his little wit.[73]

Melancholy's double life as a serious pathology and a condition of superior intellectual and artistic acumen was neither natural nor inevitable – it was created in Italy during the fifteenth century.

Chapman may not have belonged to any School of Night, but there can be no doubt at all of his devotion to another school, the Academy of Florence, headed by Marsilio Ficino (1433–99), who was largely responsible for translating into Latin and reinterpreting the work of Plato, and for bringing neo-Platonist thought into Renaissance Europe.

Ficino, knowing that he was born under the sign of 'Aquarius, Saturn's night abode',[74] considered himself to be melancholic; he wrote to the poet Giovanni Cavalcanti, a fellow member of the Florentine Academy, 'Saturn seems to have impressed the seal of melancholy on me from the beginning.'[75] The reinvention of his own affliction began with his interest in Plato's description of four kinds of madness in the *Phaedrus*, the first two being the 'prophetic' madness of oracles and madness as a relief-giving expiation of ancestral guilt. The third is what we call the 'divine madness' or 'frenzy' that is the source of poetic inspiration: 'If anyone comes to the gates of poetry and expects to become an adequate poet by acquiring expert knowledge of the subject without the Muses' madness, he will fail, and his self-controlled verses will be eclipsed by the poetry of men who have been driven out of their minds.'[76] Fourth is the divine madness that comes from seeing something or someone beautiful, leading to appreciation of a higher beauty: when one 'sees the beauty we have down here and is reminded of true beauty, then he takes wing and flutters in his eagerness to rise up, but is unable to do so; and he gazes aloft, like a bird, paying no attention to what is down below – and that is what brings on him the charge that he has gone mad'.[77]

There is nothing about melancholy here, but Ficino was also familiar with the *Problems*, a book always included amongst Aristotle's works, although most scholars attribute it to his 'school', rather than Aristotle himself. *Problem 30* begins with the rhetorical question, 'Why is it that all those who have become eminent in philosophy or politics or poetry or the arts are clearly of an atrabilious temperament?'[78] In *De vita triplici* (*Three Books on Life*), Ficino tied the Platonic notion of divine frenzy with this Aristotelian idea of the gifted melancholic, and thus he 'gave shape to the idea of the melancholy man of genius and revealed it to the rest of Europe – in particular, to the great Englishmen of the sixteenth and seventeenth centuries'.[79] Being the son of a physician, Ficino was thoroughly familiar with Galen's humoral medicine, and so was able to incorporate everything into his conception of melancholy: black bile, made of the element that penetrates to the Earth's core, encourages 'deep' thoughts, while Saturn, the highest planet (located in the sphere just below that of the fixed stars in the Ptolemaic universe) encourages 'high' ones.[80]

Chapman deserves great credit for bringing much of this together and managing to explore many forms of melancholy in one character and one scene, the visit by nearly everyone in the play to Labervele's house 'to see the humour' (7.39–40) of his son Dowsecer in action. Most regard Dowsecer as some sort of novelty act, whose madness will prove an entertaining curiosity, but the unhappy King, feeling 'quagmired in philosophy', suspects that Dowsecer 'is nothing lunatic as men suppose, but hateth company and worldly trash', and might teach him how to 'break affection' and quiet his own passions (7.12–19).

A sword, hose, codpiece, and picture of a woman – symbolic accoutrements of the life that Dowsecer has rejected – are placed in the hope that the sight of these objects will alleviate his melancholy. With the onlookers hidden, Dowsecer enters meditating upon the *Tusculan Disputations* of Cicero, extolling the virtues of the stoical, contemplative life – although he suspects 'Mark Cicero', an ambitious lawyer, of hypocrisy – and compares the present, corrupt age with a golden age of the past. Upon seeing the weapon and apparel, he takes on the role of a genuine malcontent denouncing a false one, scorning the latter's unearned superior attitude and his excesses in fashion (7.65–136). The woman's picture inspires a very interesting response: instead of the standard rejection of excessive 'painting' (cosmetics), Dowsecer defends their use (see Appendix, p. 164). Lastly, to make his withdrawal from society complete, Dowsecer denies, to his own father, the value of marriage and children.

As Oscar James Campbell notes in a 1935 article, there is 'extravagant bitterness' and 'penetrating wisdom' in Dowsecer's speeches.[81] Here Chapman offers some of his best comic writing, in that we cannot be sure if it is meant to be comic at all. I believe he used the same approach in *Ovid's Banquet of Sense*, a poem that has been subject to widely different interpretations since the 1960s. To some, it is a celebration of sensual love and a tribute to the power of beauty; others see a warning against Ovidian sensuality, possibly as a response to Shakespeare's *Venus and Adonis*.[82] To these two interpretations we might add a third: both views are correct, and Chapman intended that this be so. The ambiguity of *Ovid's Banquet* welcomes either reading, which accounts for much

of its charm – it is hard to take Ovid's delight in the sight of
Corynna's breasts seriously when he names them 'Cupid's Alps',
yet we know this dalliance will lead to his banishment. However,
the experience also inspires his composition of the mighty *Amores*:
although 'Ovid sold his freedom for a look', he might reply that
it was worth it – for every serious note, there is a comic counter-
point, and vice versa.

Dowsecer's vehement denunciation of society is delivered in an
elaborate imagery that might be acceptable from Bussy D'Ambois
or Charles, Duke of Byron, but seems absurdly pretentious in a
young scholar with no apparent experience of the world. Yet the
attitudes expressed are totally admirable: in some of the greatest
comic works – *In Praise of Folly*, *Volpone*, *Huckleberry Finn* – noble
sentiments are offered seriously, but simultaneously parodied, given
the character or diction of those offering them.

Countess Moren asks if Dowsecer is actually mad, but the King
sees the inspired melancholic of Ficino, 'This is no humour, this is
but perfect judgement...a holy fury, not a frenzy' (7.88, 200).
Meanwhile, Martia has fallen in love with him:

> Oh, were all men such,
> Men were no men but gods, this earth a heaven.
>   (7.90–1)

The crucial moment occurs when Dowsecer notices Martia:

> What have I seen? How am I burnt to dust
> With a new sun, and made a novel phoenix!
>   (7.209–10)

As interesting (and highly readable) as Ficino's *Three Books on
Life* are, their significance is minor compared with his *De amore*, a
re-creation of Plato's *Symposium*. I have noted how the *Phaedrus*
describes the divine madness initiated by seeing a beautiful object:
'the best and noblest of all the forms that possession by god can
take...when someone who loves beautiful boys is touched by this
madness he is called a lover'.[83] This is the main topic of discussion
at the *Symposium* ('banquet' or 'drinking party'), wherein Socrates
tells how Diotima instructed him in the philosophy of love, which
starts with the love of (someone else's) beautiful body. From there,
the lover moves up the scale to love of the ideal, higher beauty, 'and
gazing upon this, he gives birth to many gloriously beautiful ideas
and theories, in unstinting love of wisdom'.[84]

Ficino adopts Plato's dialogic form, indeed he claims that *De amore* is an account of his own symposium held in honour of Plato's birthday. It is a commentary, not a direct translation, but 'Tomasso Benci's' speech is quite close to that of 'Socrates'; it also incorporates Galen's eye-beams:

> The appearance of a man, which because of an interior goodness graciously given him by God, is beautiful to see, frequently shoots a ray of his splendor, through the eyes of those looking at him, into their souls. Drawn by this spark like a fish on a hook, the souls should hasten towards the one who is attracting them. This attraction, which is love, since it derives from the beautiful, good and happy, and is attracted to the same things, we do not hesitate to call Goodness, Beauty, Blessedness, and a God.[85]

De amore was instrumental in spreading 'the gospel of Platonic love throughout Europe',[86] although that gospel underwent many changes along the way (the merging of Plato's homoerotic desire into a wider programme of Platonic and courtly love is a complex topic, and outside the scope of this study). Just as Ficino restated and reinterpreted Plato, he was in turn restated and reinterpreted by others, from Castiglione in *The Courtier* to Spenser in the *Four Hymns*, informing English poetry to the Romantics and beyond.[87]

Dowsecer's reaction to Martia's beauty,

> O divine aspect,
> The excellent disposer of the mind,
> Shines in thy beauty, and thou hast not changed
> My soul to sense but sense unto my soul;
> And I desire thy pure society
> But even as angels do. To angels, fly!
>
> (7.213–18)

recalls, in its Platonic purity, the eighth of Spenser's *Amoretti*:

> Through your bright beams doth not the blinded guest,
> shoot out his darts to base affections wound;
> but angels come to lead frail minds to rest
> in chaste desires on heavenly beauty bound.
>
> (5–8)

When he exits, we might assume that Dowsecer will adopt the role of a Sir Philip Sidney, writing sonnets to the unattainable Stella. Ficino understands, however, that this highest level of love is not always attainable:

Love, as we have said, has its origin in sight. Sight is halfway between thought and touch, and hence the soul of the lover is always distracted and tossed backwards and forwards. Sometimes a desire for physical embrace arises, and sometimes a desire for chaste heavenly beauty; first the one and then the other conquers and leads.[88]

For Dowsecer to be content with the 'desire for physical embrace' is one of the most endearing things about him. When we next see him, he is intent on getting Martia away from the King and Count Moren; he then displays a different kind of self-awareness, admitting that falling for Martia has led him to realise that his former melancholy was an affectation:

> The fire of love which she hath kindled in me,
> Being greater than my heat of vanity,
> Hath quite expelled [it.]
>
> (13.56–8)

Dowsecer's conversion from a stoical denial of passion to a neo-Platonist embrace of love is somewhat ironic in that Chapman, as N. S. Brooke has observed, seemed to move in the opposite direction over his long literary career. The influence of Ficino is pervasive in *The Shadow of Night*, *Ovid's Banquet of Sense*, and the early comedies; while not disappearing, it would eventually give way to the stoic ideals found in *Bussy d'Ambois*, *The Revenge of Bussy D'Ambois*, and the two *Byron* plays.[89]

The change in Dowsecer is also highly comic in that it occurs within the space of ten lines, between his being struck by Martia's eye-beams and racing off stage to pursue a new life. Here, Chapman anticipates what has been rightly called 'comedy's greatest era': the great masterpieces of Buster Keaton and Charlie Chaplin were photographed at about eighteen frames per second, but always projected at approximately twenty-four. As Walter Kerr has written with wonderful appreciation, 'Keaton's celebrated stop-on-a dime reversals of direction and Chaplin's even more celebrated one-foot skid for a corner turn' would lose, at normal speed, their 'capacity to make us laugh with a gasp'.[90] Dowsecer's philosophical 'reversal of direction', a term associated with tragedy, is similar in its delightful quickness.

A COMEDY OF MANNERS

'I don't like your manner', Kingsley said in a voice you could have cracked a Brazil nut on. 'That's all right', I said, 'I'm not selling it'. (Raymond Chandler, *The Lady in the Lake*)

Although melancholy is the only Hippocratic humour to identify a
common character type in literature directly, Dowsecer is not the
play's only 'humorous' character. The jealousy of Labervele, Countess Moren, and the Queen, Foyes's determination to choose a
husband for his 'singular' daughter, Florilla's cold sexlessness that
melts as soon as an attractive lover presents himself – these characters represent traits as old as comedy itself, frequently appearing as
they do in Menander, Plautus, and Terence. They are also 'humorous', first in the Jonsonian sense of an overriding temperament or
idée fixe, and second in the way their underlying psychology is
understood. We notice this in the play's first speech, when Labervele
expresses his absolutely justified fear that, should Florilla see a
man 'fit to her humour' (normal temperament of a sensuous young
woman), her puritanism will evaporate and she will 'yield unto the
motion of her blood' (1.18, 20).

To introduce the play's other humours, let us return once more
to Asper in *Every Man Out*. In the final section of his speech, he
goes on to say what humour, in his opinion, is *not*:

> But that a rook, in wearing a pied feather,
> The cable hatband, or the three-piled ruff,
> A yard of shoe tie, or the Switzer's knot
> On his French garters, should affect a humour,
> O, 'tis more than most ridiculous!
>
> (Ind. 108–12)

In pointedly arguing that elaborate fashions, and by implication all
social pretensions, are not humours, Jonson (assuming Asper speaks
for him) displays what Gail Kern Paster nicely calls a 'sense of the
alarming downward mobility or diminution of the term'.[91] He is also
being more than slightly disingenuous. As Henry L. Snuggs argues
in a 1947 article, 'eccentricity and social affectation...far outnum-
ber the psychological humours' in Jonson's plays.[92] We find it in the
social-climbing pretensions of Stephano and Matheo (*F*: Stephen
and Matthew) of *Every Man In*, Fallace and Fungoso of *Every Man
Out*, the former a 'proud mincing peat', the latter someone who
'follows the fashion afar off like a spy' (Char. 55, 67–8), and in the
sublimely ridiculous affectations of just about everyone in *Cynthia's
Revels*. Indeed, the Palinode to that play provides a summary list of
the characters' 'affected humours...swaggering humours' and 'sim-
pering humours' (Pal. 2, 7, 11), concluding with the fervent prayer,
from 'all self-loving humours, good Mercury defend us' (Pal. 33–4).

Sincere or not in his earlier protestations, by 1610, when he wrote the Prologue to *The Alchemist*, Jonson appears to have surrendered:

Our scene is London, 'cause we would make known,
No country's mirth is better than our own.
No clime breeds better matter, for your whore
Bawd, squire, impostor, many persons more,
Whose manners, now called humours, feed the stage.
(Prol. 5–9)

In admitting that the distinction between the comedy of humours and the comedy of manners no longer exists, if it ever did, Jonson pays something of a tribute to Chapman; the scene of *An Humorous Day's Mirth* is not explicitly London, but the mirth is provided by characters whose 'manners' are recognisably 'our own'.

The first of these whom we meet is the young gallant Blanuel, who has an odd 'manner of taking acquaintance': whatever salutation is offered, he replies with exactly the same words, 'so long as the complements of a gentleman last, he is your complete ape' (2.24–5, 41–2). He also assumes the signature arms-folded pose of the malcontent, an amusing portrait that unfortunately is forgotten when he next appears (see below, pp. 34–5).

Blanuel serves as prelude to Labesha, the first fully developed gull to walk the English stage, a worthy predecessor to Shakespeare's Sir Andrew Aguecheek and his rival in utter ridiculousness. Some commentators believe Jonson borrowed directly from Chapman, using Labesha as a model for both Stephano and Matheo of *Every Man In*; there might be some truth in this, although Jonson was more than able to draw the type independently, from the streets of London or from other satiric portraits already in circulation.[93]

The idea of the witless gull goes as far back as the satires of Horace, Lucian, and Juvenal, but the new English model is something different. He poses as a sophisticated gallant, and often, like Sir Andrew, he woos a beautiful woman. He also wears the latest fashion, including an expensive rapier although he cannot fence, plagiarises clever oaths and sayings, and, as Labesha shows in Scene 5, is easily swayed by the most obvious flattery: 'Nay, gentlemen, look what a piercing eye he hath...Nay, look what a nose he hath...Nay, look what a handsome man he is! O nature, nature, thou never mad'st man of so pure a feature' (5.147–52). Of course, to be melancholy was also *de rigueur*: Dowsecer's abandonment of melancholy is simultaneous with Labesha's embracing it, providing us with one of the play's most hilarious moments.

Upon hearing that Martia has rejected him, Labesha grows 'marvellous malcontent' and takes 'on him the humour of the young lord Dowsecer' (10.20–4). Instead of Cicero, his text is *The Book of Burnel the Ass*; the sword, hose, and codpiece that were to 'cure' Dowsecer make way for spice-cake and cream, Labesha's favourite dish. After consuming it, he promises to hang himself, but is easily persuaded to change his mind and forget Martia by the King's promise, 'I'll get thee a wife worth fifteen of her' (13.129–30).

As splendid as Chapman's portrait of the 'fair and manly lord Monsieur Labesha' (5.191–2) is, Florilla's puritanism easily wins the prize as the most enjoyable humour in the play. Her attitude of religious severity is calculated, and there is no sense at all of sincere conviction to it; she is content to have her old husband believe she is 'too religious in the purest sort' (1.14) in order for her to have little to do with him while she waits for something better. Nobody except Labervele would be surprised to see 'her pureness...yield so soon to courses of temptations' (4.70–1).

Florilla is the English theatre's first character to be given the description 'puritan'; the stereotype, and to some degree the very idea of puritan itself, begins with her. Patrick Collinson notes that throughout the 1580s and 1590s, 'puritan' and its cognate words rarely appeared in the thousands of pages of polemical works written against those whom we now call puritans; the word was almost totally confined to plays and popular literature as an abusive term that covered a range of religious and social attitudes, from wanting to ban maypole-dancing to denouncing the word 'Christmas' as a papist abomination.[94] As far as English drama is concerned, 'puritan' was spoken only in Lyly's *The Woman in the Moon* (once) and Marlowe's *Massacre at Paris* (twice) before it was given life by Chapman and then Jonson.[95]

There were some, but not many, precedents in other forms of literature. They go back to the infamous Marprelate controversy, a cultural phenomenon that began with 'a series of pseudonymous and satirical pamphlets, seven in all, targeted principally at the bishops and professing to contain the utterances of one Martin Marprelate, [appearing] from a clandestine and migratory press between October 1588 and June 1589'.[96] The brilliant attacks of 'Martin' (his, or more likely their, identity has never been established) gave rise to a counter-attack by a number of writers hired to produce anti-Martinist tracts, including Greene, Lyly, and Nashe.[97] The Martinist and anti-Martinist pamphlets, however, were concerned mostly with the powers and duties of the clergy and with ecclesiastical government in general, along with some discussion of church doctrine; there was little satire against, or defence of, the day-to-day social behaviour of the puritan.[98]

In his 1954 book *Anti-Puritan Satire, 1572–1642*, William P. Holden sets out four character traits that came to receive the most attention. The first, that puritan extremists were bent on 'religious, social, and political revolution',[99] does not enter into our discussion, but the other three do: their insistence on the literal word of the Bible, their precisianism (adhering strictly to religious rules in everything they do), and their hypocrisy.[100]

Florilla's eagerness to quote scripture is matched only by her apparent ignorance of it; either she makes up her own quotations, or paraphrases so broadly that what she says may sound biblical, but cannot be identified with any confidence. Her precisianism is delightful, apparent upon her first entrance: realising she has dressed too warmly for the day, Florilla cannot decide whether or not to change, since the time it would take might be better spent in prayer or charitable deeds (4.1–7). She then worries about having sinned in picking up the jewels that, according to Labervele, either heaven or fairies have left for her, because (1) heaven would never approve of vain things such as jewellery, (2) fairies do not exist, having been driven away by the arrival of Christianity, and (3) the strength required to bend over

> Might have been used to take a poor soul up
> In the highway.

(4.28–9).

The main emphasis, not only for Florilla but all stage puritans who follow her, is on hypocrisy. As Collinson writes, they are

> ostensibly pious but in truth hypocritical, to the extent that 'puritan' came to be synonymous with hypocrisy. Under a cloak of specious religiosity, the puritan is three things: covetous, seditious and randy.[101]

For the puritan wife, 'randy' obviously takes precedence, and the eagerness with which Florilla agrees to have Catalian be her chaplain before Lemot arrives with a proposal to 'prove' her chastity – indeed the way she helps Labervele talk himself into allowing it and then guides Lemot through the process – these incidents offer some of the play's most humorous (in the modern sense) sequences.

Along with being, at the time, a unique character, Florilla is exceptional for the positively Brechtian cheerfulness and adaptability in everything she does. Her soliloquies, like those of a Brecht hero, seem to be directed right at us rather than internalised thinking aloud (especially effective in the relatively intimate Rose),[102] and, when her hoped-for adulterous liaison with Lemot turns into a disaster, she brazenly returns to her former self, reminding us,

> Surely the world is full of vanity.
> A woman must take heed she do not hear
> A lewd man speak.
>
> (13.88–90)

Florilla generously forgives Labervele for suspecting her of what she actually did, providing he promises never to be suspicious again, 'for what love is there, where there is no trust?' (13.114), and in a final whispered conversation with Lemot, she virtually dares him to reveal the truth with a pious 'Cursed be he that maketh debate 'twixt man and wife'. In dumbfounded admiration, Lemot can only promise, 'You have sealed up my lips' (13.140–2); we get the impression that she will soon find some other means to don 'brave attire' and indulge her 'light desires' (6.59, 61) with someone other than her husband. 'The character of Florilla', as Parrott remarks, 'is Chapman's masterpiece in this play'.[103]

Chapman gives 'the lady Martia' less to do than the 'fair countess Florilla' (8.293–4), but, for the first half of the play at least, she is a charmingly untraditional version of the traditional ingénue, burdened by her father with an idiotic suitor. She appears quite untroubled by Labesha and treats him with an amused tolerance, which carries over into her innuendo-filled conversation (including Latin puns) with Lemot (5.68–85), wherein she acquits herself extremely well. Like the King, she immediately sees what lies behind Dowsecer's melancholic pose; the 'love at first sight' aspect is conventional of course, although it seems to have more to do with Dowsecer's words than his appearance.

Martia resembles Florilla in that she happily accepts whatever the day might bring, unruffled at being ordered out of Countess Moren's house, and accompanying Florilla to the ordinary when she is supposed to be fasting with her at home. We cannot say too much about Martia after that. Fearing exposure, she flees the ordinary with Moren (9.13–14), but is captured (off stage) and brought back; we next see her there with the King. How and when she became Dowsecer's 'love, thought lost' (13.59–60), now regained, is not explained – she is betrothed to Dowsecer without ever exchanging a word with him – in this instance the explanation may lie in some text that is missing from the quarto (see 13.56–8 n.).

The task of encouraging everyone's humours, for our and his own amusement, falls to Lemot; everything that happens this day (with the exception of Dowsecer and Martia falling in love) is the result of his efforts. He is in nine of thirteen scenes, six of them (4–9) without a break. In defending *The Blind Beggar of Alexandria* against F. E. Schelling's charge that it is 'absurd and worthless', Thomas Mark Grant makes the interesting point that judging the play on the basis of the text alone is like judging a Marx Brothers film from reading the screenplay.[104] The same applies to our play, perhaps more so, in that Lemot is in so many respects an early model for Groucho. As Otis B. Driftwood in *A Night at the Opera* or Hugo Z. Hackenbush in *A Day at the Races* (titles oddly similar to *An Humorous Day's Mirth*), Groucho uses words as assault weapons to deflate the ridiculous humours of others – the haughty opera singer Rodolfo Lasparri, the society matron Mrs Claypool – indeed, could one ask for a better Countess Moren than Groucho's constant companion, Margaret Dumont?

Lemot is also akin to the intriguing slave of the Roman comedy,[105] although the differences, beyond the obvious one of class, are more important than the similarities. His tricks are at the behest of no one but himself; he is not trying to get out from some scrape or gain his freedom. Lemot's reputation, according to Labervele, is that of a rake and seducer, 'whom no man sees to enter his house but he locks up his wife, his children and his maids' (4.137–9), but he belies this characterisation; his only apparent appetite is for laughter, and he feeds this appetite through the power of speech – as he reminds us, his name 'signifies "word"' (5.67).

With Florilla's eager assistance, Lemot easily persuades Labervele that she should be subject to his proof, during which he informs her, with impeccable logic, 'madam, if you will worthily prove your constancy to your husband, you must put on rich apparel, fare daintily, hear music, read sonnets, be continually courted, kiss, dance, feast, revel all night amongst gallants' (4.230–4). This is worthy of Joseph Surface's attempt to seduce Lady Teazle in *School for Scandal*, but then, Joseph really *wants* to seduce Lady Teazle.

Later, when Florilla is ready and eager to surrender to Lemot, he scornfully sends her back to her husband; apart from biting her finger (9.46), he does her no harm. Most tellingly, he does not expose her as a fraud, even though Florilla, unlike Lady Teazle, has no intention of confessing to anything. Nor does Lemot reveal exactly what the King and Moren have been up to, for that would be much too easy – by bringing everyone to the ordinary, he gives himself the opportunity to test his skills even further, convincing the Queen that what actually happened is the direct opposite of what he told her moments ago. He deliberately unmasks the terrified Moren, disguised as a torchbearer for the lottery, and tells the Countess that he brought her to Verone's only because it would be wrong that she and her husband be apart for such a long time.

Lemot advises Florilla, 'repent, amend your life' (9.71–2), but he has no real interest in reforming anyone, indeed, he is actively opposed to it. Unlike Macilente of *Every Man Out*, who brings the 'good doting citizen' (Char. 44) Deliro to the Mitre to shock him out of his humour, Lemot makes sure Labervele will remain exactly as he is, as will the King and Queen, the Count and Countess. Otherwise, today will be the last day Lemot spends with 'humorous acquaintance' (2.10), leaving him with nothing to do the next time 'the sky hangs full of humour' (2.3).

FROM PAGE TO STAGE

An Humorous Day's Mirth has no stage history, and still awaits a modern revival; one of the aims of this edition is to show that, in the hands of a talented cast, it could provide a very humorous night's mirth in the theatre. The main plot lines of Labervele and Florilla, Labesha's pursuit of Martia, the philandering King, Moren, their jealous wives, and the progress of Dowsecer's melancholy can be hard to follow as one reads the text, but would be much clearer when communicated by actors, identified by voice and appearance rather than just a name. Lemot also provides assistance by often announcing beforehand what he is going to do (another Brechtian element to the play).

What problems there are reside chiefly in the discontinuities involving secondary characters. Lemot's plan to spend the day humorously starts well, with a display of Blanuel's odd manner of repeating *verbatim* whatever is said to him, but Blanuel is a different and inconsequential character in his subsequent appearances, just another gallant who displays no affected behaviour. In Scene 5, at Moren's house, he participates in drawing Labesha away from Martia; his arrival at Verone's ordinary is delayed because he was arrested at a local brothel and needed to arrange his release from prison. The amount of time it would take for this to happen (along with Catalian finding time for a game of tennis between Scenes 7 and 8) is not an issue, since off-stage time is always extremely fluid in plays of this period, but the inconsistency of character is too obvious to be ignored. Since Blanuel (after Scene 2) and the other young men are relatively interchangeable, an inventive director might be able to get a good effect by reassigning subsequent speeches and keeping Blanuel as a silent, rather ghostly presence, retiring 'himself to a chimney or a wall, standing, folding his arms thus' (2.45–6).

Colinet also changes: Lemot has him admit that he is 'mightily in love with lovely Martia, daughter to old Foyes' (2.70–1), but his status as a rival to Labesha never develops. When he arrives at Foyes's house to draw Martia away with an invitation from Countess Moren, he does not try to speak with her; a brief attempt in Scene 5 is quickly interrupted by Lemot, who is supposed to be supporting his cause. It is he who suggests that everyone repair to Labervele's to see Dowsecer, but this is another inconsistency: owing to a vague entry direction (7.0 SD), we cannot be sure if he arrives there, and, if he does, he is mute for the entire scene.

Taking Colinet out of Scene 7 would enable the actor to double as innkeeper Verone or his servant Jaques, although we must be very hesitant before thinking that this would have been a factor in writing the play. The idea that Elizabethan dramatists wrote with an exact number of actors in mind, therefore accounting for the seemingly early disappearance of a character to allow for a new one, represents *post hoc propter hoc* reasoning, and does not bear much scrutiny. Without doubling, *An Humorous Day's Mirth* requires fifteen men, five women, and a boy, or, in Elizabethan terms, fifteen men and six boys – not a large cast for an Admiral's play.

If we assume that the play's scenes were written in the order they appear in the text, then Chapman might have felt that he was running out of ideas during Scene 5, for the plot changes direction rather suddenly as that sequence draws to a close. The suggestion, 'Come gentlemen, let's go wait upon the King, and see the humour of the young lord Dowsecer', and Lemot's telling us, 'this wench Martia hath happy stars reigned at the disposition of her beauty, for the King himself doth mightily dote on her' (5.205–7), seem to come from nowhere.

By bringing Dowsecer into the play for a detailed look at melancholy, along with having the King lust after Martia, allowing for a second jealous wife, Chapman makes Blanuel's humour and Colinet's attachment to Martia redundant. For a playwright to add or change plot elements as he goes along is hardly unusual, and one expects that adjustments to earlier scenes would be made in the process of rehearsal, but, as is often seen in early modern texts, those adjustments do not always make their way to the printer.

Another possibility is that the play is a collaborative effort, and the printer's copy represents an early bringing together of the different writers' assignments. As Carol Chillington Rutter observes, collaboration was standard practice at the Rose, and Chapman participated: in 1598 Henslowe made a payment of £4 for a 'play book & ii acts of a tragedy of Benjamin's plot', Benjamin ('bengemen' in the original) being, of course, Ben Jonson.[106] Later, he would join with Jonson and Marston to write the celebrated *Eastward Ho*. That the quarto of *An Humorous Day's Mirth* names 'G. C.' as sole author means little, but the relative consistency of prose and verse style, including the aforementioned obscurity, would argue against a joint effort, so I would doubt that this play represents one.

Chapman exploits the conventions of the Elizabethan stage very cleverly in this play. As mentioned above, comedy works best at a rapid pace; the ease and swiftness with which the locale changes adds to that effect – not only between scenes, as we would expect, but within them. Scene 8 goes, delightfully, from Verone's to Countess Moren's house and back again within a few moments, while Scene 13 appears to start outside Verone's ordinary, and then seamlessly moves indoors without the stage clearing or any interruption in the action. Overall, the setting is not a garden or an ordinary, but simply 'the stage'.

THE TEXT

An Humorous Day's Mirth is not found in the Stationers' Register, and the quarto of 1599, published about two years after the play was first performed, is the only early edition. The play having no record of performance after its initial run at the Rose would have to be due, at least in part, to the very poor quality of this text, filled with errors and corruptions. That it is so poor is surprising, as one would expect a better effort from Valentine Simmes, the normally reliable printer who provided very good texts of a number of Shakespearean quartos, including three competent editions of *Richard II* in 1597–98.[107]

The quarto's worst feature for the editor is the printing of the entire play in prose, including even the rhymed posies Labervele leaves for Florilla (sig. A2r) and the ditty, also in rhyme, the Boy recites to introduce the lottery (sig. G4r); the only exceptions are three couplets in the posies accompanying the prizes (sig. H1r). But even a cursory reading reveals, in addition to rhymes, numerous speeches in clear, metrical verse; others could be either verse or prose, or a combination of the two. *An Humorous Day's Mirth* is not the only text of this era to present such a problem, one that is inherent in the nature of dramatic manuscripts, where the key signature of verse, a capital letter at the start of a line, was rarely used, while the 'justified right' margin of prose is impossible when using pen and paper.[108] Once drama moved away from rhyme, the compositors had extra work to do; the job required some sense of what blank verse sounded like, so perhaps we should be surprised at how often they got it right rather than how often they erred, or as might have happened on this occasion, gave up. In such instances, modern editors face a particularly daunting task, since we are required to choose either verse or prose, while in practice there is not always a clear division – blank verse is so flexible that it provides an infinitely variable range of diction, creating a large middle ground where no real distinction can, or need, be made.

Since the editing of early dramatic texts began, different approaches have been taken. A traditional one, as described by Stephen Orgel, is to assume that verse is always better than prose, and therefore to print as verse anything that looks remotely like it.[109] This is the least satisfactory alternative; English is so heavily iambic that almost any passage can be turned into verse with a little effort, and often the result is to turn elegant, rhythmic prose into bad, choppy verse. It can also lead the editor down a dangerous garden path – if we decide a passage is in verse, we must account for seriously irregular lines, and assume that the text is corrupt in some way. One must be especially wary of this with Chapman, since what appears to be a corruption might be, to quote Stanley Wells, only another 'typically cloudy effusion' for which Chapman is known.[110] On the other hand, neither will printing everything in prose do; any well trained actor knows that meaning is often derived from keys to stresses and pauses inherent in the verse structure, while prose, written in sentences rather than lines, is a different matter.

R. H. Shepherd, in his second edition (1874), was the first to tackle the problem, setting approximately 140 lines in verse. Parrott (1914) saw verse more frequently, adding another 460 lines. Shepherd provides no commentary explaining his choices, but Parrott notes the principles behind his selections:

> It seems to have been Chapman's intention to employ verse for the high places of the drama, the soliloquy with which play opens, the rhapsodies of Dowsecer, and the decisive interview between Lemot and Florilla. Prose is employed in the more familiar passages and in the scenes of lively action.[111]

This comment has an element of circularity to it: are they in verse because they are 'high places', or 'high places' because they are in verse? Yet Parrott is most helpful in suggesting that the answer may be found in dramatic context rather than just looking for iambic pentameter. I agree that Chapman does employ a method, and his versification is not arbitrary; characters usually speak in verse when they are 'humorous', e.g. Dowsecer when he is being melancholy, Labervele or Foyes jealous, Florilla puritanical, the King 'philosophical', or Labesha trying to impress others with his intelligence and social graces. They and others also use verse when indulging another's humour, e.g. Labervele and Lemot when confronted with Florilla's piety, or Lemot when telling the Queen tall tales to make her jealous.

While not a rigid rule, the pattern is sufficiently visible to use as a guiding principle in editing the text. As a result, this edition contains 495 lines of blank verse, about one-fourth of the play. A number of lines scan perfectly well, but are left as prose, since I reject the aforementioned policy of always deciding in favour of verse wherever one might find it.

Nearly as troubling as printing everything in prose is the confusion caused by the abbreviation of speech headings. Sometimes the speaker can be identified from the context, but often cannot: Co. might stand for Colinet, Count, or Countess; C. could be any of those or Catalian; La. and Lab. could mean Labervele, Labesha, or Lavel, and, since Labesha is sometimes shortened to 'Besha', Be. could be either Labesha or Berger. The similarity of Mor. and Mar. also gave the compositor no end of trouble: six of Moren's lines have the heading 'Mar.' or 'Ma.', and one of Martia's 'Mo.'.[112]

Stage directions present difficulties that are interesting and sometimes vexing. One expects to find missing or inconsistent entry and
exit directions; these are numerous but not especially troubling, but
vague directions such as *Enter the King with all the Lords* (sig. C4v),
Enter the King and another (sig. F1v), and *Enter the Queene, Lemot,
and all the rest of the lordes* (sig. F3v) make it hard to know who is
supposed to be on stage, or when.

It was once customary for an editor to use the nature of speech
headings, stage directions, and other elements of the text to place
the printer's copy into one of a limited number of categories, such
as foul papers, fair copy, or playhouse copy. These labels, as Paul
Werstine has shown, are not fully based on genuine historical prem-
ises, and they do not account for the many other ways a play might
made its way to the printer.[113] I have already noted that the quarto
text probably differs from the play as first performed in a number
of ways, but further categorisation is not warranted.

Fifteen copies of the quarto are known to exist, and many corrections were made during the press run, resulting in a great number
of variants. W. W. Greg inspected four quartos for his Malone
Society reprint of 1937; I have relied on Akihiro Yamada's brilliantly
thorough collation of fourteen copies done in 1967, and published
in *Shakespeare Studies* (Japan).[114] Allan Holaday independently
viewed ten copies for his edition, published in 1970, including the
one held at Yale University, which Yamada does not record having
seen. Although the changes are numerous, nearly all show minor
revisions in spelling or punctuation; very few have any affect on
meaning.[115]

An interesting anomaly is exclusive to only one quarto, found in
the British Library.[116] For reasons never satisfactorily explained,
sheet H, comprising the last three pages, had to be completely reset.
Only a different font requiring a slightly wider measure makes this
noticeable; resetting seems to have been done with reference to
pages already printed rather than original copy, and there are only
two substantive variants (collation 13.270 n., 325 n.). Both versions
of sheet H are in Greg's facsimile edition, the reset one as an
appendix.

CONCLUSION

Many readers will be familiar with Horace's advice from *The Art of
Poetry*,

The aim of the poet is either to benefit or to please
or to say what is both enjoyable and of service.

The context is easily overlooked – Horace is not only talking about what constitutes the best writing, but also what will draw an audience:

The senior bloc refuses plays which haven't a message:
the haughty young bloods curl their nostrils at anything dry;
Everyone votes for the man who mixes wholesome and sweet.[117]

Audience demographics may have changed since Horace's day but his advice remains sound, and overall Chapman seems to have followed it. He has produced a comedy that most assuredly benefits and pleases, one that would be as likely to do so in the twenty-first century as in the sixteenth. There is much benefit in what we learn of the way people of his time understood the workings of the human mind, what people perceive and do not perceive of the outside world, and how the never-ending battle between reason and emotion is best fought. If the play can be said to have a 'message', we benefit there as well: even the silliest behaviour, provided it does no real harm, is not to be condemned or judged.

The pleasure comes from a story, in spite of its inconsistencies and false starts, that is credible and well-constructed, and from some brilliantly drawn characters who provide more than a few moments of comedy that may be compared favourably with anything in Jonson or Molière.

Nevertheless, George Chapman, like the comedian Rodney Dangerfield, 'just can't get no respect'. To Swinburne, *An Humorous Day's Mirth* is

a crude and coarse sample of workmanship. The characters are a confused crowd of rough sketches, whose thin outlines and faint colours are huddled together on a ragged canvas without order or proportion. There is some promise of humour in the part of a Puritan adulteress, but it comes to little or nothing; and the comedy rather collapses in a tangle of incongruous imbecilities and incoherent indecencies.[118]

James Russell Lowell sees all of Chapman's comedies as 'formless and coarse'; M. C. Bradbrook dismisses Chapman with the comment, 'his chief contribution to the drama seems to have lain in the provision of models for better men', and Paul V. Kreider decries his 'almost complete lack of originality'.[119] This last observation is quite extraordinary, since Kreider's book is entitled *Elizabethan Comic*

Character Conventions; in it he relies on Chapman for nearly all his examples, conveniently ignoring the fact that usually Chapman was not following conventions but creating them.

Admittedly, the play is uneven; some of it appears to be hastily written and fails to come off. Lemot's stunt of getting each gallant to deliver whatever proverbial cliché he chooses for him is contrived and not terribly funny (8.208–52), and the two new characters added for Scene 8, Rowley and Berger, seem purely functional. But bringing the various intrigues together to play themselves out at Verone's is an inspired choice, as it also gives us a look at the normal goings on of that establishment, the fights and love affairs amongst the staff, and a brief display of social rituals undertaken by the clientele. The lottery that closes the play is also an excellent device: the fortunes of the major characters are happily resolved, with everyone, even Labesha, walking away pleased. Best of all, the sequence, indeed the entire play, is without a hint of moralising or 'feel-good' sentimentality.

Traditionally, students of the Elizabethan theatre have tended to agree with Hamlet, assuming that public taste of the time was rather low, with second-rate plays, full 'of nothing but inexplicable dumb shows and noise' (3.2.11–12) drawing great crowds, while the best works went unappreciated. However, modern productions such as Deborah Warner's *Titus Andronicus* or Terry Hands's *Tamburlaine*, both plays Rose hits in the 1590s, offer the counter-argument that a good many Elizabethans knew quality when they saw it. Readers of this edition and, I hope, spectators at some future performance, are free to decide for themselves whether or not *An Humorous Day's Mirth* is as good a play as the theatregoers of 1597 seemed to think.

NOTES

1 England was still operating under the Julian calendar at this time; for the rest of Europe the date was 13 March.
2 R. A. Foakes, ed., *Henslowe's Diary*, 2nd ed., Cambridge, 2002, pp. 56–7.
3 Foakes, p. xxxi.
4 Andrew Gurr, *The Shakespearian Playing Companies*, Oxford, 1996, p. 240.
5 Foakes, pp. 58–60.
6 Thomas Marc Parrott, ed., *The Plays of George Chapman: The Comedies*, 2 vols [sequentially paginated], New York, 1961, pp. 673–4; Martin Wiggins, *Shakespeare and the Drama of His Time*, Oxford, 2000, p. 67.

7 S. P. Ceresano, 'Edward Alleyn's "Retirement"', *Medieval and Renaissance Drama in England* 10 (1998): 98, 104.

8 Gurr, *The Shakespeare Company, 1594–1612*, Cambridge, 2004, p. 134; *Shakespearian Playing Companies*, p. 240.

9 See Peter Thomson, *Shakespeare's Theatre*, London, 1983, p. 4; Foakes, pp. 59–60; Gurr, *Shakespearian Playing Companies*, p. 109.

10 Norman Egbert McClure, ed., *The Letters of John Chamberlain*, vol. 1, Philadelphia, 1939, pp. 21, 32, 544. The spelling of this and all other early modern texts quoted in the Introduction has been silently modernised.

11 Cited E. K. Chambers, *The Elizabethan Stage*, vol. 3, Oxford, 1923, p. 246. All of Chapman's extant tragedies postdate *Palladis Tamia*, but Henslowe's payment to him for a tragedy based on a plot by Ben Jonson at about that time would argue that he had already written, or collaborated on, other tragedies, now lost (see Foakes, p. 100).

12 On 20 September 1598, another of Dudley Carleton's correspondents, Toby Mathew, tells of a German who lost 300 crowns at 'a new play called Every Man's Humour' (quoted by Martin Seymour-Smith, intro., *Every Man in His Humour*, London, 1966, p. xv). See also Robert S. Miola, ed., *Every Man in His Humour*, Manchester, 2000, pp. 1, 11–12.

13 The third story of day five tells how the 'zima' (young dandy) Riccardo seduced the wife of Francesco Vergellesi; cited Charles Read Baskervill, *English Elements in Jonson's Early Comedy*, Austin, 1911, p. 168.

14 Thomas Marc Parrott and Robert Hamilton Ball, *A Short View of Elizabethan Drama*, New York, 1943, p. 97.

15 T. S. Eliot, 'The Sources of Chapman', *Times Literary Supplement*, 10 Feb. 1927.

16 Douglas Bush, *English Literature in the Earlier Seventeenth Century: 1600–1660*, Oxford, 1962, p. 61.

17 Pierre de La Primaudaye, *The French Academie*, London, 1618, p. 4; Frances A. Yates, *The French Academies of the Sixteenth Century*, London, 1988, p. 126; see also Rolf Soellner, *Shakespeare's Patterns of Self-Knowledge*, Columbus, 1972, p. 20; Geoffrey Bullough, *Narrative and Dramatic Sources of Shakespeare*, vol. 1, New York, 1957, pp. 427–30.

18 Jonathan Bate, *Shakespeare and Ovid*, Oxford, 1993, p. 27; A. R. Braunmuller, *Natural Fictions: George Chapman's Major Tragedies*, Newark, 1992, p. 17.

19 Frank Kermode, 'The Banquet of Sense', *Bulletin of the John Rylands Library* 44 (1961): 92, 93.

20 F. S. Boas, intro., *Bussy D'Ambois and The Revenge of Bussy d'Ambois*, Boston, 1905, p. xxvi.

21 Phyllis Brooks Bartlett, ed., *The Poems of George Chapman*, New York, 1962, p. 49; see 'pervial', *OED adj.*

22 Bartlett, p. 50.

23 John Lahr, review of Tom Stoppard's *Jumpers*, *New Yorker*, 3 May 2004.

24 Quotations from Helen Ostovich, ed., *Every Man Out of His Humour*, Manchester, 2001.

25 F. David Hoeniger, *Medicine and Shakespeare in the English Renaissance*, Newark, 1992, p. 102.

26 Roy Porter, *The Greatest Benefit to Mankind: A Medical History of Humanity from Antiquity to the Present*, London, 1997, p. 56.

27 'The Nature of Man', tr. J. Chadwick and W. N. Mann, in *Hippocratic Writings,* ed. G. E. R. Lloyd, Harmondsworth, 1983; see also Hoeniger, p. 103.

28 Nogo Arikha, *Passions and Tempers: A History of the Humours*, New York, 2007, pp. 5–6.

29 Raymond Klibansky, Erwin Panofsky, and Fritz Saxl, *Saturn and Melancholy,* London, 1964, p. 127.

30 Porter, pp. 107–8.

31 Sir John Harington, *The School of Salernum*, New York, 1970, p. 132.

32 An extract is to be found in Lloyd, pp. 272–6.

33 Miola, p. 13.

34 'Confluxion' is a word Jonson appears to have invented for the action of flowing together (see Ostovich edition, p. 118).

35 Madeleine Doran, *Endeavors of Art: A Study of Form in Elizabethan Drama*, Madison, 1954, p. 122.

36 See especially Russ McDonald, 'Othello, Thorello, and the Problem of the Foolish Hero', *Shakespeare Quarterly* 30 (1979): 51–67; J. W. Lever, intro., *Every Man in His Humour: A Parallel Text Edition*, London, 1971, pp. xxiv–xxvi; Miola, pp. 65–8.

37 Quoting H. R. Woodhuysen, ed., *Love's Labour's Lost*, London, 1998, p. 70; cf. Mark Thornton Burnett, 'George Chapman', *Oxford Dictionary of National Biography*, Oxford, 2004.

38 See 1.36 n., 3.54 n., 4.137 n., 13.5 n., 13.174 n.

39 Woodhuysen, p. 72.

40 Hardin Craig, *The Enchanted Glass: The Elizabethan Mind in Literature*, New York, 1936, p. 126.

41 Craig, p. 136.

42 Plato, *Complete Works*, ed. John M. Cooper, Indianapolis, 1997, p. 1075.

43 Plato, p. 1076.

44 Donne cited Edward Dowden, *Essays Modern and Elizabethan*, New York, 1910, p. 313; Bacon, *Of the Advancement of Learning*, ed. Arthur Johnston, Oxford, 1974, p. 116; see also Murray W. Bundy, 'Shakespeare and Elizabethan Psychology', *Journal of English and Germanic Philology* 22 (1924): 520.

45 Aristotle, *Complete Works*, ed. Jonathan Barnes, 2 vols [sequentially paginated], Princeton, 1984, pp. 642, 663.

46 See Geoffrey Miles, *Shakespeare and the Constant Romans*, Oxford, 1996, esp. pp. 1–17; Arikha, pp. 39–40.

47 R. J. Hankinson, 'Stoicism and Medicine', in *The Cambridge Companion to the Stoics*, ed. Brad Inwood, Cambridge, 2003, pp. 295–309.

48 See Vivian Nutton, *Ancient Medicine,* London, 2004, pp. 216–47; Arikha, pp. 24–41.

49 Arikha, p. 38.

50 Timothy Bright, *A Treatise of Melancholy*, London, 1586, p. 35.

51 Bright, p. 45.

52 La Primaudaye, p. 414.

53 Peter Charron, *Of Wisdome: Three Bookes Written in French*, tr. Samson Lennard, London, [n.d.], p. 66.

54 La Primaudaye, p. 414.

55 Ruth Leila Anderson, *Elizabethan Psychology and Shakespeare's Plays*, 2nd ed., New York, 1966, pp. 133–4.

56 La Primaudaye, p. 415.

57 Sean Kelsey, 'Sir John Davies', *Oxford Dictionary of National Biography.*

58 Lawrence Babb, 'The Physiological Conception of Love in the Elizabethan and Early Stuart Drama', *PMLA* 56 (1941): 1022–4; Anderson, pp. 119–20, 125–6.

59 Bartlett, p. 53.

60 Thomas Lodge, *A Margarite of America*, in *Complete Works of Thomas Lodge*, vol. 3, London, 1883, p. 47.

61 Margaret Tallmadge May, ed., *Galen on the Usefulness of the Parts of the Body*, Ithaca, 1968, pp. 472–3; see also Hoeniger, pp. 95–9.

62 Pierre Boaistuau, *Theatrum mundi The theatre or rule of the world*, London, 1566, sig. O5v–O6r.

63 Charles Rosen, 'The Anatomy Lesson', *New York Review of Books*, 9 June 2005.

64 Bright, p. 244, 258; M. Andreas Laurentius [Andreas Du Laurens], *A Discourse of the Preservation of Sight, of Melancholike Diseases, of Rheumes, and of Old Age*, tr. Richard Surphlet, London, 1599, p. 108.

65 See J. B. Bamborough, 'Robert Burton', *Oxford Dictionary of National Biography*.

66 Arikha, p. 10.

67 Harington, p. 140. For discussion of this particular type of melancholy, see Bridget Gellert Lyons, *Voices of Melancholy: Studies in Literary Treatments of Melancholy in Renaissance England*, New York, 1971, pp. 26–7; Lawrence Babb, *The Elizabethan Malady: A Study of Melancholia in English Literature from 1580 to 1642*, East Lansing, 1951, pp. 96–100.

68 See 7.7 n., 7.65–6 n., 10.66–7 n.

69 Du Laurens, p. 82, cited Lyons, p. 13.

70 Levinus Lemnius, *The Touchstone of Complexions*, tr. Thomas Newton, London, 1576, fol. 146r–v.

71 See Lyons, pp. 17–121; G. B. Harrison, 'An Essay on Elizabethan Melancholy', addendum to Nicholas Breton, *Melancholike Humours*, ed. Harrison, London, 1929, pp. 64–9.

72 Everard Guilpin, *Skialethia or a Shadowe of Truth in Certqain Epigrams and Satyres*, ed. D. Allen Carroll, Chapel Hill, 1974, p. 53.

73 Robert Kreuger, ed., *The Poems of Sir John Davies*, Oxford, 1975, p. 150.

74 Klibansky et al., p. 256.

75 Cited Carol V. Kaske and John R. Clark, intro., *Three Books on Life*, p. 20 (see n. 79 below).

76 Plato, pp. 522–3.

77 Plato, p. 527.

78 Aristotle, p. 1498.

79 quoting Klibansky et al., p. 255; see also Marsilio Ficino, *Three Books on Life: A Critical Edition and Translation*, ed. and tr. Carol V. Kaske and John R. Clark, Binghamton, 1989, pp. 117–121; Mark Hutchinson, 'The Art of Melancholy', *Times Literary Supplement*, 20 Dec. 2005.

80 Klibansky et al., p. 259.
81 Oscar James Campbell, 'Jaques', *Huntington Library Bulletin* 8 (1935): 87.
82 See Kermode, pp. 68–99; Elizabeth Story Donno, intro., *Elizabethan Minor Epics*, London, 1963, pp. 13–16; A. B. Taylor, 'Sir John Davies and George Chapman: A Note on the Current Approach to *Ovids Banquet of Sence*', *English Language Notes* 12 (1975): 261–5; John Huntington, 'Philosophical Seduction in Chapman, Davies, and Donne', *ELH* 44 (1977): 40–59; Darryl J. Gless, 'Chapman's Ironic Ovid', *ELR* 9 (1979): 21–41; Steven Matthews, 'T. S. Eliot's Chapman: "Metaphysical" Poetry and Beyond', *Journal of Modern Literature* 29 no. 4 (2006): 22–42.
83 Plato, p. 527.
84 Plato, p. 493.
85 Marsilio Ficino, *Commentary on Plato's* Symposium, tr. Sears Reynolds Jayne, Columbia, 1944, p. 183.
86 Paul Shorey, *Platonism: Ancient and Modern*, Berkeley, 1938, p. 103.
87 Shorey, p. 103; Kermode, p. 79.
88 Ficino, p. 198.
89 N. S. Brooke, intro., *Bussy D'Ambois*, Manchester, 1964, pp. xx, xxii.
90 Walter Kerr, *The Silent Clowns*, New York, 1975, p. 38.
91 Gail Kern Paster, *Humoring the Body: Emotions and the Shakespearean Stage*, Chicago, 2004, p. 199.
92 Henry L. Snuggs, 'The Comic Humours: A New Interpretation', *PMLA* 62 (1947): 115.
93 See Baskervill, pp. 112–17; C. H. Herford and Percy Simpson, ed., *Ben Jonson,* vol. 1, Oxford, 1925, pp. 343–7; Miola, pp. 13–14.
94 Patrick Collinson, 'Ecclesiastical Vitriol: Religious Satire in the 1590s and the Invention of Puritanism', in *The Reign of Elizabeth I: Court and Culture in the Last Decade*, ed. John Guy, Cambridge, 1995, p. 155; Collinson, 'The Theatre Constructs Puritanism', in *The Theatrical City: Culture, Theatre, and Politics in London, 1576–1649*, ed. David L. Smith, Richard Strier, and David Bevington, Cambridge, 1995, p. 168; see also M. M. Knappen, *Tudor Puritanism: A Chapter in the History of Idealism*, Chicago, 1939, pp. 423–40.
95 Lyly, *The Woman in the Moon*, ed. Leah Scragg, Manchester, 2006 (5.1.310); Marlowe, *The Massacre at Paris*, ed. H. J. Oliver, London, 1968 (xiv.55, xix.46). My figures are based on the Chadwyck-Healey *English Drama* database.
96 Collinson, 'Ecclesiastical Vitriol', p. 156.
97 William P. Holden, *Anti-Puritan Satire: 1572–1642*, Yale Studies in English, vol. 126, New Haven, 1954, pp. 46–8.
98 Holden, pp. 44–6; Collinson, 'Ecclesiastical Vitriol', p. 157.
99 Holden, p. 40.
100 Holden, pp. 40–2.
101 Collinson, 'Ecclesiastical Vitriol', p. 167.
102 The Rose was considerably smaller than the neighbouring Globe; see Andrew Gurr, *The Shakespearean Stage 1574–1642*, 3rd ed., Cambridge, 1992, pp. 123–9.

103 Parrott, *Plays*, p. 689.
104 Thomas Mark Grant, *The Comedies of George Chapman: A Study in Development*, Salzburg, 1972, p. 41.
105 Parrott, *Plays*, p. 689.
106 Carol Chillington Rutter, *Documents of the Rose Playhouse*, 2nd ed., Manchester, 1999, pp. 26–7; 151; Foakes, p. 101.
107 Andrew Gurr, ed., *Richard II*, Cambridge 1984, p. 175; see also Alan E. Craven, 'Proofreading in the Shop of Valentine Simmes', *Papers of the Bibliographical Society of America* 68 (1974): 361–72; Terri Bourus, 'Shakespeare and the London Publishing Environment: The Publisher and Printers of Q1 and Q2 *Hamlet*', *Analytical and Enumerative Bibliography* 12 (2001): 206–28.
108 I faced a similar situation in editing *The Famous History of the Life and Death of Captain Thomas Stukeley*; see Edelman, *The Stukeley Plays*, Manchester, 2005, pp. 40–2.
109 Stephen Orgel, *The Authentic Shakespeare and Other Problems of the Early Modern Stage*, London, 2002, p. 38.
110 Stanley Wells, *Shakespeare and Co.: Christopher Marlowe, Thomas Dekker, Ben Jonson, Thomas Middleton, John Fletcher and the Other Players in His Story*, London, 2006, p. 142.
111 Parrott, *Plays*, p. 690.
112 See collation: 5.1 SH; 5.5 SH; 5.8 SH; 5.45 SH; 7.240 SH, 7.244 SH; 7.246 SH.
113 Paul Werstine, 'Narratives About Printed Shakespeare Texts: "Foul Papers" and "Bad" Quartos', *Shakespeare Quarterly* 41 (1990): 65–86.
114 Akihiro Yamada, 'Bibliographical Studies of George Chapman's *An Humorous Day's Mirth*', *Shakespeare Studies* (Japan) 5 (1967): 119–49.
115 Craven, 'Proofreading', p. 364.
116 British Library, shelfmark C.34.c.14.
117 Michael J. Sidnell, ed., *Sources of Dramatic Theory*, vol. 1, Cambridge, 1991, pp. 73, 74.
118 A. C. Swinburne, 'Essay on the Poetical and Dramatic Works of George Chapman', in *The Works of George Chapman: Poems and Minor Translations*, London, 1904, p. xxiv.
119 James Russell Lowell, *The Old English Dramatists*, London, 1892, p. 85; M. C. Bradbrook, *The Growth and Structure of Elizabethan Comedy*, Harmondsworth, 1963, p. 181; Paul V. Kreider, *Elizabethan Comic Character Conventions*, Ann Arbor, 1935, p. 5.

AN HUMOROUS DAY'S MIRTH

A pleaſant Comedy

entituled :

An Humerous dayes
Myrth.

As it hath beene ſundrie times publikely acted by
the right honourable the Earle of Nottingham Lord high Admirall
his ſeruants.

By G. C.

AT LONDON
Printed by Valentine Symes:
1599.

[Characters in the Play

LABERVELE, *a Count*
FLORILLA, *his young wife, a puritan*
DOWSECER, *his son by a previous marriage*
LAVEL, *Dowsecer's friend*
LEMOT, *a young gallant, a gentleman, and a trickster*   5
FOYES, *a Justice*
MARTIA, *his daughter*
LABESHA, *a gull, foolish suitor to Martia*
MOREN, *a Count*
COUNTESS MOREN, *a jealous wife*   10
KING *of France*
QUEEN *of France*
COLINET, *cousin to Count Moren*
CATALIAN, *a gallant, friend to Lemot*
BLANUEL, *a gallant*   15
ROWLEY, *a gallant, and cousin to Colinet*
BERGER, *a gallant*
VERONE, *proprietor of an ordinary*
A BOY, *his son*
JAQUES, *his servant*   20
JAQUENA, *his maid*
Other servants at Verone's ordinary]

Characters in the Play] *Q* and Shepherd omit a character list; Parrott's edition is the first to include one.

6. *FOYES*] probably pronounced with two syllables, 'Foy-es', as required by the metre at 13.55. His office of Justice, first mentioned at 8.223, has no bearing on the plot.

8. *LABESHA*] Perhaps a play on *la bêche*, the 'spade', or 'shovel'.

13. *COLINET*] *Q* has both Colinet and Colenet. Colinet, as a diminutive of Colin or Nicolin, is more likely.

16. *ROWLEY*] *Q* has Rowl, Rowle, and Rowlee at various points in the text. Greg prefers Rowle, but I agree with Parrott that Rowlee (modernised to Rowley) is appropriate. The actor Sam Rowley was a member of the Admiral's Men at this time, but Chapman's use of the name, if Parrott is correct, was probably coincidental.

SCENE I

Enter the Count LABERVELE *in his shirt and nightgown,*
with two jewels in his hand.

Labervele. Yet hath the morning sprinkled throughout the
    clouds
But half her tincture, and the soil of night
Sticks still upon the bosom of the air.
Yet sleep doth rest my love for nature's debt,
And through her window and this dim twilight,   5
Her maid, nor any waking I can see.
This is the holy green, my wife's close walk,

Scene 1] *This ed.*; Scene I *Parrott*; Sc. 1 *Greg*; I.i. *Holaday; not in*
Q. 1. throughout] *conj. Brereton*; throwt *Q, Holaday*; through *Shepherd*;
thr'out *Parrott.* 5. twilight] *Shepherd*; twee-light *Q.*

Scene 1] The action of this first scene takes place in Count Labervele's
garden.

    1. *throughout*] Parrott emends *Q*'s 'throwt' to 'thr'out', in order to keep
the word one syllable, but blank verse is flexible enough to allow the customary modern spelling.

    2. *tincture*] hue, colour (*OED n.* 2). In Marston's *Antonio and Mellida*,
Andrugio asks, 'Is not yon gleam the shuddering morn that flakes / With
silver tincture, the east verge of heaven?' (3.1.1–2).

    soil] stain, dark colour (*OED n.*[3] 3a). The sense seems to be that the air
has half morning's colour and half the night's darkness; omitting the second
'half' is typical of Chapman's compressed imagery.

    4.] Sleep has my wife in a death-like grasp. 'Rest' is an abbreviated form of
'arrest', also found at 7.116. 'For' should be taken in the sense of 'in the character of, equivalent to' (*OED prep* 19a); 'nature's debt' is a proverbial image for
death (Dent D168). In Marlowe's *Edward II*, Baldock advises Spencer Junior
that they should 'pay nature's debt with cheerful countenance' (4.7.109).

    6.] Neither my wife's maid nor any other person appears to be awake.
Labervele needs to be sure he is unobserved; as we learn in subsequent lines,
he intends to place jewels, engraved with verses, in his wife Florilla's private
garden, and tell her they dropped from the sky as a present from God.

    7. *holy green*] not consecrated, but 'holy' to the puritan Florilla. Accord-
ing to Philip Stubbes's *Anatomy of Abuses*, city wives were more inclined to
use their gardens for sex rather than for prayer or contemplation: 'And for
that their gardens are locked, some of them have three or four keys apiece,
whereof one they keep for themselves, the other their paramours have to go
in before them…Then to these gardens, they repair when they list with a
basket and a boy, where they meeting their sweethearts, receive their wished
desires' (pp. 136–7).

    close] private (*OED a.* 4b).

To which not any but herself alone
Hath any key – only that I have clapped
Her key in wax and made this counterfeit –   10
To the which I steal access to work this rare
And politic device.
Fair is my wife, and young and delicate,
Although too religious in the purest sort;
But pure religion, being but mental stuff   15
And sense, indeed all for itself,

---

11. To the which] *Q, Parrott;* To which *Shepherd;* By the which *conj. Brereton, Holaday.*   16. all for] *Q;* all careful for *Parrott.*

---

11. *To the which*] Brereton, assuming that Labervele refers to his key, suggests a substitution of 'by' for *Q*'s 'to', but, as Parrott notes, 'the pronoun may be regarded as referring to the holy green' (p. 695). In any event, prepositions were used far more freely in this period compared with today (see Abbott, p. 94).

rare] splendid, excellent (*OED a.*[1] 6b), but not necessarily scarce. Chapman uses the word in both senses in this play, and later puns on the difference (13.160–3).

12. *politic*] skilfully contrived (*OED a.* 2a).

13. *delicate*] delightful, charming (*OED a.* 1) without any implication of fragility.

14. *sort*] manner, way (*OED n.*[2] III); 'too religious' and 'in the purest sort' are something of a tautology, and deleting the word 'too' would render the line metrical.

15–20.] Chapman does the actor no favours by choosing the play's first speech to indulge his habit for what Swinburne (p. xiii) calls his 'incessant byplay of incongruous digressions and impenetrable allusions'. Nevertheless, a major tenet of his thought, indeed of all Renaissance psychology, is packed within these five lines, dealing as they do with the relationship of the rational to the sensitive soul (see Introduction, pp. 14–20).

15. *pure religion*] perhaps, religion 'taken by itself' (*OED pure a.* 3a), although Labervele may be referring specifically to his wife's puritanism.

stuff] often used to denote incorporeal matter, as in Iago's 'Yet do I hold it very stuff o' th' conscience / To do no contrived murder' (1.2.2–3).

16. *sense*] the sensitive soul (see Introduction, pp. 15–16).

indeed] 'in fact' or 'in reality' (*OED advb. phr.* 1), not merely an insertion to add emphasis.

all for itself] Parrott emends to 'all careful for itself' in order to keep the verse regular, but 'careful' seems an arbitrary choice. Metrics aside, there is nothing wrong with 'for itself', meaning 'for its own sake', often found in early modern texts when referring to qualities. In Marston's *Malcontent*, Malevole describes Celso as 'one of full ten millions of men / That lovest virtue only for itself' (1.4.4–5); his *Entertainment of The Dowager-Countess of Derby* is dedicated to one who 'loveth goodness for itself, not fame' (l. 166).

'Tis to be doubted that when an object comes
Fit to her humour, she will intercept
Religious letters sent unto her mind,
And yield unto the motion of her blood.   20
Here have I brought, then, two rich agates for her,
Graven with two posies of mine own devising,
For poets I'll not trust, nor friends, nor any.
She longs to have a child, which yet, alas

---

17. 'Tis] *Parrott*; Is *Q*.

---

17. *'Tis to be doubted*] Parrott's substitution of ''Tis' for *Q*'s 'Is' to start l.
17 is probably correct, 'doubted' to be taken as 'feared' (common in
Elizabethan usage).

object] An 'object' can be anything 'placed before or presented to the eyes
or other senses' (*OED n.* 1a); for it to be a beautiful man or woman is
common in this period. Corynna is the 'object' of Ovid's senses several times
in *Ovid's Banquet of Sense*.

18. *Fit to her humour*] In this context, Florilla's humour would be her
natural underlying temperament of a 'young and delicate' woman, open to
sensual appetites.

18–19. *intercept...letters*] No literal use of 'letters' as written matter suits
the situation, so Labervele must be referring to the religious ideas that Florilla will 'intercept', i.e. prevent from reaching her rational soul unaffected
by the imagination and appetite.

20. *yield...blood*] As we soon learn, Labervele is impotent; hence his
fears must centre on what Florilla might do if presented with an attractive
'object'. Blood is the humour of sexual desire, so Florilla would be affected
by its 'motion', i.e. its movement to the heart via the appetitive spirit (see
Introduction, pp. 16–18). In *Measure for Measure*, Isabella describes Antonio
'as one who never feels / The wanton stings and motions of the sense'
(1.4.58–9).

21 *agates*] precious stones often set in jewelry. Mercutio's Queen Mab
'comes / In shape no bigger than an agate stone / On the forefinger of an
alderman' (1.4.55–7).

22. *Graven...posies*] Posies are short mottoes in verse (*OED n.* 1), commonly engraved on rings and other jewellery, or embroidered into handker-
chiefs and gloves. Those on rings would be at most two or three lines, hence
Hamlet's 'Is this a prologue, or the posy of a ring?' (3.2.152). If we take
'graven' literally, then the posies are actually engraved on the stones, but at
l. 27 Labervele speaks of writing 'in', not on 'this fair jewel', and Florilla's
instruction to 'burn them' would imply that the posies are written on small
pieces of paper, placed in an ornamental setting around the stones. Edward
Arber's *An English Garner* has a large collection of posies, all of the two-line
variety (pp. 611–24); for other types see *Love's Garland, or Posies for Rings,
Hand-kercher, and Gloves, And such pretty tokens that Lovers send their Loves*
(London, 1624).

I cannot get, yet long as much as she;   25
And not to make her desperate, thus I write
In this fair jewel, though it simple be,
Yet 'tis mine own that meaneth well in nought:
    Despair not of children,
    Love with the longest;   30
    When man is at the weakest,
    God is at the strongest.
I hope 'tis plain and knowing. In this other that I write:
    God will reward her a thousandfold,
    That takes what age can, and not what age would.   35

---

28. in nought] *Q*; enough *Parrott*.   29. Despair] *subst.* *Q* *(corrected);* tis
spare *Q* *(uncorrected); see Yamada, p. 131*.   32. the] *Shepherd, Holaday; not
in Q or Parrott.*

---

25. *I cannot get*] Labervele is impotent; whether he thinks this has brought
about his wife's puritan holiness, or his wife's puritanism has caused the
impotence, is delightfully unclear. In 1614, Chapman became involved with
a notorious real-life case involving the unsatisfied wife of a supposedly
impotent husband, by writing the poem *Andromeda Liberata* to celebrate the
wedding of Frances Howard to Robert Carr, the Earl of Somerset. In order
to marry Carr, Howard was granted an annulment of her marriage to the
Earl of Essex on a trumped-up charge of impotence. In the court hearing
that followed, Essex indignantly claimed that any number of women had
found his sexual powers more than adequate; it was only when he was with
his wife that they deserted him (see *DNB* entries on Robert Devereux, third
Earl of Essex, and Frances Howard).

28. *in nought*] Parrot substitutes 'enough', but the sense seems to be that
Labervele is being properly modest about his poetic skills.

30. *with the longest*] for a very long time (*OED long a*[1] II B1h), preceding
OED's earliest citation, the 1636 translation of Florus's *Roman Histories*.
Labervele being impotent, the word 'longest' is an unfortunate choice, and
the pun might be intended.

32. *at the strongest*] *Q* reads 'at strongest', but Shepherd's insertion of 'the'
must be correct, to make the line consistent with *Q* at 4.35. Labervele might
be alluding to 2 Corinthians, 12.10: 'Therefore have I delectation in infirmi-
ties, in rebukes, in necessities, in persecutions, in anguishes for Christ's sake:
For when I am weak, then am I strong' (Bennett, p. 91).

33. *knowing*] *OED* has no definition to fit this context precisely. Perhaps
this is a nonce-word for 'knowledgeable' or 'showing intelligence'.

34-5.] Florilla will be rewarded if she accepts what her aged husband *can*
give her, rather than what he *would* give her, were he able.

I hope 'tis pretty and pathetical.

[*He lays down the jewels.*]

Well, even here,
Lie both together till my love arise
And let her think you fall out of the skies.
I will to bed again.   40

Exit.

SCENE 2

Enter LEMOT *and* COLINET.

Lemot. How like thou this morning, Colinet? What, shall we
    have a fair day?
Colinet. The sky hangs full of humour, and I think we shall
    have rain.

36.1 SD.] *This ed.; not in Q.*

Scene 2] *This ed.;* Scene II *Parrott;* Sc. ii *Greg;* I.ii. *Holaday; not in Q.*
1 SH.] *Q (this l. only).*   3 SH.] *subst. Q (this l. only).*

---

36. *pathetical*] moving, affecting (*pathetic*, OED a. 1b). In *Love's Labour's
Lost*, Armado praises Moth's 'Sweet invocation of a child, most pretty and
pathetical' (1.2.97–8). *The Fair Maid of the Exchange* has Cripple indignantly
claiming he can 'write a letter / Ditty, or sonnet with judicial phrase / As
pretty, pleasing, and pathetical / As the best Ovid-imitating dunce / In all
the town' (sig. F3r).

SD. He lays…jewels] The jewels need to be there for Florilla to discover
them in Scene 4, yet they cannot lie in the middle of the stage during Scenes
2 and 3. This type of problem, frequent in Elizabethan drama, could have
been handled in a number of ways. In this instance, the jewels might be
placed next to the pillars holding up the stage canopy—visible, surely, but
not obtrusive. The recent excavations of the Rose site indicate that these
pillars were quite far forward, so Florilla's suddenly noticing the jewels (4.8)
would be credible (see Gurr, p. 130).

37–40.] The close to this speech can be lined in any number of ways; my
choice emphasises the rhyme.

37. *even here*] now and in this place. In *The Tempest*, Alonso tells his
courtiers, 'Even here will I put off my hope' (3.3.7).

39. *you*] the jewels.

Scene 2] The dialogue offers no precise indication of the setting. Given
Lemot's promise to Colinet that an 'odd gentleman' will be brought 'hither'
(2.22), Lemot's house is likely to be the imagined locale.

3. *humour*] moisture. Lemot immediately picks up on Colinet's use of the
original meaning and plays with the other senses of the word.

Lemot. Why, rain is fair weather when the ground is dry and   5
    barren, especially when it rains humours; for then do
    men, like hot sparrows and pigeons, open all their wings
    ready to receive them.
Colinet. Why, then we may chance to have a fair day, for we
    shall spend it with so humorous acquaintance as rains   10
    nothing but humour all their lifetime.
Lemot. True, Colinet, over which will I sit like an old king in
    an old fashion play, having his wife, his counsel, his
    children, and his fool about him, to whom he will sit and
    point very learnedly as followeth: 15
      My counsel grave, and you my noble peers, my
        tender wife,
      And you my children dear, and thou my fool –
Colinet. Not meaning me, sir, I hope.
Lemot. No, sir, but thus will I sit, as it were, and point out
    all my humorous companions.   20
Colinet. You shall do marvellous well, sir.

---

5 SH.] *This ed.; Lem. Le. Q; Le. Shepherd, Holaday; Lem. Parrott.*
6. humours] *This ed.*; humor *Q.*   9 SH.] *This ed.; Col. Co. Q; Co. Shepherd,
Holaday; Col. Parrott.*

---

7. *hot sparrows and pigeons*] traditionally the most wanton of all birds,
especially the former. John Day's prose tale *Peregrinatio Scholastica* contains
a description of 'an antimasque...in the manner of a drunken dance',
including a couple 'of amorous behaviour, that like hot sparrows or Barbary
pigeons, consume and melt away in dalliance' (pp. 497–8).

13. *old fashion*] *OED*'s earliest citation for this variant of the more
common 'old fashioned'.

16–17. *My counsel grave...fool*] very likely a direct parody of Thomas
Preston's popular *The Lamentable Tragedy Mixed Full of Pleasant Mirth con-
taining the life of Cambyses, King of Persia. Cambyses* is also lampooned in *A
Midsummer Night's* Dream, with Quince and company's *Most Lamentable
Comedy and Most Cruel Death of Pyramus and Thisbe*, and in 1 *Henry IV*, as
Falstaff announces his intention to act in 'King Cambyses' vein' (2.4.390).
Like Lemot's 'old fashion play', it begins with the same three words, spoken
by the King to his counsellor and other lords: 'My counsel grave and sapient
with lords of legal train', and after the Counsellor's reply, the King's second
speech begins with the very same phrase, 'My counsel grave a thousand
thanks' (sig. A2v, A3r). If the first line of Lemot's 'quotation' is a Preston-
like fourteener, as printed here, then the second line, interrupted by Colinet,
begins with 'And', another common feature in *Cambyses* (see Edelman,
'Preston's *Cambyses, King of Persia*', *Explicator* 65 (2007): 194–7).

Lemot. I thank you for your good encouragement. But,
  Colinet, thou shalt see Catalian bring me hither an odd
  gentleman presently to be acquainted withal, who in his
  manner of taking acquaintance will make us excellent   25
  sport.

Colinet. Why, Lemot, I think thou sendst about of purpose
  for young gallants to be acquainted withal, to make
  thyself merry in the manner of taking acquaintance.

Lemot. By heaven, I do, Colinet, for there is no better sport   30
  than to observe the complement, for that's their word,
  complement. Do you mark, sir?

Colinet. Yea, sir, but what humour hath this gallant in his
  manner of taking acquaintance?

Lemot. Marry, thus, sir: he will speak the very self-same word,   35
  to a syllable, after him of whom he takes acquaintance:
  as if I should say, 'I am marvellous glad of your acquaintance', he will reply, 'I am marvellous glad of your
  acquaintance'; 'I have heard much good of your rare
  parts and fine carriage'; 'I have heard much good of your   40
  rare parts and fine carriage.' So long as the complements
  of a gentleman last, he is your complete ape.

---

31. *complement, for that's their word*] As Buffone tells Sogliardo in *Every
Man Out*, 'if you affect to be a gentleman indeed, you must observe all the
rare qualities, humours, and complements of a gentleman' (1.2.24–7).
Defined by *OED* as 'that which goes to 'complete' the gentleman; a personal
accomplishment or quality' (*n.* 7), 'complement' was a popular word
amongst would-be gallants, and derided by John Hoskins in his *Directions
for Speech and Style* (c. 1599). Hoskins's advice on writing with 'perspicuity',
incorporated by Jonson into the *Discoveries*, is 'not to cast a ring for the
perfumed terms of the time, as accommodation, complement, spirit, etc.'
(*Discoveries*, p. 86). Donne's fourth *Satire* describes the world's worst bore,
who speaks in a 'tongue, call'd complement' (l. 44).

40. *parts*] attributes, talents (*OED n.*[1] 15). In *As You Like It*, Oliver
describes Orlando as 'an envious emulator of every man's good parts' (1.1.143–
4); Macilente of *Every Man Out* is 'a man well parted' (Characters. 7).

carriage] habitual conduct or behaviour (*OED n.* 15a); often combined
with 'parts', as in Lorenzo Junior (*F*: Edward Knowell) to his cousin Stephano
of *Every Man In*, 'A gentleman of so fair sort as you are, of so true carriage,
of so special good parts, of so dear choice and estimation' (*Q*, 1.2.96–7).

41–2. *So long...gentleman last*] So long as there are gentlemanly qualities
of which to speak.

42. *ape*] literally, at this time, any simian (*OED n.*), ubiquitous as a
metaphor for a foolish imitator of others; cf. 7.127 n.

Colinet. Why, this is excellent.

Lemot. Nay, sirrah, here's the jest of it: when he is past this
    gratulation, he will retire himself to a chimney or a wall,   45
    standing, folding his arms thus. An go you and speak to
    him, so far as the room you are in will afford you, you
    shall never get him from that most gentlemanlike set or
    behaviour.

Colinet. This makes his humour perfect. I would he would   50
    come at once.

            Enter CATALIAN *and* BLANUEL.

Lemot. See where he comes! Now must I say, *lupus est in*
    fabula, for these Latin ends are part of a gentleman and
    a good scholar.

Catalian. Oh, good morrow, Monsieur Lemot. Here is the   55
    gentleman you desired so much to be acquainted withal.

Lemot. He is marvellous welcome. [*To Blanuel*] I shall be
    exceeding proud of your acquaintance.

Blanuel. I shall be exceeding proud of your acquaintance.

---

51. at once] *This ed.;* once *Q.*   55 SH.] *Q (this l. only).*   59 SH.] *This ed.;*
Blan. Bla. Q; Bla. Shepherd; Blan. Parrott.

---

44. *sirrah*] normally a term for servants or other inferiors. Lemot would
be using it ironically, as a means of expressing affection.

45. *gratulation*] greeting (*OED n.* 4). In *The Travels of the Three English
Brothers*, the Sophy of Persia welcomes his visitors with 'No gentle stranger
greets our continent, / But our arms fold him in a soft embrace: / Yet must
his gratulation first be paid / Upon our foot' (1.1.35–8).

46. *folding…thus*] the conventional pose of melancholy (see Introduction,
pp. 22–3).

An go you] if you go (see Abbott, p. 73).

48. *set*] stance, position.

51. *come at once*] *Q* reads 'come once', but Colinet must mean 'immediately', as he has already been informed that Catalian is bringing the odd
gentleman 'presently' (l. 24). *OED* offers many definitions of 'once' without
the preposition, but none fitting this context.

52–3. lupus est in fabula] 'the wolf is in the fable', equivalent to 'talk of
the devil'. This 'Latin end' appears in Terence's *Adelphi*, John Barsby noting
that it must derive from a story in which a wolf suddenly appeared while
talked about (Terence, p. 313). A similar expression is found in Plautus's
Stichus, '*atque eccum tibi lupum in sermone*', or 'there you are – the wolf in
the fable' (Plautus, p. 66). Other plays in which it appears include Jonson's
Cynthia's Revels (2.3.6–7, 68) and Middleton's *Family of Love* (l. 1816).

Lemot. I have heard much good of your rare parts and fine   60
    carriage.

Blanuel. I have heard much good of your rare parts and fine
    carriage.

Lemot. I shall be glad to be commanded by you.

Blanuel. I shall be glad to be commanded by you.   65

Lemot. I pray, do not you say so.

Blanuel. I pray, do not you say so.

Lemot. Well, gentlemen, this day let's consecrate to mirth,
    and Colinet, you know, no man better, that you are
    mightily in love with lovely Martia, daughter to old   70
    Foyes.

Colinet. I confess it; here are none but friends.

Lemot. Well, then, go to her this morning in Countess
    Moren's name, and so perhaps you may get her company,
    though the old churl be so jealous that he will suffer no   75
    man to come at her but the vain gull Labesha, for his
    living sake, and he, as yet, she will not be acquainted
    withal.

Colinet. Well, this I'll do, whatsoever come of it.

Lemot. Why nothing but good will come of it; ne'er doubt it,   80
    man.

Catalian. [*Aside to Lemot, observing Blanuel*] He hath taken up
    his stand. Talk a little further, and see an you can remove
    him.

61, 63. carriage] *Shepherd*; cariages *Q*; carriages *Parrott.* 70. lovely] *conj.*
Deighton; love by *Q.* 74. Moren's] *Shepherd*; Moris *Q.* 79. of] *This ed.*;
on *Q.* 82 SH.] *This ed.; Cata. Cat. Ca. Q; Ca. Shepherd; Cat. Parrott.*

61, 63. *carriage*] *Q* has 'cariages', but Lemot has told Colinet that he
would say 'carriage'. While both forms are found in texts of this period, the
singular is more common, as in the line from *Every Man In* quoted above
(1 40 n.), so Shepherd's emendation is appropriate.

73–4. *in Countess Moren's name*] Although no mention of it is made here,
we learn at 5.37 that Colinet is Count Moren's cousin.

76. *gull*] Of the many words for 'dupe' or 'simpleton' with an avian origin,
'gull' was the most popular in Chapman's time.

76–7. *for his living sake*] for the sake of his estate and possessions (*OED*
living n. 4). We would write 'living's', but omitting the final *s* was acceptable
in Elizabethen usage (Hope, p. 38).

82–3. *taken up his stand*] Blanuel has assumed the arms-folded pose pre-
dicted earlier.

83. *and see an*] and see if, a common form (see Abbott, p. 73).

Lemot. I will, Catalian. Now, Monsieur Blanuel, mark, I pray.   85
Blanuel. I do, sir, very well, I warrant you.
Lemot. You know the old Count Labervele hath a passing fair
    young lady that is a passing foul puritan.
Blanuel. I know her very well, sir. She goes more like a milk-
    maid than a countess, for all her youth and beauty.   90
Lemot. True, sir, yet of her is the old count so jealous that he
    will suffer no man to come at her. Yet I will find a means
    that two of us will have access to her, though before his
    face, which shall so heat his jealous humour till he be
    start mad. But, Colinet, go you first to lovely Martia, for   95
    'tis too soon for the old lord and his fair young lady to
    rise.
Colinet. *Adieu*, Monsieur Blanuel.
Blanuel. *Adieu*, good Monsieur Colinet.

                              Exit COLINET.

Lemot. Monsieur Blanuel, your kindness in this will bind me   100
    much to you.
Blanuel. Monsieur Lemot, your kindness in this will bind me
    much to you.
Lemot. I pray you do not say so, sir.
Blanuel. I pray you do not say so, sir.   105

SD. Aside to Lemot, observing Blanuel] *This ed.; Aside to Lemot Parrott; not in Q.*   85. Catalian] *Shepherd*; Cat. *Q.*   95. start] *Q, Parrott*; stark *Shepherd.*

87, 88. *passing*] exceedingly (*OED adv.*).

88. *foul puritan*] 'Puritan' was a derogatory term at this time, and 'foul' may be taken as an intensifier of Lemot's disapproval, rather than in the sense of 'dirty' or 'ugly', which would hardly apply to Florilla (see Introduction, pp. 30–2).

89–90. *like a milkmaid*] proverbial for simplicity of dress. In *The True Chronicle History of King Leir*, 'costly robes' are compared with 'a milkmaid's smock and petticoat' (sig. C2r). Sir Thomas Overbury's *Characters* has a milkmaid 'so far from making herself beautiful by art, that one look of hers is able to put all face-physic out of countenance…The lining of her apparel (which is herself) is far better than outsides of tissue: for though she be not arrayed in the spoil of the silkworm, she is decked in innocency, a far better wearing' (pp. 118–19).

95. *start mad*] We might expect 'stark mad', but 'start', while less common, can take the same meaning of 'entirely' in phrases of this type. *OED* gives some examples from this period for 'start naked' (see Greg, p. ix). The expression appears again at 4.247.

Lemot. Will't please you to go in?
Blanuel. Will't please you to go in?
Lemot. I will follow you.
Blanuel. I will follow you.
Lemot. It shall be yours.   110
Blanuel. It shall be yours.
Lemot. Kind Monsieur Blanuel!
Blanuel. Kind Monsieur Lemot!

[*Exeunt.*]

SCENE 3

Enter FOYES *and* MARTIA, *and* LABESHA.

Foyes. Come on, fair daughter, fall to your work of mind and
    make your body fit to embrace the body of this gentle-
    man's. 'Tis art! Happy are they, say I!

113.1 SD. *Exeunt*] *Holaday; Exit Q; Exit Lemot with Blanuel Parrott.*

Scene 3] *This ed.*; Scene III *Parrott*; Sc. iii *Greg*; I.iii *Holaday; not in Q.*
0 SD. LABESHA] *Parrott*; Besha *Q.*   1 SH.] *Q (this l. only).*

Scene 3] 'This scene is laid at the house of Foyes' (Parrott).
    0 SD. LABESHA] Henslowe's playhouse inventory of 'all the apparel',
taken 13 March 1598, includes '*Item*, Labesha's cloak, with gold buttons'
(Henslowe, p. 321).
    1. *fall...mind*] The construction is typically obscure, but Foyes's general
meaning seems clear enough. Martia should make herself ready, both in
mind and body, to meet her suitor Labesha. Lemot's comment at 2.77–8,
'as yet, she will not be acquainted withal', implies that Martia has so far
refused to do so.
    2. *of this gentleman's*] This form of the possessive is occasionally seen in
early modern texts, e.g. Berowne having 'framed a letter to the sequent of
the stranger Queen's' (4.2.138–9); see Hope, p. 38.
    3. *'Tis art*] Assuming the text is not corrupt, 'art' might be taken as social
skills that would complement what Martia already has by 'nature'. This
would be somewhat similar to Mercutio's use of the word when encouraging
Romeo to stop 'groaning' over Rosaline and engage in some witty conversation: 'Now art thou sociable, now art thou Romeo, now art thou what thou
art, by art as well as by nature' (2.4.88–90).
    Happy...I] perhaps the start of the proverbial saying that ends with
'whose wooing that is not long adoing' (Dent W749). Chapman uses it in
Sir Giles Goosecap, in the form 'Blest is the wooing...' (3.2.98).

Labesha. I protest, sir, you speak the best that ever I heard.
Foyes. I pray, sir, take acquaintance of my daughter.   5
Labesha. [*To Martia*] I do desire you of more acquaintance.
Foyes. [*To Martia*] Why dost not thou say, 'Yea, and I the
    same of you'?
Martia. That everybody says.
Foyes. Oh, you would be singular.   10
Martia. Single, indeed.
Foyes. 'Single, indeed'! That's a pretty toy! Your betters,
    dame, bear double, and so shall you.

---

4 SH.] *This ed.; Be. Besh. Besha Lab. La. Labe. Labesh. Q; Be. La. Shepherd;
Labes. Parrott.*   5 SH.] *Holaday; Fo. Foies Foy. Q; Fo. Shepherd; Foy. Parrott.*
6 SD.] *This ed; not in Q.*   7 SD.] *Holaday; not in Q.*   9 SH.] *This ed.; Mar.
Ma. Q; Mar. Shepherd.*   12 toy! Your] *This ed.*; toy, / Your *Q.*

4. *protest*] With his first words, Labesha confirms Lemot's description of
him as a 'vain gull' (2.76), 'protest' being a term affected by the pretentious.
In Marston's *What You Will*, the 'fusty cask' Lampatho's constant 'protests'
arouse the ire of Quadratus, who, like John Hoskins (see 2.31 n.), hates such
'perfumed' words: 'protest, protest, / Catzo! I dread these hot protests'
(ll. 451, 475, 478–9). The Nurse comments on Romeo's use of the word
with 'I will tell her, sir, that you do protest, which, as I take it, is a gentleman-
like offer' (2.4.177–8).
    6.] Nick Bottom uses exactly the same words when introduced to Cobweb,
Peaseblossom, and Mustardseed (3.1.182–96).
    10–11. *singular.../ Single*] wordplay on Martia's desire to remain single,
i.e. unmarried, and the cult of 'singularity', a studied affectation of individu-
ality in dress or behaviour, albeit usually applied to men. Jonson's character
notes to *Every Man Out* describe Puntarvolo as 'a vainglorious knight, over-
Englishing his travels, and wholly consecrated to singularity' (Characters.
13–14), while the letter Malvolio finds in Olivia's garden instructs him, 'put
thyself into the trick of singularity' (2.5.151–2).
    12. *toy*] foolish or idle notion (*OED n.* 4a). In *Eastward Ho*, Security
muses, 'A toy, a toy runs in my head i'faith' (3.2.340). The word had a much
wider variety of uses in Elizabethan times than are common today, and was
not restricted to a child's plaything (see 4.53 n.). *Q* has a line break after
'toy', which would make 11–12 the only two blank verse lines in the text,
except that neither line is in iambic pentameter (see Introduction, pp. 37–8).
    13. *bear double*] a familiar quibble on 'bear', as in bearing children, and
bearing the weight of a man in intercourse (Williams, pp. 84–5, 87–8). But
'a horse that bears double' (l. 18) also plays on a horse's carrying two riders
at once and a woman having more than one lover. In *Northward Ho*, Mayberry, thinking his wife unfaithful, objects to Bellamont saying he is jealous
without cause: 'Without cause, when my mare bears double: without cause?'
(1.3.39–40).

Labesha. Exceeding pretty! [*To Martia*] Did you mark it,
    forsooth?   15
Martia. What should I mark, forsooth?
Labesha. Your bearing double, which equivocate is and hath
    a fit allusion to a horse that bears double, for your good
    father means you shall endure your single life no longer
    – not in worse sense than bearing double, forsooth.   20
Martia. I cry you mercy. You know both, belike.
Labesha. Knowledge, forsooth, is like a horse and you, that
    can bear double: it nourisheth both bee and spider, the
    bee honeysuckle, the spider poison. I am that bee.
Martia. I thought so, by your stinging wit.   25
Labesha. Lady, I am a bee without a sting – no way hurting
    any, but good to all, and before all, to your sweet self.
Foyes. Afore God, daughter, thou art not worthy to hear him
    speak! But who comes here?

---

14 SD.] *This ed.; not in Q.*   17. allusion] *Shepherd*; illusion *Q, Holaday.*

---

17. *equivocate*] *OED* offers no definition as an adjective, its first citation
for 'equivocal' being 1601. The verb 'equivocate', which Dr Johnson neatly
defines as 'to mean one thing and express another', was just coming into
fashion, so it is appropriate that Labesha, trying to impress, would use it as
something of a malapropism, perhaps for 'equivalent'.
    21. *cry you mercy*] beg your pardon; very common in this era.
belike] in all likelihood (*OED adv.*).
    23–4. *the bee honeysuckle, the spider poison*] Labesha does not mean the
flower honeysuckle, but honey 'sucked' or gathered by bees (*OED n.* 7),
sometimes spelled 'honeysuck'. In *Serpents* (1608), Edward Topsell notes
that bees 'have a fore-feeling and understanding of rain and winds aforehand,
and do rightly prognosticate of storms and foul weather, so that then, they
fly not far from their own homes, but sustain themselves with their honeysuck already provided' (p. 75). The idea that spiders derived their poison in
the same manner that bees got their nourishment is proverbial (Dent B208),
e.g. Sir Politic's comment to Peregrine in *Volpone*, 'the spider and the bee
oft-times / Suck from one flower' (2.1.30–1). Topsell, however, attempts to
debunk the myth: 'All these spiders are venomous even naturally, for that is
so settled and deeply fastened in them, as can by no means be eradicated
or taken away. Neither suck they this venom and poisonous quality from
plants or herbs, as many men think' (p. 249).
    26. *without a sting*] Labesha unwittingly says that he lacks a penis; a sting
is a pole, or staff (*OED n.* 1) as well as an insect's sharp-pointed weapon.
Shakespeare puns on this in *The Taming of the Shrew*, when Katherine warns
'If I be waspish, best beware my sting' and Petruchio replies, 'My remedy
is then to pluck it out' (2.1.210–11).

Enter COLINET.

Colinet. God save you, sir.   30
Foyes. You are welcome, sir, for aught that I know yet.
Colinet. I hope I shall be so still, sir.
Foyes. What is your business, sir? And then I'll tell you.
Colinet. Marry, thus, sir, the Countess Moren entreats your
    fair daughter to bear her company this forenoon.   35
Foyes. This forenoon, sir? Doth my lord or lady send for her,
    I pray?
Colinet. My lady, I assure you.
Foyes. My lady, you assure me? Very well, sir. Yet that house
    is full of gallant gentlemen, dangerous thorns to prick   40
    young maids, I can tell you.
Colinet. There   are   none   but   honest   and   honourable
    gentlemen.
Foyes. All is one, sir, for that. I'll trust my daughter with any
    man, but no man with my daughter, only yourself, Mon-   45
    sieur Besha, whom I will entreat to be her guardian and
    to bring her home again.
Colinet. I will wait upon her, an it please you.
Foyes. No, sir, your weight upon her will not be so good.
    Here, Monsieur Besha, I deliver my daughter unto you   50
    a perfect maid, and so I pray you look well unto her.
Colinet. Farewell, Monsieur Foyes.
Labesha. I warrant I'll look unto her well enough. Mistress,
    will it please you to preambulate?
Martia. With all my heart.   55

Exeunt.

---

36. *my lord*] Count Moren.
40–1. *thorns…maids*] The bawdy pun on 'thorns' and 'prick' is obvious.
44. *All is one*] It doesn't matter.
46. *Besha*] Labesha. Chapman uses the two forms of the name
indiscriminately.
48–9.] Colinet's use of the familiar 'wait upon' in the sense of 'escort'
allows for Foyes's 'weight upon', as in sexual intercourse, similar to the pun
on 'bear double'.
54. *preambulate*] walk or go before, or in front (*OED v.* 1); distinct from
'perambulate', which is to travel through or walk about an area. A pretentious word, it is also spoken by Armado to Holofernes in *Love's Labour's
Lost*: 'Arts-man, preambulate' (5.1.81).

SCENE 4

Enter [FLORILLA,] *the puritan.*

Florilla. What have I done? Put on too many clothes?
   The day is hot, and I am hotter clad
   Than might suffice health.
   My conscience tells me that I have offended,
   And I'll put them off.   5
   That will ask time that might be better spent;
   One sin will draw another quickly so.
   See how the devil tempts! [*Seeing the jewels*] But what's
     here? Jewels? [*Taking them up*]
   How should these come here?

Enter LABERVELE.

Labervele. Good morrow, lovely wife. What hast thou there?   10
Florilla. Jewels, my lord, which here I strangely found.
Labervele. That's strange indeed. What, where none comes
   But when yourself is here? Surely the heavens

Scene 4] *This ed.*; Scene IV *Parrott*; Sc. iv *Greg*; I.iv *Holaday; not in Q.*
0 SD. *Enter* FLORILLA *the*] *Parrott; Enter the Q.*   1 SH.] *This ed.*; Florila,
Flo. *Q*; Flo. *Shepherd.*   8 SDs.] *This ed.; not in Q.*   10 SH.] *This ed.; Lab.*
La. *Q; La. Shepherd; Lab. Parrott.*

   Scene 4] 'Like Scene 1, this scene is laid in Florilla's private garden'
(Parrott).
   6.] Florilla evokes Paul's admonition, 'Take heed therefore how ye walk
circumspectly: not as unwise, but as wise, redeeming the time, because the
days are evil' (Ephesians, 5.15–16). As Paul A. Jorgensen notes, the philosophy of advising us to make the best use of the time given us on earth informs
Prince Hal's promise in 1 *Henry IV*, 'I'll so offend to make offence a skill, /
Redeeming time when men think least I will' (1.2.216–17). That Florilla
would apply Paul's dictum to the time required to change her clothes shows
the ridiculousness of her puritan pretensions (see Jorgensen, pp. 231–42).
   13. *Surely*] Labervele is 'humouring' Florilla's puritanism by using this
word, seemingly everywhere in the Bible, from the beginning of the Old
Testament, 'And surely your blood of your lives will I require' (Genesis,
9.5), to the penultimate verse of the New Testament, 'He which testifieth
these things, saith, surely, I come quickly' (Revelation 22.20). Florilla
repeats it several times, and only when she is adopting her 'puritanical'
attitude (4.24, 4.57, 9.36; 13.88, 13.109).

Have rained thee jewels for thy holy life
And using thy old husband lovingly;   15
Or else do fairies haunt this holy green,
As evermore mine ancestors have thought.
Florilla. Fairies were but in times of ignorance,
Not since the true pure light hath been revealed;
And that they come from heaven I scarce believe.   20
For jewels are vain things; much gold is given
For such fantastical and fruitless jewels,
And therefore heaven, I know, will not maintain
The use of vanity. Surely I fear
I have much sinned to stoop and take them up,   25
Bowing my body to an idle work;
The strength that I have had to this very deed
Might have been used to take a poor soul up
In the highway.
Labervele. You are too curious, wife. Behold your jewels!   30
What, methinks there's posies written on them:
     (*Then he reads*)
  Despair not of children,
  Love with the longest;
  When man is at the weakest,
  God is at the strongest.   35
Wonderful rare and witty, nay divine!

18.] The tradition that Christianity's arrival in England drove out all the fairies began long before the rise of puritanism. At the beginning of her tale, Chaucer's Wife of Bath speaks of 'th' olde dayes of the Kyng Arthour', when 'Al was this land fulfild of fayerye'. This was before the arrival of the Christian religion, with its 'lymytours and othere hooly freres / That serchen every lond and every streem', and so 'maketh that ther ben no fayeryes' (ll. 859–72). Bishop Richard Corbett (1582–1635) offers similar sentiments in his poem, *The Fairies' Farewell*: 'But since of late Elizabeth / And later James came in, / They never danced on any heath / As when the time had been' (cited Parrott, p. 691).

28–9. *take…highway*] Florilla probably refers to the story of the Good Samaritan (Luke 10.25–37), although this is not a direct quote.

30. *curious*] particular, cautious (*OED a.* 2b).

31. *there's posies*] The plural subject taking a singular verb is common in early modern usage (Abbott, pp. 234–40).

Why this is heavenly comfort for thee, wife.
What is this other? [*He reads*]
   God will reward her a thousandfold,
   That takes what age can, and not what age would.   40
The best that ever I heard! No mortal brain,
I think, did ever utter such conceit
For good plain matter and for honest rhyme.
Florilla. Vain poetry! I pray you burn them, sir.
Labervele. You are to blame, wife. Heaven hath sent you them   45
To deck yourself withal like to yourself,
Not to go thus like a milkmaid.
Why, there is difference in all estates
By all religion.   ·
Florilla.   There is no difference!
Labervele. I prithee wife, be of another mind,   50
And wear these jewels and a velvet hood.

---

38 SD.] *This ed.; not in Q.*

42. *conceit*] a fanciful, ingenious, or witty notion or expression (*OED n.* 8).

46. *To deck yourself withal*] Labervele refers not just to the poems but to the 'jewels' in which they are set.

47. *like a milkmaid*] See 2.89–90 n.

48–9.] Labervele believes that Florilla, being a countess, should dress as befits her social class, and that such distinctions are proper to all Christians. What the different levels of society were authorised to wear was set out by royal proclamations; although Florilla insists that that any superfluity in dress is ungodly, for most people the decrees were, as Hamlet says of a different royal proclamation, 'more honoured in the breach than the observance' (1.4.16).

51. *velvet hood*] Velvet was one of the fabrics reserved for the aristocracy. Queen Elizabeth's proclamation of 1597 reaffirms the rules she set out in 1562, and again in 1574: 'none shall wear...velvet in gowns, cloaks, safeguards, or other uppermost garments; embroidery with silk, netherstocks of silk, under the degree of knight's wife, except gentlewomen of the privy chamber, the maidens of honour, and such whose husbands or themselves may dispend £200 by the year for term of life in possession above all charges' (*Proclamations*, 3: 178). That such strictures were routinely ignored is shown by Stubbes's condemnation of such 'capital ornaments, as French hood, hat, cap, kercher, and such like, whereof some be of velvet, some of taffeta, some

Florilla. A velvet hood! Oh, vain, devilish device!
　A toy made with a superfluous flap,
　Which being cut off, my head were still as warm.
　Diogenes did cast away his dish　　　　　　　　　55
　Because his hand would serve to help him drink.
　Surely these heathens shall rise up against us.
Labervele. Sure, wife, I think thy keeping always close,
　Making thee melancholy, is the cause
　We have no children, and therefore, if thou wilt,　60
　Be merry and keep company, i' God's name.

(but few) of wool, some of this fashion, some of that, according to the variable fantasies of their serpentine minds. And to such excess it is grown that every artificer's wife, will not stick to go in her hat of velvet every day' (p. 113).

　52.] In rejecting the velvet hood, Florilla follows the preacher Thomas Becon, whose catechism *The Jewel of Joy* (c. 1547) reads, 'Here, even from the beginning, do we learn both what garments were given unto man of God, and for what purpose. Neither with fine cloth, nor with satin, damask, velvet, nor with cloth of gold, did God apparel Adam, neither did he trim and set forth our grandmother Eve with sumptuous apparel of cloth of silver, or cloth of gold, neither did he set upon her head a French hood with an edge of gold, besides pearls and precious stones, and such other trim-trams...but he clothed them both with simple garments of leather, not that they should rejoice and be proud of them, but to use them as things necessary to cover their wretched nakedness, and to defend them from the cruel storms and fierce tempests of wind, rain, snow, hail, etc.' (p. 437).

　53. *toy*] something of little or no value, a trifle (*OED n.* 5), as Macbeth says in a far more serious context, 'There's nothing serious in mortality / All is but toys' (2.3.92–3); cf. 3.12 n.

　55–6.] one of the best known stories of the Cynic philosopher Diogenes of Sinope (c. 412–323 BC). As his namesake Diogenes Laertius relates in *Lives of Eminent Philosophers*, 'one day, observing a child drinking out of his hands, he cast away the cup from his wallet with the words, "A child has beaten me in the plainness of living"' (2: 39).

　57. *against*] in comparison with us (*OED prep.* 16), or, by way of confuting us. Heathen philosophers such as Diogenes put us Christians to shame.

　58. *close*] shut in, at home, as in Pistol's farewell to the Hostess in *Henry V*, 'Let huswifery appear. Keep close, I thee command' (2.3.62–3); cf. 1.7 n.

　59. *melancholy*] the first time the word is spoken in the play, used here in the general sense of 'sad'.

Florilla. Sure, my lord, if I thought I should be rid
    Of this same banishment of barrenness,
    And use our marriage to the end it was made,
    Which was for procreation, I should sin   65
    If by my keeping house I should neglect
    The lawful means to be a fruitful mother;
    And therefore if it please you I'll use resort.
Labervele. [*Aside*] God's my passion, what have I done? Who
    would have thought her pureness would yield so soon to   70
    courses of temptations? [*To Florilla*] Nay, hark you, wife,
    I am not sure that going abroad will cause fruitfulness in
    you. That, you know, none knows but God himself.

---

63. banishment] *Q, Holaday*; punishment *Shepherd.*   69 SD.] *Parrott; not*
in Q.   71 SD.] *This ed.; not in Q.*

---

63. *banishment*] Holaday (p. 129) rejects Shepherd's emendation, 'punishment', noting that *Q*'s 'banishment' is consistent with the puritan sense
of 'isolation from grace'.
    65. *procreation*] Chapman has a wonderful time with this word as the play
proceeds.
    66. *keeping house*] remaining at home, similar to 'keeping always close' at
l. 58, perhaps with the added meaning of performing domestic duties (*OED
house n.*[1] 18).
    67. *the lawful means*] 'Any of' or 'all of' the lawful means seems to be the
sense.
    68. *use resort*] The more common form is 'make' or 'have' resort, i.e. to
go to some place for a specific purpose (*OED resort n.* 4), as in Chapman's
Iliad, 'To th' altars of the gods they made divine resorts' (11.723). There
might also be a quibble on 'house of resort' being a brothel, e.g. Mistress
Overdone's lament in *Measure for Measure*, 'But shall all our houses of resort
in the suburbs be pulled down?' (1.2.101–2), and Marina's demanding of
Lysimachus in *Pericles*, 'And do you know this house to be a place / Of such
resort and will come into't?' (4.6.79–80). Labervele's concerns are similar
to those expressed by Thorello (*F*: Kitely) in *Every Man In*, who doubts his
wife Bianca's fidelity 'where there is such resort / Of wanton gallants and
young revellers' (1.4.164–5), although in this case the men are coming to his
wife, rather than the other way around. Florilla's acquiescence to the idea
of going out 'to be merry and keep company' is all too quick for Labervele,
and his rapid shifting back and forth from wanting and not wanting his wife
to stay at home would be very funny in the hands of a skilled actor.
    69. *God's my passion*] a mild oath, also found in Rowley's *A Shoemaker,
A Gentleman*: 'Hence you whore-master! Knave! God's my passion, got a
wench with child, thou naughty pack!' (4.2.64–5).
    72. *abroad*] out of one's house (*OED adv.* 3). At this time there was no
necessary implication of going to a foreign country.

Florilla. I know, my lord, 'tis true, but the lawful means must
    still be used.   75
Labervele. Yea, the lawful means indeed must still, but now
    I remember that lawful means is not abroad.
Florilla. Well, well, I'll keep the house still.
Labervele. Nay, hark you, lady, I would not have you think –
    marry, I must tell you this – if you should change the   80
    manner of your life, the world would think you changed
    religion too.
Florilla. 'Tis true. I will not go.
Labervele. Nay, if you have a fancy.
Florilla. Yea, a fancy, but that's no matter.   85
Labervele. Indeed, fancies are not for judicial and religious
    women.

            Enter CATALIAN, *like a scholar.*

Catalian. God save your lordship, and you, most religious
    lady.
Labervele. Sir, you may say 'God save us' well indeed, that   90
    thus are thrust upon in private walks.
Catalian. A slender thrust, sir, where I touched you not.
Labervele. Well, sir, what is your business?
Catalian. Why, sir, I have a message to my lady from Mon-
    sieur Du Bartas.   95

94–5. Monsieur Du Bartas] *Parrott*; Monsier du Barto *Q, Holaday*; Monsieur du Barte *Shepherd*.

---

86. *judicial*] judicious, showing sound judgement (*OED a.* 5), not
restricted to matters of law.

86.1 SD. like a scholar] wearing an academic gown.

91. *thrust upon*] intruded upon (*OED thrust v* 8a).

92.] In saying that the intrusion is small or insignificant (*OED slender a*
4), Catalian puns on 'thrust', which, like 'touched', is a fencing term. The
latter is synonymous with 'hit', as in Hamlet's 'Another hit. What say you?'
and Laertes' reply, 'A touch, a touch, I do confess't' (5.2.285–6).

94–5. *Monsieur Du Bartas*] Guillaume de Salutes Du Bartas (1544–90),
whose poetic retelling of Genesis, *Les Sepmaines* (*The Divine Weeks*), was
widely read in both France and England. Chapman drew on Du Bartas's
philosophy in such works as *The Shadow of Night* (Schoell, pp. 39–42); see
following note.

Labervele. To your lady! Well, sir, speak your mind to your
   lady!

Florilla. You are very welcome, sir, and I pray, how doth he?

Catalian. In health, madam, thanks be to God, commending
   his duty to your ladyship, and hath sent you a message   100
   which I would desire your honour to hear in private.

Florilla. 'My ladyship' and 'my honour'! They be words
   which I must have you leave. They be idle words, and
   you shall answer for them, truly. 'My duty to you' or 'I
   desire you' were a great deal better than 'my ladyship',   105
   or 'my honour'.

Catalian. I thank you for your Christian admonition.

Florilla. Nay, thank God for me. Come, I will hear your
   message with all my heart, and you are very welcome, sir.

Labervele. [*Aside*] 'With all my heart and you are very welcome   110
   sir', and go and talk with a young lusty fellow able to
   make a man's hair stand upright on his head! What purity
   is there in this, trow you, ha? What wench of the faculty
   could have been more forward? Well sir, I will know your
   message. [*To Catalian*] You, sir, you, sir, what says the   115

---

110 SD.] *Parrott; not in Q.*   113. you, ha? What] *This ed.;* you? ha, what *Q,
subst. Parrott.*   115 SD.] *This ed.; not in Q.*

97–101.] Chapman is being light-hearted in having Catalian claim to be
a disciple of the famous poet, who died seven years before the play was
performed. We might assume that Catalian chose the first scholarly name
that came to mind, and Florilla, eager to have some company, is happy to
play along. Alternatively, she might just be ignorant of who the real Du
Bartas is, or was.

111. *lusty*] a word with a range of meanings, including 'hearty', 'handsome', and 'full of lust or sexual desire' (*OED* a.).

113. *trow you, ha?*] think you, do you suppose? (*OED v.*), very common
in this period. Previous editors, following *Q*, have 'What purity is there in
this, trow you? Ha, what wench…', but I take 'ha' as part of the interroga-
tive, as in Chapman's *May-Day*, 'When shall's have a rouse, ha?' (2.1.602),
not as an exclamation introducing the next phrase. Chapman is fond of the
construction, using it twice more in *May-Day* (2.1.626, 3.1.131) and again
in *Sir Giles Goosecap* (4.2.66).

wench of the faculty] prostitute, similar to the 'daughters of the game' and
'sisters of the hold-door trade' in *Troilus and Cressida* (4.5.63, 5.10.51). A
'faculty' can be any trade or profession (*OED n.* 8).

holy man, sir? Come, tell true, for by heaven or hell I will
have it out.

Catalian. Why, you shall, sir, if you be so desirous.

Labervele. Nay, sir, I am more than 'so desirous'! Come, sir,
study not for a new device now.   120

Catalian. Not I, my lord, this is both new and old. I am a
scholar, and being spiritually inclined by your lady's most
godly life, I am to profess the ministry and to become her
chaplain, to which end Monsieur Du Bartas hath com-
mended me.   125

Labervele. Her chaplain, in the devil's name? Fit to be vicar
of hell!

Florilla. My good head, what are you afraid of? He comes
with a godly and neighbourly suit. What, think you his
words or his looks can tempt me? Have you so little faith?   130
If every word he spake were a serpent as subtle as that
which tempted Eve, he cannot tempt me, I warrant you.

Labervele. Well answered for him, lady, by my faith. Well,
hark you, I'll keep your chaplain's place yonder for a
while, and at length put in one myself.   135

---

124. Monsieur Du Bartas] *Parrott*; monsier du Barte *Q*; Monsieur du Barte
Shepherd; Monsier du Barto *Holaday.*

---

116. *holy man*] Apart from being a poet, Du Bartas was a soldier and
counsellor to Henry of Navarre. Perhaps Labervele, not willing to admit he
has never heard of him, assumes Catalian, if he is actually a scholar, would
be studying with a cleric.

120. *study*] search, cast about for (*OED v.* 2f).

128. *head*] husband, as in Paul to the Ephesians, 'Wives, submit your-
selves unto your own husbands, as unto the Lord: For the husband is
the head of the wife, even as Christ is the head of the Church: and he
is the saviour of the body' (Ephesians, 5.22–3). This sentiment is repeated
in countless texts, most famously in *The Taming of the Shrew*, 'Thy
husband is thy lord, thy life, thy keeper / Thy head, thy sovereign'
(5.2.146–7).

131. *If*] Even if.

133. *for him*] as far as he (Catalian) is concerned.

134–5 *I'll keep…myself.*] Labervele seems to be telling Florilla that he will
'keep', in the sense of 'save', the chaplain's lodgings (*OED place n.*[1] 9 a) on
his estate until he is ready to make his own appointment.

Enter LEMOT[, *as* CATALIAN *moves to the side of the stage*].

What, more yet? God's my passion, whom do I see? The
very imp of desolation, the minion of our king, whom no
man sees to enter his house but he locks up his wife, his
children and his maids, for where he goes he carries his
house upon his head like a snail. [*To Lemot*] Now, sir, I   140
hope your business is to me.

Lemot. No, sir, I must crave a word with my lady.

Labervele. These words are intolerable, and she shall hear no
more!

Lemot. She must hear me speak!   145

Labervele. Must she, sir? Have you brought the King's warrant
for it?

Lemot. I have brought that which is above kings.

Labervele. Why, every man for her sake is a puritan! The
devil, I think, will shortly turn puritan, or the puritan will   150
turn devil.

Florilla. What have you brought, sir?

135.1 SD. *Enter* LEMOT] *right margin* Q.   *as* CATALIAN *moves to the side of
the stage*] *This ed.; not in* Q.   138. locks] *Shepherd;* lookes *Q.*   140
SD.] *This ed.; not in* Q.

135.1 SD.] Catalian has nothing more to say for the rest of the scene, but
his continued presence is implied by Lemot's address to 'sirrah' at l. 248. It
makes sense for Catalian to remain, as an unobserved observer.

137. *imp*] literally, a shoot of a plant or tree, often used figuratively to
mean a child of the devil (*OED n.* 1, 4).

desolation] dissolution. In Scene 6, Labervele uses the word 'desolate'
(*OED a.* 7) in this sense (6.24, 28). *Love's Labour's Lost* has Costard speaking
of the 'the merry days of desolation' he has seen (1.2.151); although prone
to malapropisms, Costard might be taken literally, with the same meaning.

minion] favourite, close companion (*OED n.* 1 1). In early use, there was
sometimes a connotation of a homosexual relationship, but that is not
implied here.

139–40. *where he goes...like a snail*] The 'he' of this clause is the man
who needs to lock up the women of his house should Lemot pay a visit; a
snail 'that carries his house upon his head' is proverbial for a cuckold (Dent
S580). In *Northward Ho*, Greenshield, assuming Mayberry is a cuckold,
claims 'I think when he comes home, poor snail, he'll not dare to peep forth
of doors lest his horns usher him' (5.1.88–90).

148. *above kings*] a commonplace, although Lemot does not appear to be
quoting any biblical or proverbial source directly.

Lemot. Marry, this, madam: you know we ought to prove one
  another's constancy, and I am come in all chaste and
  honourable sort to prove your constancy.   155
Florilla. You are very welcome, sir, and I will abide your
  proof. It is my duty to abide your proof.
Labervele. You'll bide his proof? It is your duty to bide his
  proof? How the devil will you bide his proof?
Florilla. My good head, no otherwise than before your face in   160
  all honourable and religious sort. I tell you I am constant
  to you, and he comes to try whether I be so or no, which
  I must endure. [*To Lemot*] Begin your proof, sir.
Lemot. Nay, madam, not in your husband's hearing, though
  in his sight; for there is no woman will show she is   165
  tempted from her constancy, though she be a little. Withdraw yourself, sweet lady.

                              [*They withdraw.*]
Labervele. Well, I will see, though I do not hear. Women may
  be courted without offence, so they resist the courtier.
Lemot. Dear and most beautiful lady, of all the sweet, honest   170
  and honourable means to prove the purity of a lady's

---

163 SD.] *This ed.; not in Q.*   167.1 SD.] *Parrott; not in Q.*

153. *we ought to prove*] we all need to test (*OED v.* 1).

154. *constancy*] a loaded word. Florilla is not only to prove that she is
'constant' (l. 161) to her husband in the specific sense of being faithful in
marriage, but needs to demonstrate that she has the moral virtue of constancy so prized by the stoics: the ability to remain calm and unmoved of
mind, not subject to the passions. In *All's Well*, Lafeu says of Helen, 'I have
spoke / With one that in her sex, her years, profession, / Wisdom and
constancy, hath amazed me more / Than I dare blame my weakness'
(2.1.82–4).

155. *sort*] See 1.14 n.

156–7. *abide your proof*] withstand your trial.

158. *bide*] While Labervele is repeating his wife's statement, there is no
need to emend Q to 'abide', since 'bide' is an equally common form,
with the same meaning. The discrepancy might be intended, since Florilla's
word, 'abide', is used very frequently in the 1559 edition of the *Book of
Common Prayer* and the *Geneva Bible*, while 'bide' appears only a few
times.

160. *no otherwise*] in no other way (*OED otherwise n.* 1). This form, now
obsolete, was common in Chapman's time.

169. *so*] provided that.

constancy, kisses are the strongest. I will therefore be
bold to begin my proof with a kiss.

Florilla. No, sir, no kissing!

Lemot. No kissing, madam? How shall I prove you then suf-   175
ficiently, not using the most sufficient proof? To flatter
yourself by affection of spirit, when it is not perfectly
tried, is sin.

Florilla. You say well, sir. That which is truth is truth.

Lemot. Then do you well, lady, and yield to the truth.   180

Florilla. By your leave, sir, my husband sees. Peradventure it
may breed an offence to him.

Lemot. How can it breed an offence to your husband to see
your constancy perfectly tried?

Florilla. You are an odd man, I see, but first I pray tell me   185
how kissing is the best proof of chaste ladies.

Lemot. To give you a reason for that, you must give me leave
to be obscure and philosophical.

Florilla. I pray you be. I love philosophy well.

Lemot. Then thus, madam: every kiss is made as the voice is,   190
by imagination and appetite, and, as both those are presented to the ear in the voice, so are they to the silent
spirits in our kisses.

---

172. *kisses are the strongest*] In the *Paradoxes*, Donne writes of kissing as
'the divinest touch of all...the strange and mystical union of souls' (*Paradox*
2, ll. 11–12); *Ovid's Banquet of Sense* devotes several stanzas to the 'perpetual-
motion-making-kiss' Corynna gives Ovid (99.5).

177–8. *affection...sin*] The word 'sin' suggests that Lemot is bringing
Florilla's puritan pretensions into the argument, implying that she might be
flattering herself by affecting, i.e. 'putting on', an appearance of 'spirit' in
the religious sense. This anticipates the 'philosophical' play on 'spirits' as
purveyors of imagination and appetite (ll. 190–200).

179. *truth is truth*] a common proverb (Tilley T381). Taken together,
Florilla's answer and Lemot's statement that provoked it could be a reference to 1 John, 1.8: 'If we say that we have no sin, we deceive ourselves, and
the truth is not in us.'

180. *do you well*] i.e. act on the principle you have just enunciated.

188. *obscure and philosophical*] For Chapman, the two words always
go together; perhaps this is a 'dig' at his critics (see Introduction,
pp. 7–8).

190–1. *every kiss...appetite*] concepts central to the 'philosophy' of the
soul that Lemot brings to the argument (see Introduction, pp. 16–18).

Florilla. To what spirit mean you?

Lemot. To the spirits of our blood.   195

Florilla. What if it do?

Lemot. Why then, my imagination and mine appetite, working
upon your ears in my voice and upon your spirits in my
kisses, piercing therein the more deeply, they give the
stronger assault against your constancy.   200

Florilla. Why then, to say 'prove my constancy' is as much as
to say 'kiss me'.

Lemot. Most true, rare lady.

Florilla. Then prove my constancy.

Lemot. Believe me, madam, you gather exceeding wittily   205
upon it.

                                        [*He kisses her.*]

Labervele. [*To himself*] Oh, my forehead! My very heart aches
at a blow! What dost thou mean, wife? Thou wilt lose thy
fame, discredit thy religion, and dishonour me forever.

Florilla. [*Aloud*] Away, sir. I will abide no more of your proof,   210
nor endure any more of your trial.

Lemot. Oh, she dares not, she dares not. I am as glad I have
tried your purity as may be. You, the most constant lady
in France? I know an hundred ladies in this town that
will dance, revel all night amongst gallants, and in the   215
morning go to bed to her husband as clear a woman as
if she were new christened; kiss him, embrace him and
say, 'no, no, husband, thou art the man', and he takes
her for the woman.

---

199. more deeply] *Q (corrected); most deeply Q (uncorrected); see Yamada,
p. 132.* 206.1 SD.] *subst. Parrott; not in Q.* 207 SD.] *This ed.; not in
Q.* 210 SD.] *This ed.; not in Q.*

---

195. *spirits of our blood*] another expression of the Galenic theory by which
the spirits travelled through the body along with the humours. In this case,
as at 1.20, the humour is blood, responsible for the sexual appetite.

205. *gather*] reason, draw conclusions (*OED v.* 10).

209. *fame*] reputation (*OED n.* 2).

212. *she dares not*] Lemot might be pretending to address himself, but
loudly, for Labervele's benefit.

218. *the man*] the only one she loves, as in *Twelfth Night*, with Viola's
rueful 'I am the man' (2.2.25), and *As You Like It*, when Touchstone asks,
'And how, Audrey, am I the man yet?' (3.3.2–3).

Florilla. And all this can I do.   220
Labervele. Take heed of it, wife.
Florilla. Fear not, my good head, I warrant you, for him.
Lemot. Nay, madam, triumph not before the victory. How
        can you conquer that against which you never strive, or
        strive against that which never encounters you? To live   225
        idle in this walk, to enjoy this company, to wear this habit
        and have no more delights than those will afford you, is
        to make Virtue an idle huswife, and to hide herself in
        slothful cobwebs that still should be adorned with actions
        of victory. No, madam, if you will worthily prove your   230
        constancy to your husband, you must put on rich apparel,
        fare daintily, hear music, read sonnets, be continually
        courted, kiss, dance, feast, revel all night amongst gal-
        lants. Then if you come to bed to your husband with a
        clear mind and a clear body, then are your virtues *ipsis-* 235
        sima; then have you passed the full test of experiment and

---

228. in] *Shepherd; not in Q.*   230. worthily] *conj. Brereton;* unworthily *Q.*

223. *triumph...victory*] proverbial (Dent V50). Triumph is used in its
original sense of a Roman general celebrating a victory with a march through
the city, an honour granted by the Senate.
226. *habit*] costume (*OED n.* 1), not necessarily associated with a religious order.
228. *Virtue*] Dame Virtue; such personifications are typically female.
idle huswife] 'Huswife' and 'housewife' were interchangeable; perhaps the
former spelling, which we find in *Q*, carries more connotation of a light or
loose character, especially if accompanied by an adjective such as 'idle'. In
Whetstone's *Promos and Cassandra, Part* 1, those accusing Lamia of harlotry
claim that all the city 'doth ring of her lewd life / Indeed she is known for
an idle huswife' (sig. D4r).
230. *worthily*] *Q* reads 'unworthily', but as Brereton (p. 57) notes, the
context requires 'worthily'.
232. *fare*] dine (*OED v.* 8). Faring 'daintily' or deliciously would be hard
for a sincere puritan, given Luke's parable of 'a certain rich man, which
was clothed in purple and fine white, and fared very deliciously every day'.
He ended up in hell, while the beggar Lazarus, who 'laid at his gate full
of sores...was carried by the angels into Abraham's bosom' (Luke,
16.19–21).
235–6. ipsissima] genuine, their true selves, as in the legal expression
ipsissima verba, 'the very words'.

you shall have an hundred gallants fight thus far in blood
for the defence of your reputation.

Labervele. O vanity of vanities!

Florilla. O husband, this is perfect trial indeed!   240

Labervele. And you will try all this now, will you not?

Florilla. Yea, my good head, for it is written, 'We must pass
   to perfection through all temptation'. Habakkuk, the
   fourth.

Labervele. Habakkuk! Cuck me no cucks! In-a-doors, I say!   245
   Thieves, puritans, murderers! In-a-doors, I say!

                    [*Exeunt* LABERVELE *and* FLORILLA.]

Lemot. So now is he start mad, i'faith. [*To Catalian*] But
   sirrah, as this is an old lord jealous of his young wife, so
   is ancient Countess Moren jealous of her young husband.
   We'll thither to have some sport, i'faith.   250

                    Exit [*with* CATALIAN].

SCENE 5

Enter LABESHA, *hanging upon* MARTIA['s] *sleeve,*
and the Lord MOREN *comes to them.*

Moren. I prithee, Besha, keep a little off. Hang not upon her
   shoulders thus, for shame.

243, 245. Habakkuk] *Parrott*; Abacuke *Q, Holaday*; Abacuk *Shep-
herd.*   246.1 SD.] *subst. Parrott*; Exit *Q.*   247. start] *Q, Parrott*; stark
Shepherd.   SD. *To Catalian*] *This ed.; not in Q.*   250.1 SD. *Exit with*
CATALIAN] *Parrott; Exit Q; Exeunt Holaday.*

Scene 5] *This ed.*; Scene V *Parrott*; Sc. v *Greg*; I.v *Holaday; not in Q.*
0 SD. LABESHA] *This ed.; Besha Q.*   MARTIA'S] *Shepherd; Martia Q.*
1 SH.] *This ed.*; Mar. *Q*; Mor. *Parrott.*

243–4. *Habakkuk, the fourth*] As Parrott notes, the Book of Habakkuk has
only three chapters, but, more pertinent to the 'humorous' nature of Florilla's puritanism, her theological knowledge being mere pretence, is that
nothing in Habakkuk bears even the slightest resemblance to the words she
supposedly quotes.

246. *Thieves, puritans, murderers*] There seems no explanation to this
exclamation, other than to assume that Labervele is over-excited. He cries
out again against puritans and murderers at 9.1.

247. *start mad*] See 2.95 n.

Scene 5] This scene takes place at the house of Count and Countess Moren.

Labesha. My lord, *pardonnez moi*, I must not let her talk alone
  with anyone, for her father gave me charge.
Moren. Oh, you are a goodly charger for a goose.   5
Labesha. A goose! You are a gander to call me goose. I am a
  Christian gentleman as well as you.
Moren. Well, sirrah, get you hence, or by my troth I'll have
  thee taken out in a blanket, tossed from forth our hearing.
Labesha. In a blanket? What, do you make a puppy of me?   10
  By skies and stones, I will go and tell your lady.   *Exit.*
Moren. Nay, but Besha –
Martia. Nay, he will tell, my lord.

        Enter the COUNTESS MOREN *and* LABESHA.

Countess. Why, how now, my lord? What, thought you I was
  dead, that you are wooing of another thus? Or are you   15
  laying plots to work my death?
Moren. Why, neither, sweet bird. What need you move these
  questions unto me, whom you know loves you above all
  the women in the world?

---

3. *pardonnez moi*] subst. *Parrott; Pardon a moy Q.* 5 SH.] *This ed.*;
Mar. *Q*; Mor. *Parrott.* 8 SH.] *This ed.; Mar. Q; Mo. Shepherd.* 12 SH.]
This ed.; Mor. Lord. Lor. Mo. Me. Q; Mo. Shepherd; Mor. Parrott.
13.1 SD. LABESHA] *Parrott; Besha Q.* 14 SH.] *This ed.; Coun. Con. C. Co.
Count. Cou. Q; Coun. Shepherd, Holaday; Count. Parrott.*

   5.] Moren puns on Labesha having a 'charge' or responsibility (l. 4) by
likening him both to a 'charger', i.e. a large platter (*OED n.* 1) fit for serving
a roast goose, and then to the goose itself.
   8. *by my troth*] by my good faith, honesty – one of the most common
expressions of the period.
   9. *out in a blanket, tossed*] a very old form of mild punishment applied to
both dogs and humans, and ubiquitous in early modern drama, e.g. Ballurdo
in Marston's *Antonio and Mellida*, 'That I'll toss love like a dog in a blanket'
(4.1.273), or Lickfinger warning Pennyboy Senior in Jonson's *The Staple of
News*, 'Go, Sir, / You will be tossed like Block [his dog] in a blanket else'
(4.3.79–80).
   11. *By skies and stones*] Labesha uses this expression, which I have not
found elsewhere, here and at 8.321; it could be that he is trying to coin new
oaths, something a would-be gallant is encouraged to do. Jonson has fun
with this in *Every Man In*, with Cob's admiration of Bobadilla, 'Oh, I have
a guest, he teacheth me, he doth swear the best of any man christened'
(*Q*, 1.3.72–4).
   17. *sweet bird*] a common expression of endearment, employed by both
Sir Diaphanous Silkworm and Master Needle in Jonson's *The Magnetic Lady*
(2.5.78, 5.7.38).

Countess. How he can flatter, now he hath made a fault!   20
Labesha. He can do little, an he cannot cog.
Moren. Out, you ass!
Countess. Well, come tell me what you did entreat.
Moren. Nothing, by heaven, sweet bird; I swear, but to entreat
   her love.   25
Countess. But to entreat her love!
Moren. Nay, hear me out.
Countess. Nay, here you are out, you are out too much,
   methinks, and put me in.
Moren. And put you in?   30
Countess. In a fair taking, sir, I mean.
Moren. Oh, you may see what hasty taking is. You women
   evermore scramble for our words, and never take them
   mannerly from our mouths.
Countess. Come, tell me what you did entreat.   35
Moren. I did entreat her love to Colinet.

---

21. *cog*] flatter, wheedle his way out (*OED v.* 5). Falstaff declares his love
to Mistress Ford in *Merry Wives* with 'Come, I cannot cog and say thou art
this and that like a-many of these lisping hawthorn-buds that come like
women in men's apparel' (3.3.64–7). Originally the term referred to cheating
at dice.

22. *Out*] an expression of impatience, leading to the delightful play on
the word over the next few lines (see following n.).

28–31.] The Countess answers her husband's 'hear me out' by first saying
that he is out, in the sense of being 'out' of his part, as an actor who has
forgotten his lines – the induction to *Cynthia's Revels* has a child actor assuring his nervous colleague, 'be not out, and good enough' (Ind. 203–4). She
then extends the wordplay to Moren's being out (away from home) too
much, but offers an unwitting sexual pun on Moren having his penis 'out'
too often: with 'and put me in', she means to say, colloquially, 'put (or keep)
me indoors', but this is also a way of saying 'put it in me'. In Fletcher's *A
Wife for a Month*, each of three citizens' wives says to the fool, Tony, 'put
me in', as in 'help me gain entry to the wedding'. He responds with demurs
about his sexual stamina: 'a trick of legerdemain, to put ye all in / 'Twould
pose a fellow that had twice my body' (2.4.1–11); see 3.26 n., Williams,
p. 1121.

31. *fair taking*] 'pretty pickle' (Parrott), as Pharamond says of Galatea and
the other ladies in Beaumont and Fletcher's *Philaster*, 'If they should all
prove honest now, I were in a fair taking' (2.2.4–5).

32. *hasty taking*] jumping to conclusions.

34. *mannerly*] decently, in a seemly manner (*OED adv.* 1). Moren gets
full value from his wife's 'and put me in'.

Countess. To Colinet? Oh, he is your dear cousin, and your
  kind heart, i'faith, is never well but when you are doing
  good for every man. Speak, do you love me?

Moren. I'faith, sweet bird.   40

Countess. Best of all others?

Moren. Best of all others.

Countess. That's my good bird, i'faith.

Labesha. O mistress, will you love me so?

Martia. No, by my troth, will I not.   45

Labesha. 'No, by my troth, will I not.' Why, that's well said.
  I could never get her to flatter me yet.

          Enter LEMOT, BLANUEL, *and* CATALIAN, *and* COLINET.

Lemot. Good morrow, my good lord, and these passing lovely
  ladies.

Countess. So now we shall have all manner of flattering with   50
  Monsieur Lemot.

Lemot. You are all manner of ways deceived, madam, for I
  am so far from flattering you that I do not a whit praise
  you.

Countess. Why do you call us passing lovely, then?   55

Lemot. Because you are passing from your loveliness.

Martia. Madam, we shall not have one *mot* of Monsieur
  Lemot, but it shall be as it were a moat to drown all our
  conceit in admiration.

---

41. others?] *Shepherd*; others. *Q.* 42. others.] *Shepherd*; others? *Q.*
45 SH.] *subst. Shepherd; Mor. Q.* 50 SH.] *conj. Brereton; Cat. Q; Ca. Shepherd.* 58. moat] *Shepherd*; mote *Q, Holaday.*

---

53. *not a whit*] not at all (*OED whit n.*¹).

56.] Lemot denies he is a flatterer with a pun on 'passing'. The ladies are
not 'passing lovely' in the sense of 'very beautiful', but are nearly past the
age of their good looks.

57. mot] word (Fr.), as Lemot explains at l. 67.

58. *moat*] either a ditch surrounding a castle or fort, typically filled with
water, or simply a pond (*OED n.*¹). Martia is a match for Lemot in the
ensuing punning contest on *mot*.

59. *conceit*] apprehension, understanding (*OED n.* 2; cf. 4.42 n.). Rosalind, as Ganymede, tells Orlando he is 'a gentleman of good conceit'
(5.2.51–2).

admiration] wonder, astonishment. In describing the Ghost's appearance,
Horatio asks of Hamlet, 'Season your admiration for a while' (1.2.192).

Lemot. See what a mote her quick eye can spy in mine, before   60
    she looks in it.

Martia. So mote I thee, thine answer is as good as mought
    be.

Lemot. Here's a poor name run out of breath quickly.

Countess. Why, Monsieur Lemot, your name is run out of   65
    breath at every word you speak.

Lemot. That's because my name signifies 'word'.

Martia. Well hit, Monsieur *Verbum.*

Lemot. What, are you good at Latin, lady?

Martia. No, sir, but I know what *verbum* is.   70

Lemot. Why 'tis green bum – *ver* is green, and you know what
    bum is, I am sure of that.

Martia. No, sir, 'tis a verb, and I can decline you.

Lemot. That you can, I'll be sworn.

Martia. What can I do?   75

Lemot. Decline me, or take me a hole lower, as the proverb
    is.

Martia. Nay, sir, I mean plain grammatical declination.

Lemot. Well, let's hear your scholarship, and decline me.

---

60. *mote*] We have gone from 'word' to 'water-filled ditch' to 'particle of
dust' (*OED n.*[1] 1); 'Why seest thou a mote in thy brother's eye, but perceivest
not the beam that is in thine own eye?' (Matthew, 7.3).

62. *So mote I thee*] As I hope to prosper. Martia continues the game by
using 'mote' in its archaic form: a verb, sometimes spelled 'mought', expressing possibility or wish (*OED v.*[1]), while 'thee' is an archaic form of 'thrive'
or 'prosper' (*OED v.*[1] 1). In *The Faerie Queene*, the Red Cross Knight tells
the Palmer, 'But you, fair Sir, whose pageant next ensues / Well mote ye
thee, as well can wish your thought / That home ye may report thrice happy
news' (Bk. 2, 1.33).

68. *Monsieur* Verbum] 'Mister Word'.

71. *green bum*] The punning gets indecent over the next few lines; green
is associated with virginity (hence 'green sickness') and sexuality in general
(see Williams, pp. 620–3).

76. *decline*] Strictly speaking, one conjugates, not declines, a verb, but as
OED notes, this colloquial usage is common. It also allows for the puns that
follow.

76–7.] Lemot uses 'decline' in the sense of 'bring down', or 'lower' (*OED
v.* 17), to play on both the proverbial 'to take a [button] hole lower' or 'take
one down a peg' (Dent P181), and the bawdy sense of hole as vagina
(Williams, pp. 671–3).

Martia. I will, sir: *moto, motas.*   80
Labesha. Oh, excellent! She hath called him 'ass' in Latin.
Lemot. Well, sir, forward.
Martia. Nay, there's enough to try both our scholarships.
Lemot. Moto, motas: nay, faith, forward to *motavi* or *motandi.*
Martia. Nay, sir, I'll leave when I am well.   85
Countess. Why, Monsieur Lemot, your name being in word
general, is in ninny, or in hammer, or in cock, or in
buzzard.

---

80. moto, motas] Martia puns on 'Lemot' by declining the Latin verb
motare, 'to move'.

82.] Labesha having interjected, Lemot asks him to continue.

83. *there's enough*] that is sufficient, as Duke Frederick to Rosalind, 'Thou
art thy father's daughter – there's enough' (1.3.58).

84. motavi *or* motandi] the first person perfect and the gerund of *motare*.

85. *leave…well*] let well alone (Dent W260).

87. *in ninny, or in hammer*] The Countess begins a short contest with
Lemot in naming words associated with jealousy, cuckoldry, or just general
stupidity, both the avian and human variety. 'Hammer' may be taken as
an abbreviation of 'ninnyhammer' (ninny, or simpleton) or 'yellowhammer', a common species of bunting very common in England (Newton,
p. 61). It also applies to cuckolds or other easily fooled men; in Middleton's *The Family of Love*, Mistress Glister warns her husband, 'I say you
are a ninnyhammer, and beware the cuckoo' (l. 1644). Middleton also
plays on these words by naming his goldsmith Yellowhammer in *A Chaste
Maid in Cheapside*, while in Dekker and Webster's *Westward Ho*, Mistress
Birdlime promises to teach the 'yellow-hammer' Justiniano 'that there's a
difference between a cogging bawd and an honest motherly gentlewoman'
(2.2.19–21).

cock] here, a woodcock, proverbially easy to snare. The most notable
woodcock in English drama would have to be Malvolio, 'Now is the woodcock near the gin' (2.5.83).

88. *buzzard*] another common metaphor for 'fool'. In Jonson's *The Case
Is Altered*, Valentine remarks on the drunk and overdressed Juniper and
Onion: 'Oh, here's a sweet metamorphosis, a couple of buzzards turned to
a pair of peacocks' (5.6.4–5).

Lemot. Or in wagtail, or in woodcock, or in dotterel, or in
    dizzard.   90
Martia. Or in clot, or in head, or in cow, or in baby.
Lemot. Or in malkin, or in trash, or in pap, or in lady.
Countess. Or indeed in everything.
Lemot. Why, then, 'tis in thing.
Martia. Then, good Monsieur Thing, there let it rest.   95
Lemot. Then, above all things, I must have a word with you.
Labesha. Hands off, sir, she is not for your mowing.

---

89. *wagtail*] Erasmus, citing the tenth-century Byzantine encyclopaedia,
The Suda, notes that the wagtail is 'a bird of the seacoast, light in weight
and with almost no body, which has a peculiar habit of constantly jerking
its tail feathers', and is 'proverbially used by country people as a name for
the very poor, who had no home or anything else they could call their own'
(33: 116). Early modern writers commonly used it for a slight or contemptible
person, as we see in Kent's opinion of Oswald, 'Spare my grey beard, you
wagtail?' (2.2.67).

    dotterel] According to *OED*, we cannot be sure whether the silly bird is
named after the silly person, or the other way around. Jonson's *The Devil Is
an Ass* features Fabian Fitzdottrel, the foolish Squire of Norfolk.

    90. *dizzard*] defined by *OED* as a fool, in the sense of jester, or more
generally as a blockhead. Unlike the other epithets in this line, there is no
apparent reference to bird life.

    92. *malkin*] wench, sluttish woman (*OED n.* 1). Chaucer's Host asks the
Man of Laws to begin his tale immediately, since time, once lost, 'wol nat
come agayn, withouten drede / Namore than wole Malkynes maydenhede /
Whan she hath lost it in hir wantownesse' (29–31).

    trash] then, as now, frequently applied to women of low morals. By
naming the gingerbread-woman of *Bartholomew Fair* Joan Trash, Jonson
implies that she sells more than gingerbread.

    pap] in this period, either breast (*OED n.*[1] 1), such as 'that left pap'
where Bottom, as Pyramus, repeatedly and gloriously stabs himself
'thus, thus, thus' (5.1.298–300), or a cereal-based food suitable for babies
(*OED n.*[2]).

    95. *Monsieur Thing*] Martia tops Lemot with the familiar pun on 'thing'
and 'penis' (see Williams, pp. 1379–81).

    97. *mowing*] jesting, bantering (*OED v.* 2b), also a bawdy pun (Wil-
liams, pp. 919–20); cf. Lodge's *Wit's Misery*, 'I am not for your mowing'
and *A Margarite of America*, 'this is no meat for your mowing'. These
expressions are given a splendidly delicate gloss in the 1883 edition of
Lodge's *Works*: ' "mowing" means carnal acquaintance, and the phrases
mean to convey that there is no equality between the speakers' (4: 38;
3: 28; 4: 50).

Lemot. She is for your mocking.

Labesha. And she mock me, I'll tell her father.

Lemot. That's a good child; thou smellest of the mother, and   100
she was a fool, I warrant you.

Labesha. Meddle with me, but do not meddle with my
mother.

Lemot. That's a good child. [*To Martia*] Come, I must needs
have a word with you.   105

Labesha. You shall do none of your needs with her, sir.

Catalian. Why, what will you do?

Labesha. What will I do? You shall see what I'll do.

                                        Then he offereth to draw.

Blanuel. Go to, you ass. Offer to draw here, and we'll draw
thee out of the house by the heels.   110

Labesha. What, three against one? Now was ever proper hard-
favoured gentleman so abused? Go to, mistress Martia,
I see you well enough. Are you not ashamed to stand
talking alone with such a one as he?

Lemot. How, sir? With such a one as I, sir?   115

Labesha. Yea, sir. With such a one as you, sir.

Lemot. Why, what am I?

---

104 SD.] *Holaday; not in Q.*   108.1 SD.] *Left margin Q.*

---

98. *mocking*] Lemot turns Labesha's 'mowing' into the proverbial
'mocking and mowing', i.e. 'making faces' (Dent M1030). When Prospero's
'strange shapes' remove the illusory banquet, they do so 'with mocks and
mows' (3.3.82 SD).

100. *thou smellest of the mother*] a play on either, or both, of two expressions. To have 'much of the mother', as Horace says of Crispinus in *Poetaster*
(3.1.155), is to act like a woman suffering from hysteria, while 'smelling of
the lamp' is an accusation of laboriously studied speech or writing (*OED*
smell v 9c). As Erasmus relates in the *Adages*, 'it used to be a common criti-
cism of Demosthenes that his arguments smelt of the lamp, because his
speeches were all written and thought out before he left home' (32: 110);
the court prologue to Jonson's *The Staple of News* promises the royal audience, 'A work not smelling of the lamp, tonight / But fitted for your Majesty's
disport' (Prol. 1–2).

109. *Go to*] a common expression of contempt or anger (cf. l. 118 n.).

109–10. *Offer to draw...draw thee out*] Blanuel plays on drawing a sword
and drawing, i.e. pulling or dragging, Labesha out of the house.

111–12. *hard-favoured*] *OED* defines this as 'ugly', similar to the more
common 'ill-favoured', but Labesha probably means, or at least intends to
mean, that he is lacking in favour, i.e. ill-treated.

Labesha. What are you, sir? Why, I know you well enough.

Lemot. Sirrah, tell me what you know me for, or else by
heaven I'll make thee better thou hadst never known how   120
to speak.

Labesha. Why, sir, if you will needs know, I know you for an
honourable gentleman and the King's minion, and were
it not to you, there's ne'er a gentleman in Paris should
have had her out of my hands.   125

Martia. Nay, he's as tall a gentleman of his hands as any is
in Paris.

Colinet. [*To Lemot*] There's a favour for you, sir.

Lemot. But I can get no favour for you, sir.

Blanuel. [*To Moren*] I pray, my lord, entreat for your cousin   130
Colinet.

Moren. Alas, man, I dare not for my wife.

Catalian. Why, my lord, she thinks it is for nothing but to
speak for your cousin.

Moren. [*To Countess*] I pray you, bird, give me leave to speak   135
for my cousin.

Countess. I am content for him.

Moren. Then one word with you more, courteous lady Martia.

Labesha. Not an you were my father.

Moren. Gentlemen, for God's sake thrust this ass out of the   140
doors.

---

128 SD.] *This ed.; not in Q.*   130 SD.] *This ed.; not in Q.*   135 SD.] *This
ed.; not in Q.*

---

118. *know you well enough*] proverbial, said to supposed knaves or villains
(Dent K171.1), e.g. Falstaff to the Hostess in 1 *Henry IV*, 'Go to, I know
you well enough' (3.3.64).

126. *tall…of his hands*] valorous and skilful at fighting. The newly gentri-
fied Clown promises Autolycus in *The Winter's Tale*, 'I'll swear to the prince
thou art a tall fellow of thy hands and that thou wilt not be drunk' (5.2.161–
3). Martia plays on Labesha's 'out of my hands', l. 125.

129.] One easily forgets by this time that Lemot is supposedly trying to
help Colinet gain favour with Martia.

131. *for my wife*] because of my wife's jealousy.

137.] I do not mind your speaking on my cousin's behalf.

139.] No, even if you were my father. Labesha takes his chaperon's role
very seriously.

Lemot. Nay, by'r Lady, he'll run home and tell her father.

Catalian. Well, go to her; I warrant he shall not trouble you.
[*To Labesha*] Kind gentleman, how we dote on thee! –
Embrace him, gentlemen.   145

Blanuel. O sweet Besha, how we honour thee!

Colinet. Nay, gentlemen, look what a piercing eye he hath.

Labesha. An eye? I have an eye an it were a polecat.

Catalian. Nay, look what a nose he hath.

Labesha. My nose is neat crimson.   150

Blanuel. Nay, look what a handsome man he is! O nature,
nature, thou never mad'st man of so pure a feature!

Labesha. Truly, truly, gentlemen, I do not deserve this
kindness.

Catalian. O lord, sir, you are too modest. Come, shall we   155
walk?

Labesha. Whither? To the alehouse?

Lemot. [*To Countess*] Hark you, madam, have you no more
care of the right of your husband than to let him talk thus
affectionately with another?   160

Countess. Why, he speaks not for himself, but for his cousin
Colinet.

Lemot. God's my life, he tells you so. Nay, an these excuses
may serve, I have done.

---

144 SD.] *Parrott; not in Q.*   147 SH.] *subst. Holaday; Co. Q; Ca. Shepherd;
Cat. Parrott.*   151 SH.] *subst. Q, Holaday; Ca. Shepherd; Cat. Parrott.*
158 SD.] *This ed.; not in Q.*

144–52.] The gallants are distracting Labesha, enabling Moren to speak
with Martia. The separate conversations that follow might be spoken at more
or less the same time, interspersed with one another, in the style of a Caryl
Churchill play.

147 SH. Colinet] Shepherd and Parrott give this line to Catalian, but *Q*'s
speech heading of *Co.* could refer to Colinet, who would be taking part in
the distraction.

148. *polecat*] The European polecat is known for its fetid smell, but here
the falsely modest Labesha would be alluding to the dark mask across its eyes.

151 SH. Blanuel] As at l. 134, Shepherd and Parrott assign this to
Catalian, but *Q*'s heading of *Blan.* is acceptable. They all participate in the
mock praise of Labesha (see Holaday, p. 129).

163. *God's my life*] an oath found frequently in plays of this era.

164.] *Q* has the direction *Enter Lemot* in the right margin, adjacent to
this line, although he has been on stage since l. 47. Holaday's explanation

Countess. By the mass, now I observe him, he looks very   165
    suspiciously indeed. Ne'er trust me if his looks and his
    gesture do not plainly show himself to swear, 'by this light
    I do love thee'.

Lemot. By'r Lady, madam, you guess shrewdly indeed. But
    hark you, madam, I pray let not me be the author of   170
    discord between my good lord and you.

Countess. No, no, Monsieur Lemot, I were blind if I could
    not see this. I'll slit her nose, by Jesus.

Moren. How now, what's the matter?

Countess. What's the matter? If I could come at your mistress,   175
    she should know what's the matter.

Moren. My mistress?

Countess. Yea, your mistress! Oh, here's fair dissimulation.
    [*To Martia*] O ye impudent gossip, do I send for you to
    my house to make you my companion, and do you use   180
    me thus? Little dost thou know what 'tis to love a man
    truly, for if thou didst, thou wouldst be ashamed to
    wrong me so.

Martia. You wrong me, madam, to say I wrong you.

Countess. Go to, get you out of my house.   185

Martia. I am gone, madam.

Moren. [*To Countess*] Well, come in, sweet bird, and I'll per-
    suade thee there's no harm done.

---

179 SD.] *Parrott; not in Q.*   187 SD.] *This ed.; not in Q.*

(p. 129) is both ingenious and persuasive: he notes that this direction, which
is found at the lower right corner of sig. C2r in *Q*, is identical to that inserted
in the same position on sig. B2r (4.135 in this text). When setting the type
for inner C, the compositor must have neglected to remove this direction
from the skeleton of inner B.

   173. *slit her nose*] Chapman himself was almost the recipient of this rather
painful form of punishment. In his *Conversations* with William Drummond,
Ben Jonson relates how, after the scandalous performance of *Eastward Ho*,
he 'voluntarily imprisoned himself with Chapman and Marston, who had
written it amongst him. The report was that they should then had their ears
cut and noses' (*Conversations*, p. 12).

   175. *your mistress*] Countess Moren is convinced her husband is having
an affair with Martia.

Countess. Well, we shall hear your persuasions.

[*Exeunt* COUNTESS *and* MOREN.]

Lemot. Well, God knows, and I can partly guess, what he   190
must do to persuade her. Well, take your fair charge, fair
and manly lord Monsieur Labesha.

Colinet. [*To Martia*] One word with you more, fair lady.

Lemot. Not a word. No man, on pain of death, not a word.
He comes upon my rapier's point that comes within forty   195
foot on her.

Labesha. Thanks, good Lemot, and thanks gentlemen all, and
her father shall thank you.

[*Exeunt* LABESHA *and* MARTIA.]

Colinet. Much good do it you, sir. Come gentlemen, let's go
wait upon the King, and see the humour of the young   200
lord Dowsecer.

Lemot. Excuse me to the King, and tell him I will meet him
there.

[*Exeunt* COLINET, CATALIAN, *and* BLANUEL.]

So, this is but the beginning of sport between this fine
lord and his old lady. But this wench Martia hath happy   205
stars reigned at the disposition of her beauty, for the King
himself doth mightily dote on her. Now to my puritan,
and see if I can make up my full proof of her.

[*Exit.*]

189.1 SD.] *Parrott; not in Q.*   192 lord] *Parrott; L. Q.*   194 SH.] *subst. Q,*
Parrott; Mo. Shepherd.   SD. *To Martia*] *This ed.; not in Q.*   199 SH.] *subst.*
Q, Parrott; Mo. Shepherd.   203.1 SD.] *Parrott; not in Q.*   208.1 SD.] *Parrott;*
not in Q.

195–6. *forty foot*] a proverbial expression for a large distance (Dent F581),
as in Goshawk's generous appraisal of Laxton's talents in *The Roaring Girl*,
'Life, I think he commits venery forty foot deep: no man's aware on't'
(2.1.25–6).

199–201. *Come...Dowsecer*] If this invitation were to be delivered by
Catalian, then Colinet's presence is not required at all in Scene 7, with the
effect of resolving some of the ambiguities in the entry stage direction (see
7.0 SD n., Introduction, pp. 35–6).

200. *wait upon*] attend.

202–3. *Excuse...there*] Presumably the gallants plan to join the King at
his palace and travel with him to Labervele's house, where Lemot will
meet them, although this is inconsistent with their entrance at the start
of Scene 7.

205–6. *this...reigned*] Martia was born under a favourable star sign. The
syntax is odd to the modern ear, but common in Chapman's day (see
Abbott, pp. 164–6).

SCENE 6

Enter [FLORILLA] *the puritan in her best attire.*

Florilla. Now am I up and ready. Ready, why?
Because my clothes once on, that call we ready.
But readiness, I hope, hath reference
To some fit action for our several state.
For when I am attired thus, countess-like,   5
'Tis not to work; for that befits me not;
'Tis on some pleasure, whose chief object is
One man's content, and he my husband is.
But what need I thus be attired,
For that he would be pleased with meaner weed?   10

Scene 6] *This ed.*; Scene VI *Parrott*; Sc. vi *Greg*; II.i *Holaday; not in Q.*
o SD. Florilla] *Parrott; not in Q or Holaday.*

Scene 6] The action is at Count Labervele's house, perhaps in the garden.
1–22.] Florilla's speech on wifely duty and pleasure, like Falstaff's on honour in 1 *Henry IV* (5.1.127–41), is a rich parody of English sermons and other forms of religious instruction, especially the repetitive question–answer format known as the catechism. In his Christmas sermon of 1605, preached before James I at Whitehall, the famed orator Lancelot Andrewes asks (and answers): 'And what is the seed of Abraham, but as Abraham himself is? And what is Abraham? Let him answer himself: "I am dust and ashes". What is Abraham? Let me answer in the persons of all the rest; *dicens, putredini, &c.* saying to rottenness, "Thou art my mother", and to the worms, "ye are my brethren". 1. They are Spirits; now, what are we – what is the seed of Abraham? Flesh. And what is the very harvest of the seed of the flesh? What, but corruption, and rottenness, and worms? There is the substance of our bodies' (Andrewes, p. 4).
4. *our several state*] the particular circumstances of us puritans.
10. *meaner weed*] more humble apparel. 'Weed' is common in both the singular, as here, and in the plural, e.g. Orsino to Viola in *Twelfth Night*, 'let me see thee in thy woman's weeds' (5.1.273). Thomas Becon (see 4.52 n.) would approve of Florilla's contentment with 'meaner weed': 'It is sufficient also for honest married wives, that they be so apparelled that they please their husbands: they that deck themselves to please the fancies of other, and to make themselves gazing-stocks to the world, practise rather the madness of whores, than the conditions of honest women. There is nothing that doth better adorn, garnish, and set forth an honest woman, than sobriety, shame-facedness, cleanness of life, honest conversation, integrity of manners, silence, fear toward God, loving obedience toward her husband, comely behaviour in countenance, in looking, in going, in speaking, in doing, and at the last to wear such apparel as serveth for her state and degree' (p. 439).

Besides, I take no pleasure thus to please him.
I am content, because it is my duty,
To keep to him and not to seek no further.
But if that pleasure be a thing that makes
The time seem short, if it do laughter cause,   15
If it procure the tongue but heartily
To say, 'I thank you', I have no such thing.
Nor can the godliest woman in the world
Against her nature please her sense or soul.
She may say, 'this I will', or 'this I will not',   20
But what shall she reap hereby? Comfort in
Another world, if she will stay till then.

Enter [LABERVELE] *her husband behind her.*

Labervele. [*Aside*] Yea, marry, sir, now I must look about.
Now if her desolate prover come again,
Shall I admit him to make farther trial?   25
I'll have a dialogue between myself

22.1 SD. LABERVELE] Parrott; *not in Q or Holaday.*   23 SD.] *This ed.; not in Q.*

---

13. *not to seek no further*] The double negative for emphasis is common in Elizabethan English (Abbott, p. 295).

14. *that pleasure...thing*] Florilla refers back to 'some [particular] pleasure' (l. 6); there may be some further punning, unintended by the speaker, on 'thing' and 'penis', both here and at l. 17 (see 3.26 n.).

15. *time seem short*] proverbial (Dent H747).

16. *procure*] prevail upon, persuade (*OED v.* 6).

19. *her sense or soul*] When the singular 'sense' and 'soul' are placed in contradistinction, as they are here, the former can be taken as the sensitive soul, the seat of the passions, the latter as the rational soul (see Introduction, pp. 14–15).

22. *stay*] wait (*OED v.*[1] 2c)

24. *desolate*] dissolute; cf. 4.137 n.

prover] one who tries, tests, or puts to the proof (*OED n.*); a rare usage.

26–34.] Labervele's 'dialogue' with Reason is similar to Launcelot Gobbo's with 'the fiend' in *The Merchant of Venice* (2.2.1–32); like Gobbo, Labervele imagines himself a character in a moral interlude. Reason is personified in *A Goodly Interlude of Nature, The Comedy of Patient and Meek Grissel,* and *The Marriage of Wit and Science.*

And manly reason to that special end:
'Reason, shall I endure a desolate man to come
And court my wife, and prove her constancy?'
Reason: 'To court and prove her you may bear, my lord,   30
For perfect things are not the worse for trial;
Gold will not turn to dross for deepest trial.'
Before God, a comfortable saying!
Thanks, gentle Reason, I'll trouble you no more.
[*To Florilla*] God save, sweet wife. Look up, thy
  tempter comes.   35
Florilla. Let him, my lord. I hope I am more blest
 Than to relent in thought of lewd suggestion.
Labervele. But if by frailty you should yield in thought,
 What will you do?
Florilla.   Then shall you keep me close
 And never let me see man but yourself.   40
 If not, then boldly may I go abroad.
Labervele. But how shall I know whether you yield or no?

---

35 SD.] *This ed.; not in Q.*

27. *manly reason*] rationality, the highest of the soul's three parts (see Introduction, pp. 14–15). In Chapman's *Revenge of Bussy D'Ambois*, Clermont defends the St Bartholomew massacre, saying it was heinous only 'to a brutish sense / But not a manly reason' (2.1.206–7); Brooke's *Romeus and Juliet* has the Friar demanding of the banished Romeus, 'Thy crying, and thy weeping eyes denote a woman's heart. / For manly reason is quite from off thy mind outchased / And in her stead affections lewd and fancies highly placed' (1354–6).

28, 30.] These long lines are accounted for by the extrametrical vocative, 'Reason'.

32.] a play on the proverbial sayings 'gold is tried in the fire' and 'no gold without dross' (Dent G284, G289). Dross, in its precise meaning, is 'scum, recrement, or extraneous matter thrown off from metals in the process of melting' (*OED n.* 1).

33. *comfortable*] encouraging, reassuring (*OED a.* 1a).

37. *relent…suggestion*] soften, or yield in my convictions, by the effect of Lemot's words. The original meaning of 'relent' was to melt or soften under heat (*OED v.* 1); 'suggestion', originally, was synonymous with 'temptation' (*OED n.* 1).

38. *frailty*] lack of constancy (see 4.154 n.). Labervele apparently agrees with Hamlet that women are prone to it.

Florilla. Hear us yourself, my lord.

Labervele.   Tut, that were gross,
    For no woman will yield in her husband's hearing.

Florilla. Then to assure you if I yield or no,   45
    Mark but these signs: as he is proving me,
    If I do yield, you shall perceive my face
    Blush and look pale, and put on heavy looks.
    If I resist, I will triumph, and smile,
    And when I hold but up my finger,   50
    Stop his vain lips, or thrust him on the breast,
    Then is he overthrown both horse and foot.

Labervele. Why, this doth satisfy me mightily.
    See, he is come.

[Enter LEMOT.]

Lemot. Honour to my good lord, and his fair young lady.   55

Labervele. Now, Monsieur Satan, you are come to tempt
    And prove at full the spirit of my wife.

Lemot. I am, my lord, but vainly, I suppose.

Labervele. You see she dares put on this brave attire,
    Fit with the fashion, which you think serves much   60
    To lead a woman into light desires.

Lemot. My lord, I see it, and the sight thereof
    Doth half dismay me to make further proof.

54.1 SD.] *Parrott; not in Q.*

43. *gross*] lacking in delicacy of perception, dull, stupid (*OED a.* 13a).

48. *heavy looks*] sad expression, as in Romeo's 'Love goes toward love as schoolboys from their books / But love from love, toward school with heavy looks' (2.2.158–9).

51. *Stop his vain lips*] put my finger against his lips.

52. *both horse and foot*] literally, both cavalry and infantry, a very common metaphor for 'completely'. In *Captain Thomas Stukeley*, young Thomas is confident of success with Nell Curtis: 'she's mine, horse and foot' (2.183).

57. *spirit*] Labervele probably means her 'particular character, disposition, or temper' (*OED n.* 8a), but of course Lemot is more interested in the humoral spirits set off by Florilla's 'piercing glancings' (l. 72).

59. *brave*] showy, elaborate (*OED a.* 2).

63. *dismay*] discourage, dishearten (*OED v.*¹ 1).

Labervele. Nay, prove her, prove her, sir, and spare not.
What, doth the witty minion of our king   65
Think any dame in France will say him nay?
But prove her, prove her, sir, and spare not.
Lemot. Well, sir, though half discouraged in my coming,
Yet I'll go forward. – Lady, by your leave.
                                          [*He withdraws with* FLORILLA.]
Florilla. Now, sir, your cunning in a lady's proof.   70
Lemot. Madam, in proving you I find no proof
Against your piercing glancings,
But swear I am shot thorough with your love.
Florilla. I do believe you. Who will swear he loves,
To get the thing he loves not? If he love,   75
What needs more perfect trial?
Lemot.   Most true, rare lady.
Florilla. Then are we fitly met; I love you too.
Lemot. Exceeding excellent.
Florilla. Nay, I know you will applaud me in this course.
But to let common circumstances pass,   80
Let us be familiar.

---

64. sir] *Parrott;* see *Q.*   69.1 SD.] *Parrott; not in Q.*   73. thorough] *Parrott,*
thorow *Q*; through *Shepherd.*

64.] Q's 'see and spare not' does make sense, but Parrott's emendation
to 'sir' is justified, in that Labervele, in his excitement, would repeat l. 64;
the compositor seems to have read 'sir' as 'see' again at l. 112.
    71–3.] effective wordplay on 'proof' and 'proving', in the sense of the trial
Florilla is undergoing, and 'proof' as armour of sufficient hardness to withstand the shot of a longbow or musket (see Edelman, pp. 270–2).
    72. *piercing glancings*] eye-beams, an important component of Galenic
humours theory (see Introduction, pp. 19–20). In the contest for Florimell's
girdle in *The Faerie Queene*, Sir Triamond presents Canacee, 'Whose beauty's beam eftsoons did shine so bright, / That daz'd the eyes of all, as with
exceeding light' (Bk 4, 5.10).
    73. *thorough*] through. Q's form is retained for metric purposes. 'Through'
and 'thorough' were interchangeable in Elizabethan usage. Shakespeare
often employs the latter when two syllables are required, as in *Julius Caesar*,
where Cassius asks Brutus, 'You are contented to be led in triumph / Thorough the streets of Rome?' (5.1.108–9).
    80. *circumstances*] circumlocutions, beating about the bush (*OED n.* 6).
In *The Merchant of Venice*, Antonio replies to Bassanio's tale of shooting two

Lemot. Dear life, you ravish my conceit with joy.
Labervele. [*Aside*] I long to see the signs that she will make.
Florilla. I told my husband I would make these signs:
    If I resisted, first hold up my finger,   85
    As if I said, 'i'faith, sir you are gone',
    But it shall say, 'i'faith, sir, we are one'.
                      [*She holds up a finger.*]
Labervele. [*Aside*] Now she triumphs, and points to heaven, I
    warrant you.
Florilla. Then must I seem as if I would hear no more   90
    And stop your vain lips. Go, cruel lips,
    You have bewitched me, go!
           [*She places her hand against Lemot's lips.*]
Labervele. [*Aside*]   Now she stops in
    His scornèd words, and rates him for his pains.
Florilla. And when I thrust you thus against the breast,
    Then are you overthrown both horse and foot.   95
Labervele. [*Aside*] Now is he overthrown both horse and foot.
Florilla. Away, vain man, have I not answered you?
Lemot. [*Speaking aloud*] Madam, I yield, and swear I never
    saw
    So constant nor so virtuous a lady.
Labervele. [*To Lemot*] Now speak, I pray, and speak but truly,   100
    Have you not got a wrong sow by the ear?
Lemot. My lord, my labour is not altogether lost,
    For now I find that which I never thought.

---

83 SD.] *Parrott; not in Q.*   87.1 SD.] *This ed.; not in Q.*   88 SD.] *Parrott; not in Q.*   90. more] *Shepherd*; moret *Q.*   92.1 SD.] *This ed.; not in Q.*   93 SD.] *Parrott; not in Q.*   96 SD.] *Parrott; not in Q.*   98 SD.] *This ed.; not in Q.*   100 SD.] *Parrott; not in Q.*

---

arrows with 'You know me well, and herein spend but time / To wind about my love with circumstance' (1.1.153–4).

   82. *ravish my conceit*] fill my thoughts (see 5.59 n.).

   92. *stops in*] keeps in, prevents from escaping. Florilla has, as planned, placed her hand against Lemot's lips.

   93. *rates*] scolds (*OED v.*² 1).

   101. *wrong sow by the ear*] not exactly the best proverb (Dent S685) to use when referring to one's wife.

   103.] a clever double meaning in this line. While admitting to Labervele that he did not expect to fail in his assault on Florilla's con-

Labervele. Ah, sirrah, is the edge of your steel wit
    Rebated then against her adamant?   105
Lemot. It is, my lord. Yet one word more, fair lady.
Labervele. Fain would he have it do, and it will not be. [*Aside
    to Florilla*] Hark you, wife, what sign will you make me
    now, if you relent not?
Florilla. [*Aside to Labervele*] Lend him my handkerchief to   110
    wipe his lips of their last disgrace.
Labervele. [*Aside to Florilla*] Excellent, good! – Go forward,
    sir, I pray.
Florilla. [*Speaking apart with Lemot*] Another sign, i'faith,
    love, is required.
Lemot. Let him have signs enough, my heavenly love.   115
    Then know there is a private meeting
    This day at Verone's ordinary,
    Where, if you will do me the grace to come,
    And bring the beauteous Martia with you,

107–8 SD.] *This ed.; not in Q.*   110. SD.] *This ed.; not in Q.*   112 SD.] *This
ed.; not in Q.*   sir] *Parrott*; see *Q*   114 SD.] *This ed.; not in Q.*

---

stancy, Lemot is telling her (and us) that he did not expect to succeed
so easily.

105. *Rebated*] dulled or blunted, referring to edged weapons in the literal
sense (*OED rebate v*^{1} 4), often abbreviated to 'bated'. The most important
sword in all of English drama is one that should have been rebated but was
not, as the dying Laertes tells Hamlet, 'The treacherous instrument is in thy
hand / Unbated and envenom'd' (5.2.316–17).

adamant] a name given to a variety of stones distinguished by their
hardness (*OED*). Lysander, in Chapman's *The Widow's Tears*, has 'a
heart of adamant' (3.1.1), as does Countess Marcellina of *Monsieur D'Olive*
(1.1.207).

107. *Fain...not be*] Labervele thinks Lemot has given up, and expresses
his delight in a typically Chapmanesque, i.e. difficult, way. 'Have it do', if
not a compositor's error, might be understood as 'have done', or 'make an
end of it'. 'It will not be' is a common way of saying, 'it cannot be done',
as in Venus's vain attempts to arouse Adonis in Shakespeare's poem: 'But
all in vain, good queen! It will not be; / She hath assayed as much as may
be proved' (ll. 607–8).

117. *ordinary*] an inn or tavern were meals were provided at a fixed price
(*OED n.* 12c), and where gambling often occurred; see Zwager (pp. 61–82)
for a fascinating description of these establishments.

I will provide a fair and private room   120
Where you shall be unseen of any man,
Only of me, and of the King himself,
Whom I will cause to honour your repair
With his high presence.
And there with music and quick revellings   125
You may revive your spirits so long time dulled.
Florilla. I'll send for Martia, then, and meet you there,
And tell my husband I will lock myself
In my close walk till supper-time.
                    [*She gives her handkerchief to Lemot.*]
[*Speaking aloud*] We pray, sir, wipe your lips of the
          disgrace   130
They took in their last labour.
Lemot. Marry, the devil was never so despited.
                              [*He starts to go.*]
Labervele. Nay, stay, sir.
Lemot. No, no, my lord, you have the constantest wife
That ever – well, I'll say no more.   135
                                   Exit.
Labervele. Never was minion so disminioned! Come, con-
     stancy, come my girl, I'll leave thee loose to twenty of
     them, i'faith.
                         Then he sighs.
Florilla. Come, my good head, come.
                            [*Exeunt.*]

129. close] *Parrott*; choise *Q*; choice *Shepherd*.   129.1 SD.] *This ed.; not in Q.*   130 SD.] *This ed.; not in Q.*   132.1 SD.] *This ed.; not in Q.*
133. sir] *Parrott*; see *Q*.   138.1 SD.] *left margin, Q.*   139.1 SD. Exeunt*]
Holaday; Exit Shepherd; Exit with Labervele Parrott; not in Q.

123. *repair*] visit, sojourn (*OED n.*[1]), similar to the earlier use of 'resort' (see 4.68 n.).
125. *quick*] lively.
132. *despited*] spited (*OED despite v.*).
136. *never…disminioned*] Never was a favourite of the King so discomfited; a nicely put, if deluded, reference to Labervele's former description of Lemot as 'the minion of our king' (l. 65).

SCENE 7

Enter the KING *and all the lords* [LEMOT, COLINET, CATALIAN,
and BLANUEL, *to the sound of*] *trumpets.*

King. Why sound these trumpets, in the devil's name?
Catalian. To show the King comes.
King. To show the King comes?
　　Go hang the trumpeters! They mock me boldly,
　　And every other thing that makes me known,　　　　　　　5
　　Not telling what I am, but what I seem:
　　A king of clouts, a scarecrow full of cobwebs,
　　Spiders and earwigs, that sets jackdaw's long tongue
　　In my bosom and upon my head;

Scene 7] *This ed.*; Scene VII *Parrott*; Sc. vii *Greg*; II,ii *Holaday; not in Q.*
0 SD. LEMOT, COLINET, CATALIAN, *and* BLANUEL, *to the sound of*] *This
ed.; with the Q.*　2 SH.] *subst.* Shepherd, *Holaday; C. Q; Col. Parrott.*

Scene 7] This scene, like the preceding, is at Count Labervele's house.

0. SD.] *Q*'s stage direction, *Enter the King and all the lords, with the Trum-
pets*, is not very clear in determining who, other than Lemot, enters with the
King. Catalian speaks in the scene, so he must be present. At the end of
Scene 5 everyone seemed to agree to meet at Labervele's, so Blanuel and
Colinet might also be included, although both are mute (see following n.).
As noted previously, reassigning Colinet's lines at 5.199–201 would allow
his absence from this scene, freeing the actor to double in another role.
This is one of those loose ends in *Q* that cannot be resolved completely (see
5.199–201 n., Introduction, p. 35).

2. SH.] *Q*'s speech heading of *C.* could be either Colinet or Catalian; I
follow Shepherd in selecting Catalian, as he speaks at 7.119, while Colinet's
presence is less certain.

4–11.] The King's humour, as he arrives at Labervele's house to observe
Dowsecer's melancholy, is one of dissatisfaction with the trappings of
royalty, since he is beset with 'the affections of love' (l. 10).

7. *clouts*] patches, shreds (*OED n.*[1] 1). In the *Q*1 version of *Hamlet*, the
Prince describes Claudius as 'a king of clouts, of very shreds' (11.44). Parrott
(p. 692) speculates that Chapman might be parodying the lost 'ur-*Hamlet*'
(cf. 7.65–6 n., 10.66–7 n.).

8. *earwigs*] insects, *Forficula auricularia*, so called from the notion that
they penetrate into the head through the ear (*OED n.*)

jackdaw's long tongue] The jackdaw, or daw, a member of the crow family,
is 'noted for its loquacity and thievish propensities' (*OED n.* 1). In Chapman's *All Fools*, Valentine compares a youth who boasts of his romantic
conquests to 'a jackdaw that, when he lights upon / A dainty morsel, caws
and makes his brags' (3.1.364–5); cf. l. 134 n.

> And such are all the affections of love   10
> Swarming in me, without command or reason.
>
> *Lemot.* How now, my liege? What, quagmired in philosophy,
> bound with love's whipcord and quite robbed of reason?
> And I'll give you a receipt for this presently.
>
> *King.* Peace, Lemot. They say the young lord Dowsecer is   15
> rarely learned and nothing lunatic as men suppose, but
> hateth company and worldly trash. The judgement and
> the just contempt of them have in reason arguments that
> break affection, as the most sacred poets write, and still
> the roughest wind. And his rare humour come we now   20
> to hear.   [*Lemot and the King speak privately.*]

---

21 SD.] *This ed.; not in Q.*

---

10. *affections*] with 'passions' and 'appetites', one of the most common words for the spirits arising from the sensitive soul (see Introduction, pp. 16–18).

13. *whipcord*] *OED*'s primary definition is 'a thin tough kind of hempen cord, of which whip-lashes or the ends of them are made', but notes that it could signify fine cord for 'whipping', or binding something closely. The latter sense is used here, as in Greene's *Friar Bacon and Friar Bungay*, where Rafe promises to send to the Isle of Ely for four or five dozen geese, and 'have them tied six and six together with whipcord' (5.9–10).

14. *receipt*] medical prescription (*OED n.* 1b).

16. *nothing*] not at all (*OED adv.* 1a).

17. *worldly*] earthly, mundane (*OED a.* 1).

judgement] the rational soul, as we read in *The French Academy*: 'The faculty and virtue of the soul, so necessary in man and which is able to judge of things imagined and perceived by the other senses...to know whether they be good or bad and what is to be embraced or eschewed, is called the judging or discoursing faculty, namely reason' (La Primaudaye, p. 416, cited Miola, ed., *Every Man In*, 1.4.214 n.).

18. *them*] 'company and worldly trash'.

18–19. *arguments that break affection*] According to Sir Francis Bacon, reason's main weapon in its conflict with the sensitive soul is the art of rhetoric: 'If the affections in themselves were pliant and obedient to reason, it would be true there should be no great use of persuasions and insinuations to the will more than of naked propositions and proofs; but in regard of the continual mutinies and seditions of the affections...reason would become captive and servile if eloquence of persuasions did not practise and win the imagination from the affections' part' (Bacon, pp. 140–1; cf. Bundy, p. 523).

19. *sacred*] respected, revered, but not necessarily in a religious sense (*OED a.* 4), often used in reference to poets. Marlowe's translation of Ovid's tribute to Tibullus in the *Elegies* asks, 'Thee sacred Poet could sad flames destroy? / Nor feared they thy body to annoy?' (3.8.41–2).

Lemot. Yea, but hark you, my liege, I'll tell you a better
 humour than that. Here presently will be your fair love
 Martia to see his humour, and from thence fair countess
 Florilla and she will go unto Verone's ordinary, where 25
 none but you and I and Count Moren will be most merry.
King. Why, Count Moren, I hope, dares not adventure into
 any woman's company but his wife's.
Lemot. Yes, as I will work, my liege, and then let me alone to
 keep him there till his wife comes. 30
King. That will be royal sport. See where all comes. –
 Welcome, fair lords and ladies!

> *Enter* LABERVELE, LABESHA, *and all the rest* [MOREN,
> COUNTESS MOREN, FOYES, *and* MARTIA].

Labervele. My liege, you are welcome to my poor house.
Lemot. [*Indicating Labesha*] I pray, my liege, know this gentleman especially. He is a gentleman born, I can tell you. 35
King. With all my heart. What might I call your name?
Labesha. Monsieur Labesha, Seigneur de Foulasa.
King. De Foulasa! An ill-sounding barony, of my word. But
 to the purpose: Lord Labervele, we are come to see the
 humour of your rare son, which by some means, I pray, 40
 let us partake.
Labervele. Your highness shall too unworthily partake the
 sight which I with grief and tears daily behold, seeing in
 him the end of my poor house.
King. You know not that, my lord. Your wife is young, and 45
 he perhaps hereafter may be moved to more society.

32.1–2 SD. MOREN, COUNTESS MOREN, FOYES, and MARTIA] *This ed.; not
in* Q. 34 SD.] *This ed.; not in* Q. 37. Seigneur de Foulasa] *Parrott; siniora
defoulasa* Q, *Holaday; Signor de Foulasa Shepherd.* 38. De Foulasa] *Shepherd; Defoulasa* Q, *Holaday.* barony] *Parrott;* barrendrie Q.

---

29. *let me alone*] leave it to me.
32.1 SD.] Q's entry direction is *Enter Labervele, Labesha, and all the rest.*
Having accounted for those who enter at the beginning of the scene (see 7.0
SD n.), *all the rest* would be Count and Countess Moren, Foyes, and Martia.
37. *Foulasa*] Perhaps a compound of the French *fou* (fool) and *las* (weary),
hence something like 'wearisome fool'.
44. *end...house*] We soon learn that Dowsecer rejects the idea of marriage and children.

Labervele. Would to God he would, that we might do to your
   crown of France more worthy and more acceptable
   service.

King. Thanks, good my lord. See where he appears.   50

     Enter LAVEL *with a picture* [*of a woman*],
     a pair of large hose, a codpiece, and a sword.

   Say, Lavel, where is your friend, the young lord
   Dowsecer?

Lavel. I look, my liege, he will be here anon; but then I must
   entreat your majesty and all the rest to stand unseen, for
   he as yet will brook no company.   55

King. We will stand close, Lavel. But wherefore bring you
   this apparel, that picture and that sword?

50.1 SD. *of a woman*] *This ed.; not in* Q.   53 SH.] *This ed.*; La. Lav. Q; Lav.
Shepherd; La. *Holaday.*

50.2 SD. a pair of large hose] No part of the Elizabethan man's apparel
was as subject to the whim of fashion as was the hose, or breeches. As we
read in that still indispensable reference, *Shakespeare's England*, at the time
Elizabeth ascended the throne, 'the upper hose or breeches, which in Mary's
reign had been short and melon-shaped, now assumed, by reason of excessive padding, most absurd proportions'. In 1562, the Queen issued a proclamation 'touching the excess of apparel', which included measures 'for the
reformation of the use of the monstrous and outrageous greatness of hose',
ordaining that 'no tailor, hosier, or other person, whatsoever he shall be,
after the day of the publication hereof, shall put any more cloth in any one
pair of hose for the outside than one yard and a half, or at the most one yard
and three quarters of a yard of kersey or of any other cloth, leather, or of
any other kind of stuff above that quantity'. Such orders, of course, had as
much effect as King Canute's instructions to the ocean; by the 1590s 'the
upper hose was...enormous, reaching from the hips to just above the knee
and fastened to the stockings by broad garters of silk or velvet trimmed with
gold fringes' (*Shakespeare's England* 2: 103–4; *Proclamations* 2: 189–90).

   codpiece] a bagged appendage to the front of the close-fitting hose or
breeches worn by men from the 15th to the 17th c., often conspicuous and
ornamented (*OED n.* 1). In Webster's *The Devil's Law-Case*, Winifred
reckons her age by remembering 'the loss of Calais, and the first coming up
/ Of the breeches with the great codpiece' (4.2.434–5), placing the fashion's
beginnings early in the reign of Henry VIII. The tasselled codpiece worn by
Reginald Denny as Benvolio in George Cukor's 1936 film of *Romeo and Juliet*
must be seen to be believed.

   53. *look*] expect (*OED v.* 3c).

   55. *brook*] tolerate.

   56. *stand close*] stay concealed, out of sight, as Oberon to Puck, 'Stand
close. This is the same Athenian' (3.2.41).

Lavel. To put him, by the sight of them, in mind of their
brave states that use them, or that at the least of the true
use they should be put unto.   60
King. Indeed, the sense doth still stir up the soul, and, though
these objects do not work, yet it is very probable in time
she may. At least we shall discern his humour of them.
Lemot. See where he comes, contemplating. Stand close.

> [*They stand aside.*]

Enter DOWSECER.

Dowsecer. *Quid enim videatur ei magnum in rebus humanis, cui*   65
aeternitas omnis totiusque mundi nota sit magnitudo.

64.1 SD.] *This ed.; not in* Q.   65 SH.] *This ed.;* Dow. *Parrott; not
in* Q.   65–6.] *This ed.; Quid Dei potes videri magnum in rebus humanis
quæ æterni omnes to thy ousque notas sic omnibus magna tutor* Q; *Quid ei potest
videri magnum in rebus humanis cui aeternitas omnis totiusque nota sit mundi
magnitudo* Parrott.

---

59. *brave*] See 6.59 n.

61. *the sense...the soul*] another statement of the psychological theories
informing the play (see Introduction, pp. 14–20).

63. *she*] the sense; see 4.228 n.

65–6.] The Latin, which Dowsecer translates in the ensuing lines, is
completely mangled in Q (see collation). It derives from book four of
Cicero's *Tusculan Disputations*; Parrott only partially restored the original,
surmising that Chapman is quoting from an imperfect memory. As Holaday
observes, however, the problem may have resided with a befuddled compositor, and so I see no reason why the lines should not be exactly as found in
Erasmus's edition, *Marci Tullii Ciceronis quaestiones Tusculanae*, printed in
1577. T. W. Baldwin notes that the *Disputations* were part of the English
grammar school curriculum, so Dowsecer might have memorised the
passage, but he is more likely to be reading aloud. Lemot's description of
his mood, 'contemplating', does not preclude his carrying a book with him,
consistent with what was, or would become, standard behaviour for the
melancholy student, including the most famous of all: '*Enter Hamlet reading
on a book*' (2.2.167 SD). Baldwin argues that Hamlet's book is the very same
Disputations, so like 'king of clouts' (see 7.7 n.), this might be another parody
of the lost *Hamlet* play, although Chapman and Shakespeare could both be
drawing on what was by then a common tradition. In any case, a studious
melancholic's book, as Bridget Gellert Lyons notes, 'was generally related
to the subject of his preoccupations; Dowsecer's affected ruminations
about the decay of the world...are touched off by his reading of Cicero'.
See Parrott, p. 692; Holaday, pp. 129–30; Erasmus 32: 601–10; Cicero,

'What can seem strange to him on earthly things,
To whom the whole course of eternity
And the round compass of the world is known?'
A speech divine, but yet I marvel much   70
How it should spring from thee, Mark Cicero,
That sold for glory the sweet peace of life
And made a torment of rich nature's work,
Wearing thyself by watchful candlelight,
When all the smiths and weavers were at rest,   75

---

73. made] *Shepherd*; make *Q*.

Disputations, p. 367; Baldwin, 2: 229–31; Lyons, pp. 26–7; Introduction, pp. 20–1.

67–9.] John Dolman's translation, *Those five Questions, which Mark Tully Cicero, disputed in his manor of Tusculanum* (London, 1561), has 'For what may seem great to him, in thy world, who museth on eternity, and knoweth the largeness of the wide world' (sig. W1r). The 1927 translation of J. E. King reads 'For what can seem of moment in human occurrences to a man who keeps all eternity before his eyes and knows the vastness of the universe?' (Cicero, *Disputations*, p. 368). Chapman's version is very literal given that it is in verse.

67. *strange*] exceptionally great (*OED a.* 9a), as in *Antony and Cleopatra*, 'I did not think to draw my sword' gainst Pompey / For he hath laid strange courtesies and great / Of late upon me' (2.2.153–5).

71. *Mark Cicero*] i.e. Marcus Tullius Cicero.

72–3.] Cicero grew up in the small town of Arpinum, but, as we find in North's Plutarch, 'he being by nature ambitious of honour, and pricked forward also by the persuasion of his father and friends, in the end he began to plead [practise law], and there obtained not the chiefest place by little and little, but so soon as he fell to practise, he was immediately esteemed above all other orators and pleaders in his time, and did excel them all' (p. 72).

74.] According to Plutarch, it was Demosthenes, more than Cicero, who would stay up all night working on his speeches: 'thereof came the opinion men had of him, that he had no very quick capacity by nature, and that his eloquence was not natural, but artificially gotten with extreme labour'. Unwilling to speak 'unless he had first studied the matter well', Demosthenes's work, said his critics, 'smelled of the lamp' (see 5.100 n.). Cicero, on the other hand, was far from his best after working late: on one occasion, he 'took no rest all night' preparing for an important case, and 'what through watching, and the trouble of his mind he was not very well, and was not so well liked for his pleading' (Plutarch, pp. 51, 52, 93).

And yet was gallant ere the day-bird sung,
To have a troop of clients at thy gates,
Armed with religious supplications,
Such as would make stern Minos laugh to read.
Look on our lawyer's bills, not one contains   80
Virtue or honest drifts, but snares, snares, snares.
For acorns now no more are in request,
But when the oak's poor fruit did nourish men,
Men were like oaks, of body tough and strong.

---

81. snares, snares, snares] *Parrott*; he cares, he cares, he cares *Q*.   82. no more] *Parrott; not in Q*.   83. when] *Parrott; not in Q*.

---

76. *gallant*] finely dressed (*OED a.* 1a).

sung] This and other past indicative tenses with *u* rather than *a* were common in this period (Abbott, p. 241).

77.] Cicero 'gave his father's chief mansion house to his brother, and went to dwell himself in the mount Palatine, because such as came to wait upon him and do him honour, should not take the pains to go so far to see him. For, he had as many men daily at his gate every morning, as either Crassus had for his wealth, or Pompey for his estimation among the soldiers...Yea furthermore, Pompey's self came unto Cicero, because his orations stood him to great purpose, for the increase of his honour and authority' (Plutarch, p. 74).

78. *religious*] scrupulous, exact (*OED a.* 4).

79. *stern Minos*] Minos and his two fellow judges of the dead, Rhadamanth and Aechus, are often characterised as 'stern' or 'grim'. They do not frighten Hercules in Thomas Heywood's *Silver Age*, who boasts that when he enters the underworld, 'Stern Minos, Aeacus, and Rhadamanth / Shall from the dreadful sessions kept in hell / Be rous'd by us' (p. 145).

81. *snares, snares, snares*] *Q*'s 'he cares, he cares, he cares' is not entirely without sense, but as Parrott notes (p. 697), the verse is fairly regular here, so his substitution of 'snares' is reasonable. In *De Officiis* (p. 119), Cicero deplores sharp legal practices, especially fraudulent dealing in real estate, when a 'For Sale' sign in front of a house is *tamquam plagam*, 'just like a snare'.

82. *acorns*] In the *Metamorphoses*, Ovid writes of a lost age when 'men were content with nature's food', living on 'strawberries...cherries and the clutching bramble's fruit / And acorns fallen from Jove's spreading tree' (1.103–5). Chapman revisited this 'golden world' in his translation of *The Georgics of Hesiod* (sig. B3v–B4r).

no more] *Q* does not have these two words, but as Parrott (p. 697) notes, without them, or something similar, the line 'is deficient by one foot, and means, as it stands, exactly the opposite of what it should'.

Men were like giants then, but pygmies now,   85
Yet full of villainies as their skin can hold.
Lemot. How like you this humour, my liege?
King. This is no humour; this is but perfect judgement.
Countess. Is this a frenzy?
Martia. Oh, were all men such,   90
Men were no men but gods, this earth a heaven.
Dowsecer. [*Seeing the sword*] See, see the shameless world,
That dares present her mortal enemy
With these gross ensigns of her lenity:
Iron and steel, uncharitable stuff,   95
Good spital-founders, enemies to whole skins,

---

92 SH.] *This ed.; Do. Dow. Q; Do. Shepherd; Dow. Parrott.   SD. Seeing the
sword] Parrott; not in Q.   94. lenity] Q, Holaday; levity Parrott.*

85. *Men...then*] an oft-quoted passage from Genesis: 'But there were
giants in those days in the earth: yea and after that the sons of God came
unto the daughters of men, and had begotten children of them, the same
became mighty men of the world, and men of renown' (6.4).

pygmies] the mythical race of very small people, also called 'three-span
men', as they never grew taller than twenty-seven inches, a 'span' being the
average distance of nine inches from thumb to little finger (*OED n.*¹).
According to Pliny, they lived 'at the extreme boundary of India...in the
most outlying mountain region' (2: 523). They are described by Homer as
being constantly at war with cranes: in Chapman's *Iliad*, the Trojans brought
their troops into battle formation shouting like 'cranes that fill with harsh
confusion / Of brutish clangs all the air and in ridiculous war /...Visit the
ocean and confer the Pygmy soldier's death' (3.3–6).

89. *frenzy*] The Countess asks if Dowsecer is simply mad, but later in the
scene (l. 200) the King makes a distinction between this type of frenzy and
the 'holy fury', i.e. Plato's 'divine madness', that he recognises in Dowsecer
(see Introduction, pp. 23–4).

93. *her mortal enemy*] 'Dowsecer himself, as satirist of the world's customs'
(Parrott).

94. *ensigns*] emblems or flags, especially the colours of a military company
(see Edelman, pp. 124–6).

lenity] mildness, mercy (*OED n.*). Parrott substitutes 'levity', but since
Dowsecer is speaking of weapons, an ironic delivery of *Q*'s 'lenity' seems
more apt.

96. *spital-founders*] 'Spital' is a form of the word 'hospital', an institution
made necessary, according to Dowsecer, by weapons of iron and steel. The
Spitalfields, an area surrounding London's Hospital of Saint Mary, are
mentioned in a number of Elizabethan plays (Sugden, p. 483).

As if there were not ways enough to die
By natural and casual accidents,
Diseases, surfeits, brave carouses, old aqua-vitae and
    too base wines
And thousands more. Hence with this art of murder!   100
                    [*Seeing the hose and codpiece*]
But here is goodly gear: the soul of man,
For 'tis his better part. Take away this,
And take away their merits and their spirits.
Scarce dare they come in any public view
Without this countenance-giver;   105
And some dares not come, because they have it, too,
For they may sing, in written books they find it.

---

99. wines] *Holaday*; wives *Q.*   100.1 SD.] *Parrott; not in Q.*

---

98. *natural and casual accidents*] strangely similar to Horatio's promise to tell 'Of carnal, bloody, and unnatural acts / Of accidental judgements, casual slaughters' (5.2.334–5).

99.] Chapman's inclusion of such an extensive list makes for a very unmetrical line; Peele runs into a similar problem in *The Battle of Alcazar* (4.1.38–42).

surfeits] excesses (*OED n.*), as in King Harry's rejection of Falstaff at the end of 2 *Henry IV*, 'I have long dreamt of such a kind of man / So surfeit-swelled, so old, and so profane' (5.5.49–50).

aqua-vitae] distilled alcoholic spirits (*OED*).

101–6.] Dowsecer's thoughts would be clearer without 'too' at the end of l. 106: he seems to say that some men dare not appear without elaborate and expensive hose and codpiece, while others are reluctant to appear *with* the same articles, since they have yet to pay for them. In Dekker's *The Gull's Hornbook*, we learn that 'the first suit of apparel that ever mortal man put on came neither from mercer's shop nor the merchant's warehouse. Adam's bill would have been taken then sooner than a knight's bond now; yet he was great in nobody's books for satin and velvet' (p. 77).

105. *countenance-giver*] provider of one's standing in society (*countenance OED n.* 10).

107.] As Parrott surmises (p. 692), the 'written books' would be tailors' account books, filled with unpaid bills. This reading is consistent with Chapman's use of the same phrase in *The Widow's Tears*, where Tharsalio says, 'marry, if you ask how we come by this new suit, I must take time to answer it; for as the ballad says, "In written books I find it"' (1.1.33–5). Tailors' accounts, it seems, were as realistic as broadside ballads, the 'supermarket tabloids' of the day, which alternated moral tales and indecent ditties with lurid accounts of natural disasters, murders, or monsters, all set to popular tunes. They would often conclude with a statement that the story must be

What is it then, the fashion or the cost?
The cost doth much, but yet the fashion more;
For, let it be but mean, so in the fashion,   110
And 'tis most gentleman-like. Is it so?
Make a hand in the margin, and burn the book.
A large hose and a codpiece makes a man;
A codpiece, nay indeed, but hose must down.
Well, for you gentle forgers of men,   115

---

109. much] *Parrott*; match *Q.*   113, 114. hose] *Parrott*; house *Q.*   115.
you] *Parrott*; your *Q.*

---

true, as it came from a book: *A most Miraculous, Strange, and True Ballad*,
about a young man wrongfully hanged, but who miraculously survived, ends
with 'The truth of this strange accident / men need not far to look, / For 'tis
confirmed by good men's hands, / and printed in a book' (Clark, p. 163).
Similarly, in *The Winter's Tale*, Mopsa hopes the Clown will buy some of
Autolycus's ballads: 'I love a ballet in print, a-life, for then they are sure to
be true' (4.4.260–1); cf. Rollins, p. 330.

109. *much*] Parrott's emendation from Q's 'match' seems sensible, especially if we remember that the word was sometimes spelled 'mutch', e.g. in
Q of Chapman's *All Fools*, 'I tell you Marc-Antonio there is mutch / In that
young boy my sonne' (sig. G4v).

110–11.] Wearing the latest style is so important that even if one's apparel
be 'but mean' (of inferior material), having to replace it constantly is going
to run up a debt with the tailor.

112.] This line is difficult, since we cannot be sure to whom Dowsecer's
imperative is directed. Assuming the 'book' is the tailor's account book, he
might be addressing the imagined fashionable gentleman. A 'hand in the
margin' may be the familiar symbol of a small hand with pointing finger that
Renaissance readers often drew in a book to mark an interesting passage (see
Sherman, pp. 25–52). Alternatively, it may be his signature as a promise of
payment (*OED hand n.* 17). Then, instead of kissing the book, as one does
when swearing an oath, he should burn it, since he has no intention of ever
paying. In *The Family of Love*, Lipsalve, Purge, and Gudgeon must 'kiss
the book' (l. 1995) as they testify to Mistress Purge's supposed wrongdoings,
and of course Shakespeare plays delightfully on the expression in *The
Tempest*, the book being Stephano's bottle of sack.

113. *a codpiece makes a man*] a point not lost on cross-dressing heroines
such as Julia of *Two Gentlemen of Verona*, who is reminded by Lucetta, 'A
round hose, madam, now's not worth a pin, / Unless you have a codpiece
to stick pins on' (2.7.55–6).

114. *hose must down*] One must have a codpiece to make (look like) a
man, but needs to remove one's breeches to have sex and thereby make
(produce) a man.

115–16.] The 'for you' in l. 115 means 'as for you'; in l. 116 it may be
taken as 'because you'.

And for you come to rest me into fashion,
I'll wear you thus, and sit upon the matter.
Labervele. And he doth despise our purposes.
Catalian. Bear with him yet, my lord. He is not resolved.
Lavel. I would not have my friend mock worthy men,   120
For the vain pride of some that are not so.
Dowsecer. I do not here deride difference of states,
No, not in show, but wish that such as want show
Might not be scorned with ignorant Turkish pride,
Being pompous in apparel and in mind.   125
Nor would I have with imitated shapes;
Men make their native land the land of apes,

---

118. And he] *Q*; And so he *Parrott.*

---

116. *rest*] arrest, seize as at 1.4, or perhaps 'wrest' (twist) is intended.

117.] Parrott suggests that Dowsecer removes his own hose and puts on the new pair 'hind side foremost, or in some such fashion shows his contempt for the "goodly gear"'.

118. *And he doth*] I do not adopt Parrott's metrical insertion of 'so' before 'he'. The comments of the onlookers, out of Dowsecer's hearing, are not necessarily in verse (see Introduction, pp. 36–8).

122.] These sentiments may be compared with those expressed by Florilla in Scene 4.

123. *such as want show*] those who do not believe in outward display, such as Hamlet: 'I have that within which passes show' (1.2.85).

124–5.] The opulence of the Turkish court was legendary, but George Sandys's account of his visit to Constantinople in 1610 shows that, while their clothes were made of the richest fabrics, the Turks were not overly fashion-conscious: 'They never alter their fashions, not greatly differing in the great and vulgar, more than in the richness. Cloth of tissue, of gold and silver, velvet, scarlet, satin, damask, camlet, lined with sables, and other costly furs, and with martins, squirrels, foxes and cony-skins; worn according to their several qualities. But the common wear is violet cloth. They retain the old world's custom in giving change of garments, which they may aptly do, when one vest fitteth all men, and is of every man's fashion' (Purchas, p. 141).

127. *the land of apes*] The English obsession with foreign fashion is a constant theme of early modern texts. A good example is found in Dekker's pamphlet *News from Hell*, wherein the travels of a wandering knight are described: 'The next place he call'd in at was France, where the gentlemen, to make apes of Englishmen, whom they took daily practising all the foolish tricks of fashions after their Monsieur-ships, with yards instead of leading staves, mustered all the French tailors together ... [they would] sweat out their very brains, in devising new French cuts, new French colours, new French codpieces, and new French panes in honour of Saint Denis, only to

Living like strangers when they be at home,
And so perhaps bear strange hearts to their home;
Nor look a-snuff like a pianet's tail,   130
For nothing but their curls and formal locks,
When like to cream bowls, all their virtues swim
In their set faces, all their in-parts, then,

---

131. curls] *conj. Brereton*; tails *Q*.

---

make the giddy-pated Englishmen consume his revenues in wearing like clothes' (2: 114).

128. *strangers*] foreigners (*OED n.* 1).

129. *strange hearts*] foreign feelings and behaviour. As in the previous lines, 'strange' is more precisely 'foreign', rather than 'unfamiliar' or 'odd'. In *As You Like It*, Rosalind gives Jaques instructions in how to act like a traveller: 'Look you lisp and wear strange suits; disable all the benefits of your own country; be out of love with your nativity, and almost chide God for making you that countenance you are' (4.1.33–7).

130. *look a-snuff*] adopt an indignant or contemptuous attitude, similar to the more common 'take it in snuff', and to the much later 'turn up one's nose'. *OED* conjectures that the expression originally came from the physical reaction to the smoking snuff of a candle.

pianet's tail] Amongst the distinguishing features of the European variety of the pianet, more commonly known as the pie or magpie, is its long tail, often of multi-coloured plumage. Hence, like the peacock's tail, it is a metaphor for proud or ostentatious appearance.

131. *curls and formal locks*] Brereton's suggestion of 'curls' for *Q*'s 'tails' is very apt; 'formal' is often used to denote a symmetrical or very regular hair style, as in the description of the maid in *A Lover's Complaint*: 'Her hair, nor loose nor tied in formal plait / Proclaimed in her a careless hand of pride' (ll. 29–30). Greene derides the Englishman's need to have the latest coiffure in his *Quip for an Upstart Courtier*, where a barber asks, 'Sir will you have your...hair cut after the Italian manner, short and round, and then frounced with the curling irons, to make it look like a half moon in a mist? or like a Spaniard long at the ears, and curled like to the two ends of an old cast periwig? or will you be Frenchified with a love lock down to your shoulders, wherein you may wear your mistress's favour?' (11: 246–7).

132–3. *When...faces*] Dowsecer's description is similar to Gratiano's in *The Merchant of Venice*: 'There are a sort of men whose visages / Do cream and mantle like a standing pond, / And do a wilful stillness entertain' (1.1.88–90); both liken the layer of cream atop a bowl of milk, especially as it turns sour, to a stagnant pond. Such a man has no inner qualities worth considering: his 'virtues', which are not virtues at all, are on the surface of his 'set' face, i.e. fixed with a predetermined expression. In *The Revenge of Bussy D'Ambois*, Clermont speaks of 'these painted men / All set on out-side, look upon within, / And not a peasant's entrails shall you find / More foul and measled, nor more starv'd of mind' (2.1.192–5).

    Fit to serve peasants or make curds for daws.
                          [Seeing the picture]
    But what a stock am I thus to neglect   135
    This figure of man's comfort, this rare piece?
Labervele. Heavens grant that make him more humane and
    sociable!
King. Nay, he's more humane than all we are.
Labervele. I fear he will be too sharp to that sweet sex.   140
Dowsecer. She is very fair. I think that she be painted;
    And if she be, sir, she might ask of me,
    'How many is there of our sex that are not?'
    'Tis a sharp question, marry, and I think
    They have small skill. If they were all of painting,   145
    'Twere safer dealing with them; and, indeed,
    Were their minds strong enough to guide their bodies,
    Their beauteous deeds should match with their
        heavenly looks.
    'Twere necessary they should wear them,
    And would they vouchsafe it, even I   150
    Would joy in their society.
Martia. And who would not die with such a man?
Dowsecer. But to admire them as our gallants do,
    'Oh, what an eye she hath! Oh, dainty hand!
    Rare foot and leg!' and leave the mind respectless,   155
    This is a plague that in both men and women
    Make such pollution of our earthly being.

134.1 SD.] *Parrott; not in Q.*

    134. *make curds for daws*] People kept jackdaws as pets and often fed them
curds. In *Shoemaker's Holiday*, Firk derides Lacy's attempt at a Dutch
accent: 'he speaks yawing like a jackdaw, that gapes to be fed with cheese
curds' (4.98–9).
    135. *stock*] literally, a log, a block of wood (*OED n.*¹ 1 b).
    137. *humane*] civil, courteous, as befits a man (*OED a.* 1).
    141–51.] See Appendix (pp. 164–6) for discussion of Dowsecer's rather
unconventional attitude to the use of cosmetics.
    145. *If...painting*] if all women used cosmetics.
    149. *should wear them*] should adorn themselves with their (painted) heav-
enly looks.
    150. *vouchsafe it*] bestow this favour (*OED vouchsafe v.* 1).
    155. *respectless*] unobserved, or unregarded (*OED respect v.* 2).

Well, I will practise yet to court this piece.

Labervele. O happy man! Now have I hope in her.

King. Methinks I could endure him days and nights.   160

Dowsecer. Well, sir, now thus must I do, sir, ere it come to
    women. Now, sir – a plague upon it, 'tis so ridiculous, I
    can no further! What poor ass was it that set this in my
    way? Now if my father should be the man – God's pre-
    cious coals, 'tis he!   165

                [*Labervele approaches Dowsecer,*
                    while the others remain apart.]

Labervele. Good son, go forward in this gentle humour.

    Observe this picture; it presents a maid

    Of noble birth and excellent of parts,

    Whom for our house and honour sake I wish

    Thou wouldst confess to marry.   170

Dowsecer. To marry, father? Why, we shall have children.

Labervele. Why, that's the end of marriage, and the joy of
    men.

Dowsecer. Oh, how you are deceived! You have but me,

    And what a trouble am I to your joy!

    But, father, if you long to have some fruit of me,   175

165.1–2 SD.] *This ed.; not in Q.*

158.] Dowsecer will practise the art of courtly conversation with the
woman in the picture.

159. her] One is tempted to emend to 'him', but Labervele's hope might
reside in womankind, as represented by the picture.

161–2.] The attempt at pretended courtship lasts only a few moments
before Dowsecer abandons it.

164–5. *God's precious coals*] a mild exclamation, found elsewhere (in later
plays) without 'God's', probably due to the 1606 Act to Restrain the Abuses
of Players.

169. *honour sake*] Most early modern texts have the expected 'honour's',
but this form is sometimes seen, and is closer to what an actor would actually
say if he is not to slow his delivery; cf. 2.76–7 n.

170. *confess*] OED offers no definition in the sense of 'consent'; perhaps
the latter word was intended.

175–91.] Dowsecer's comparison of parenthood with farming is similar to
a passage in Plutarch's essay 'On Affection for Offspring' from the *Moralia*:
'He that plants a vineyard in the vernal equinox gathers the grapes in the
autumnal; he that sows wheat when the Pleaides set reaps it when they rise;
cattle and horses and birds bring forth young at once ready for use; but as
for man, his rearing is full of trouble, his growth is slow, his attainment of

See, father, I will creep into this stubborn earth
And mix my flesh with it, and they shall breed
Grass to fat oxen, asses, and such like;
And when they in the grass the spring converts
Into beast's nourishment,   180
Then comes the fruit of this my body forth.
Then may you well say,
Seeing my race is so profitably increased,
'That good fat ox and that same large-eared ass
Are my son's sons, that calf with a white face   185
Is his fair daughter'; with which, when your fields
Are richly filled, then will my race content you.
But for the joys of children, tush, 'tis gone;
Children will not deserve, nor parents take it.
Wealth is the only father and the child,   190
And but in wealth no man hath any joy.
Labervele. Some course, dear son, take for thy honour sake.
Dowsecer. Then, father, here's a most excellent course.
Labervele. This is some comfort yet.

---

185. son's sons] *Shepherd*; sonne sonnes *Q, Holaday.*

---

excellence is far from distant and most fathers die before it comes' (p. 351).
Parrott sees a link with Hieronimo's speech in the additions to *The Spanish
Tragedy* (1606): 'What is there yet in a son / To make a father dote, rave or
run mad?...He must be fed / Be taught to go, and speak. Ay? or yet? / Why
might man love not a calf as well?' (3rd addition, 9–14).
    177. *they shall breed*] the earth and my flesh shall combine to generate
grass (Parrott).
    178. *oxen, asses*] The ox and the ass are inextricably linked by the tenth
Commandment: 'Thou shalt not covet thy neighbour's house, neither shalt
thou covet thy neighbour's wife, nor his man servant, nor his maid, nor his
ox, nor his ass, or whatsoever thy neighbour hath' (Exodus, 20.17). Petruchio, immediately after marrying Katherina, announces 'She is my goods,
my chattels, she is my house, / My household-stuff, my field, my barn, / My
horse, my ox, my ass, my anything' (3.2.230–2).
    179. *when they in*] when they 'bring in', i.e. harvest, the grass. *OED* (*in
v.* 2) cites several examples of this usage.
    185. *calf with a white face*] perhaps an indirect allusion to the proverb,
'you would have the calf with the white face', meaning 'you must have
everything' (Dent C19).
    190.] Wealth is everything, one's inheritance and legacy; not as pithy as
Spike Milligan's 'All I ask is the chance to prove that money can't make me
happy'.
    192. *honour sake*] See l. 169 n., above.

Dowsecer. If you will straight be gone and leave me here,   195
    I'll stand as quietly as any lamb
    And trouble none of you.
Labervele. Ah, hapless man!
Lemot. How like you this humour yet, my liege?
King. As of a holy fury, not a frenzy.   200
                      [*Dowsecer notices the other onlookers.*]
Moren. See, see, my liege, he hath seen us, sure.
King. Nay, look how he views Martia and makes him fine.
Lemot. Yea, my liege, and she, as I hope well observed, hath
    uttered many kind conceits of hers.
King. Well, I'll be gone, and when she comes to Verone's   205
    ordinary, I'll have her taken to my custody.
Lemot. I'll stay, my liege, and see the event of this.
King. Do so, Lemot.   *Exit the King.*
Dowsecer. What have I seen? How am I burnt to dust
    With a new sun, and made a novel phoenix!   210
    Is she a woman that objects this sight,
    Able to work the chaos of the world

---

198. Ah] *Parrott;* An *Q, Holaday.* 200.1 SD.] *This ed.; not in Q.*
203. hope] *Q;* hath *conj. Greg, Holaday.* 204. hers] *Q;* her *conj. Brereton;*
him *conj. Greg.*

---

195. *straight*] immediately (*OED adv.* 2a).
198. *Ah*] Parrot's substitution of 'Ah' for Q's 'An' is sensible.
200. *holy fury, not a frenzy*] The King believes Dowsecer's 'frenzy' to be
the 'divine madness' Plato describes in the *Phaedrus* (see Introduction, pp.
23–4).
202. *makes him fine*] makes himself attractive, perhaps by striking a manly
pose.
203–4. *and she…of hers*] Greg (p. xii) suggests that the line should be
'and she, as I have well observed, hath uttered many kind conceits of him',
but it is sufficiently clear as it stands in *Q*. Lemot hopes that Dowsecer has
'well observed' the approving things Martia has uttered about him, the final
'of hers', while sounding strange to modern ears, can be taken as 'of her
own'.
207. *event*] outcome.
209–18.] For the philosophical history behind Dowsecer's rather sudden
change in attitude, see Introduction, pp. 25–7.
211. *objects*] 'projects', or 'throws forth', a rare usage from the Latin,
also found in *Q* of *Every Man In*, 'Yea, every look or glance mine eye

> Into digestion? O divine aspect,
> The excellent disposer of the mind,
> Shines in thy beauty, and thou hast not changed   215
> My soul to sense but sense unto my soul;
> And I desire thy pure society
> But even as angels do. To angels, fly!   *Exit.*

Martia. Fly, soul, and follow him!

Labervele. I marvel much at my son's sudden strange   220
  behaviour.

Lemot. Bear with him yet, my lord, 'tis but his humour.
  Come, what, shall we go to Verone's ordinary?

Labervele. Yea, for God's sake, for I am passing hungry.

Moren. Yea, come, Monsieur Lemot, will you walk?   225

Countess. What, will you go?

Moren. Yea, sweet bird, I have promised so.

Countess. Go to, you shall not go and leave me alone.

Moren. For one meal, gentle bird; Verone invites us to buy
  some jewels he hath brought of late from Italy. I'll buy   230
  the best and bring it thee, so thou wilt let me go.

---

213. digestion] *Parrott*; gestion *Q, Holaday.*

---

objects, / Shall check occasion' (1.4.183–4). Martia's eye-beams have taken effect.

    213. *digestion*] As Parrott notes in emending *Q*'s 'gestion', 'digestion' is a word often employed by Chapman to denote 'methodizing and reducing to order' (*OED n.* 8). It represents a contradistinction to the 'indigest' or 'formless' (*OED a.*) first state of the Earth, as Ovid describes it in the *Metamorphoses: quem dixere Chaos, rudis indigestaque moles,* 'what they call Chaos, a rough indigest mass' (1.7). In *The Shadow of Night,* the moon goddess Cynthia is addressed as 'Sorrow's dear sovereign, and the queen of rest, / That when unlightsome, vast, and indigest / The formless matter of this world did lie, / Filled'st every place with thy divinity' (29–32); *The Revenge of Bussy D'Ambois* has Bussy's ghost ascending 'from the chaos of eternal night / To which the whole digestion of the world / Is now returning' (5.1.1–3). Dowsecer's 'digestion' is Plato's pure, eternal form of beauty, which the sight of Martia's physical beauty has inspired in him (see Introduction, pp. 25–7, Parrott, p. 693, Bartlett, p. 413.).

    214. *disposer*] governor, ruler (*OED n.* 2).

    216. *soul to sense*] See 6.19 n.

    229–30. *invites...jewels*] a 'false start', not quite consistent with the lottery Verone organises at the play's end, with jewels as some of the prizes. The discrepancy is minor.

Countess. Well said, flattering Fabian, but tell me, then, what
    ladies will be there?

Moren. Ladies? Why, none!

Lemot. No ladies use to come to ordinaries, madam.   235

Countess. Go to, bird, tell me now the very truth.

Moren. None, of mine honour, bird. You never heard that
    ladies came to ordinaries.

Countess. Oh, that's because I should not go with you.

Moren. Why, 'tis not fit you should.   240

Countess. Well, hark you, bird, of my word you shall not go,
    unless you will swear to me you will neither court nor
    kiss a dame in any sort till you come home again.

Moren. Why, I swear I will not.

Countess. Go to, by this kiss.   245

Moren. Yea, by this kiss.

Foyes. Martia, learn by this when you are a wife.

Labesha. I like the kissing well.

Florilla. My lord, I'll leave you. Your son Dowsecer hath
    made me melancholy with his humour, and I'll go lock   250
    myself in my close walk till supper time.

Labervele. What, and not dine today?

Florilla. No, my good head. Come, Martia, you and I will fast
    together.

Martia. With all my heart, madam.   255
                    Exeunt [FLORILLA *and* MARTIA].

Labervele. Well, gentlemen, I'll go see my son.   *Exit.*

240, 244, 246 SH.] *This ed.; Mar. Q; Mor. Parrott.* 255.1 SD. *Exeunt*
FLORILLA *and* MARTIA] *subst. Parrott; Exit Q.*

---

232. *flattering Fabian*] Chapman's variant of 'flaunting Fabian'. Florio's
Italian–English dictionary, A *World of Words*, defines *bravazzo* as 'a swash-
buckler, a swaggerer, a cutter, a quarreller, a roister, a flaunting Flabian',
and *sfoggiatore* as a 'riotous, lavish, flaunting Fabian, a careless fellow, an
unthrift'. The original Fabians were members of the Roman gens, or clan,
of the Fabia (*OED*); their identification with riotous behaviour might
derive from the good time the Fabian priests of Pan had at the
Lupercalia.

235 *use*] make it their practice; cf. 8.69 n.

237. *of mine honour*] 'On' is the more common preposition in phrases of
this type, but this form is frequently found.

241. *of my word*] See previous n.

Foyes. By'r Lady, gentlemen, I'll go home to dinner.

Labesha. Home to dinner? By'r Lord, but you shall not. You
  shall go with us to the ordinary, where you shall meet
  gentlemen of so good carriage and passing complements   260
  it will do your heart good to see them. Why, you never
  saw the best sort of gentlemen if not at ordinaries.

Foyes. I promise you, that's rare! My lord, and Monsieur
  Lemot, I'll meet you there presently.

Lemot. We'll expect your coming.   265

Exeunt all.

SCENE 8

Enter VERONE *with his napkin upon his shoulder, and
his man* JAQUES *with another, and [a* BOY,*] his son,
bringing in cloth and napkins.*

Verone. Come on, my masters. Shadow these tables with their
  white veils, accomplish the court-cupboard, wait dili-

Scene 8] *This ed.*; Scene VIII *Parrott*; Sc. viii *Greg*; III.i *Holaday; not in Q.*
0 SD. *a* BOY] *This ed.; not in Q.*   1 SH.] *This ed.; Ver. Ve. Host Ho. Q;
Ver. Ve. Host Shepherd; Ver. Parrott.*

---

258. *By'r Lord*] far less common than 'By'r Lady' in the previous line,
but sometimes seen in medieval and early modern plays.

263. *I promise you, that's rare*] I assure you, that would be wonderful!

Scene 8] The action now moves to Verone's ordinary, the first time that
life at one of these typically Elizabethan establishments was depicted on the
London stage (see Introduction, p. 6).

0.2 SD. with another] The second servant remains mute throughout the
play; he is also required as a torchbearer in the lottery (13.137 SD).

his son] i.e. Verone's son. Family relationships are vague at this point.
Except for this stage direction, which of course spectators in the theatre
cannot read, there is no indication that the Boy is Verone's son until 13.147,
and throughout the play he is addressed only as 'Boy' by his father. Since
that, in essence, is his name, I retain *Q*'s speech heading; Henslowe's playhouse inventory contains the item, 'Verone's son's hose' (Henslowe, p. 318).

1. *masters*] good sirs, meant ironically (*OED n.*[1] 20).

Shadow] cover.

2. *accomplish*] equip, make ready, as in *Henry V*, 'the armourers, accom-
plishing the knights' (4.Cho.12).

court-cupboard] a movable sideboard or cabinet used to display plate, etc.
(*OED n.*). In *Romeo and Juliet*, as the time for Capulet's guests to arrive
approaches, Peter directs, 'Away with the joint-stools, remove the court-
cupboard, look to the plate' (1.5.6–7).

gently today for my credit and your own, that if the meat
should chance to be raw, yet your behaviours, being
neither rude nor raw, may excuse it. Or if the meat should   5
chance to be tough, be you tender over them in your
attendance, that the one may bear with the other.

Jaques. Faith, some of them be so hard to please, finding fault
with your cheer and discommending your wine, saying
they fare better at Horn's for half the money.   10

Boy. Besides, if there be any chebules in your napkins, they
say your nose or ours have dropped on them, and then
they throw them about the house.

Verone. But these be small faults. You may bear with them;
young gentlemen and wild heads will be doing.   15

Enter [JAQUENA] *the Maid.*

Jaquena. Come, whose wit was it to cover in this room, in
the name of God, I trow?

Boy. Why, I hope this room is as fair as the other.

---

8 SH.] *This ed.; Iaq. Ia. Q; Ja. Shepherd; Jaq. Parrott; Iaq. Holaday.*
10.Horn's] *This ed.*; Verones *Q*; Valere's *Shepherd.*   15.1 SD. JAQUENA] *This ed.; not in Q.*   16 SH.] *This ed.; Maid Ma. Q; Maid Shepherd.*   16–17. in the name] *Parrott;* name in the *Q.*

---

10. *Horn's*] Obviously, *Q*'s 'Verones' cannot be correct. Shepherd substitutes 'Valere's', given that *Q* has 'Valeres', referring to an ordinary, at 9.18, and again at 13.78, but in both instances it is quite obvious that the compositor misread 'Verone's' (see 9.18 n., 13.78 n.). Therefore, innkeeper Valere disappears from our text, and we are left with the task of finding a name for Verone's rival. Chapman could well have used 'Horn's', short for the popular London ordinary, the Horn on the Hoop, mentioned in *Every Man Out*, 'He's a lieger at Horn's ordinary yonder' (4.3.81–2), and in numerous other texts of the period. 'Hornes', as it is spelled in the folio version, could easily be misread as 'Verones' in Elizabethan handwriting—in some respects it is closer than 'Valeres', since an 'h', in both upper and lower case, often went below the line, making it similar to a 'v'. My emendation would be less acceptable were it the only local reference in a play ostensibly set in Paris, however London-like, but later in the scene we hear of 'Lucilla's House' (cf. ll. 82–3 n.; Chalfant, p. 99; Zwager, p. 63).

11. *chebules*] literally, the dried prune-like astringent fruit of *Terminalia Chebula*, a tree of Central Asia (*OED*); a worthy addition to the English language's long list of synonyms for 'snot'.

16. *cover*] cover the tables for dining.

Jaquena. In your foolish opinion! You might have told a wise
    body so and kept yourself a fool still.   20
Boy. I cry you mercy. How bitter you are in your proverbs!
Jaquena. So bitter I am, sir.
Verone. [*Aside*] O sweet Jaquena, I dare not say I love thee.
Jaques. Must you control us, you proud baggage you?
Jaquena. Baggage? You are a knave to call me baggage.   25
Jaques. A knave? My master shall know that.
Verone. [*Aside*] I will not see them.
Jaques. Master, here is your maid uses herself so saucily that
    one house shall not hold us two long, God willing.
Verone. Come hither, huswife. [*Aside to Jaquena*] Pardon me,   30
    sweet Jaquena. I must make an angry face outwardly,
    though I smile inwardly.
Jaquena. [*Aside to Verone*] Say what you will to me, sir.
Verone. [*Aloud*] Oh, you are a fine gossip! Can I not keep
    honest servants in my house, but you must control them?   35
    You must be their mistress?
Jaquena. Why, I did but take up the cloth because my mis-
    tress would have the dinner in another room, and he
    called me baggage.
Jaques. You called me knave and fool. I thank you, small   40
    bones.

---

23 SD.] *Parrott; not in Q.* 23. Jaquena] *Parrott;* Sateena *Q.* 27
SD.] *Parrott; not in Q.* 30 SD.] *subst. Parrott; not in Q.* 33 SD.] *This ed.;*
not in Q. 34 SD.] *This ed.; not in Q.*

19–20.] a play on the traditional, 'a fool may sometimes give a wise man
counsel' (Dent F469).
    26. *shall know that*] shall know what you said.
    30. *huswife*] hussy, loose woman. Verone is pretending to be angry with
her (see 4.228 n.).
    37. *take up the cloth*] remove the tablecloth, similar to Mistress Newcut's
orders in Middleton's *Your Five Gallants*: 'Take hence the cloth you unlucky
maple-fac'd rascal' (ll. 2272–3).
    40–1. *small bones*] Dictionaries of slang and other references offer no
precise definition of this curious expression, but Jaques's insult may be something akin to 'little bastard', or a maid who is carrying one. We find an interesting analogue in Christopher Anstey's 1795 ballad *The Monopolist*, wherein
a country squire complains to his travelling companion, 'Plague on all
women volk!—what sights / Of small-bones we have had! / 'Tis theesome
Soldiers, I do think / Make all the wenches mad' (77–80). Later, at an inn,
their Host offers a toast to 'no tax, no 'xcise, no plaguey brats / To crowd a

Jaquena. Go to, go to, she were wise enough would talk with
     you.
Boy. Go thy ways for the proudest harlotry that ever came in
     our house.   45

> [*Exit* JAQUENA.]

Verone. Let her alone, boy; I have schooled her, I warrant
     thee. She shall not be my maid long, if I can help it.
Boy. No, I think so, sir. But what, shall I take up the cloth?
Verone. No, let the cloth lie. Hither they'll come first, I am
     sure of it. Then, if they will dine in the other room, they   50
     shall.

> *Enter* ROWLEY.

Rowley. Good morrow, my host. Is nobody come yet?
Verone. Your worship is the first, sir.
Rowley. I was invited by my cousin Colinet to see your jewels.
Verone. I thank his worship and yours.   55
Rowley. Here's a pretty place for an ordinary. I am very sorry
     I have not used to come to ordinaries.
Verone. I hope we shall have your company hereafter.
Rowley. You are very like so.

45.1 SD.] *subst. Holaday; not in* Q.   51.1 SD. ROWLEY] *Parrott; Rowl.* Q;
Rowle. Holaday.   52 SH.] *This ed.; Ro. Row.* Q, *Ro. Shepherd, Row. Parrott.*

---

body's door' (159–60), while Jenny, the tavern maid, is busy trying to steal a
bottle of beer by tying it to her garter. When her body heat causes the beer to
explode, she is threatened with arrest, and responds with a whispered threat
of her own: 'She spake of things.../ To small-bones appertain'd, / Those
pleaguy brats, of which so much / His Worship had complain'd' (217–20).
Although our play was written two hundred years earlier than Anstey's dog-
gerel, there may be a connection, especially as we are later told that 'Verone
loves his maid, and she is great with child' (13.280); see Powell, pp. 235–6.
     42–3.] Anyone would be a fool to talk with you.
     44. *Go thy ways*] Away with you, be on your way.
     harlotry] harlot, as in *Othello*, 'He sups tonight with a harlotry' (4.2.233),
also used as a general epithet for lower-class women.
     45.1 SD.] Holaday inserts the needed exit direction for Jaquena. Since
she does not reply to the Boy's parting shot, it is likely that she is moving
towards the door as he speaks.
     59. *like so*] likely to do so, to have my company.

Enter BERGER.

Berger. Good morrow, my host. Good morrow, good Mon-   60
    sieur Rowley.

Rowley. Good morrow to you, sir.

Berger. What, are we two the first? Give's the cards here.
    Come, this gentleman and I will go to cards while dinner
    be ready.   65

Rowley. No, truly, I cannot play at cards.

Berger. How? Not play? Oh, for shame, say not so. How can
    a young gentleman spend his time but in play and in
    courting his mistress? Come, use this, lest youth take too
    much of the other.   70

Rowley. Faith, I cannot play, and yet I care not so much to
    venture two or three crowns with you.

Berger. Oh, I thought what I should find of you. I pray God
    I have not met with my match.

Rowley. No, trust me, sir, I cannot play.   75

                [They begin to play cards.]

Berger. Hark you, my host, have you a pipe of good tobacco?

---

60 SH.] *This ed.; Ber. Be. Q; Ber. Parrott.*   75.1 SD.] *This ed.; not in Q.*

69. *mistress*] a woman loved and courted by a man (*OED n.* 6a), but
without any necessary sexual implication; cf. 5.175 n.

use this] act accordingly, behave in this manner, i.e. play cards. This
construction is found in numerous texts, e.g. *Bartholomew Fair*, when John
Littlewit thinks his wife has called him a 'fool-John', and Quarlos tells him,
'She may call you apple-John, if you use this' (1.3.48). In *Volpone*, Sir
Peregrine responds to Lady Politic's antics with 'This is fine, i'faith! / And
do you use this often?' (4.2.63–4).

69–70. *take too much of the other*] absorb too much time in wooing one's
mistress.

71–2. *I care...venture*] I don't mind betting.

72. *crowns*] A crown was a gold coin worth 5s (*OED n.* 8).

74. *met with my match*] proverbial (Dent M745).

76. *a pipe of good tobacco*] Except for Chapman's *Blind Beggar of Alexandria*, this is the earliest extant play with any reference to tobacco. As we read in
The Gull's Hornbook, by this time it was not only obligatory for a young gallant
to smoke, but, like 'wine-snobs' today, he had to display his great knowledge
of the product. After passing through Paul's Churchyard, 'you should
blow yourself into the tobacco ordinary, where you are likewise to spend your

Verone. The best in the town. – Boy, dry a leaf.
Boy. [*Aside to him*] There's none in the house, sir.
Verone. [*Aside to the Boy*] Dry a dock leaf.

[*Exit* BOY.]

Berger. My host, do you know Monsieur Blanuel?   80
Verone. Yea, passing well, sir.
Berger. Why, he was taken learning tricks at old Lucilla's
house, the muster-mistress of all the smocktearers in

---

78 SD. *Aside to him*] *This ed.; Aside Parrott; not in Q.*   79 SD. *Aside to the Boy*] *This ed.; Aside Parrott; not in Q.*   79.1 SD. *Exit* BOY] *Parrott; Boy exits and returns with pipe Holaday; not in Q.*

---

judgment like a quacksalver upon that mystical wonder to be able to discourse whether your cane or your pudding be sweetest, and which pipe has the best bore and which turns black, which breaks in the burning, etc.' (p. 109). The subject is soon dropped here, but Jonson takes it up to great effect in *Every Man In* and *The Alchemist*, as does Chapman again in *Monsieur D'Olive* (2.2.252–81), wherein the title character offers an eloquent panegyric to the plant that rivals Falstaff's tribute to 'good sherris-sack' (2*H4*, 4.3.96–125).

79. *dock leaf*] Dock, a coarse, weedy herb used as an antidote for nettle-stings (*OED n.*[1] 1), is presumably not ideal for smoking. Jonson puns on this in *The Masque of Augurs*, where Notch, a clerk employed at a brewery near Saint Katherine's docks, is accused of stinking 'like so many bloat-herrings'. He responds, 'Sir, we do come from among the brewhouses in Saint Katherine's, that's true, there you have smoked us—the dock comfort your nostrils' (ll. 57–63).

82. *taken*] arrested.

tricks] then, as now, slang for sexual acts, although *OED* restricts this defi-nition to American usage, starting in the 1920s (see Williams, pp. 1421–2).

82–3. *Lucilla's house*] possibly an actual London brothel. Lodge's satire *A Fig for Momus* tells of 'Lucillas daughter, she that keeps the Swan / That saw her mother dally with her man; / Steal privy sports, for sweet meats hazard fame / Scarce twelve years old begins to do the same' (3: 35). The Swan was a Bankside bawdy-house, not far from the theatre of the same name (Burford, p. 108).

83. *muster-mistress*] a neat turn on 'muster-master', the person in charge of recruiting, enlisting, and training soldiers. The greatest muster-master in all literature is Justice Robert Shallow of 2 *Henry IV* (see Edelman, pp. 230–4).

smocktearers] frequenters of brothels. A smock being 'a woman's under-garment, a shift or chemise' (*OED n.* 1), it lends itself to a number of clever expressions: in Dekker's The *Honest Whore, Part* 2, Matheo's 'servant' (his father-in-law in disguise) is an 'arrant...smell-smock' (4.1.102), while in Chapman's *Widow's Tears*, Tharsalio promises the panderess Arsace, 'thou shalt hold thy tenement to thee and thine heirs for ever, in free smockage, as of the manner of panderage' (1.3.183–5).

Paris, and both the bawd and the pander were carried to
   the dungeon.   85
Verone. There was dungeon upon dungeon. But call you her
   the muster-mistress of all the smocktearers in Paris?
Berger. Yea, for she hath them all trained up afore her.

Enter BLANUEL.

Blanuel. Good morrow, my host; good morrow, gentlemen
   all.   90
Verone. Good morrow, Monsieur Blanuel. I am glad of your
   quick delivery.
Blanuel. Delivery? What, didst thou think I was with child?
Verone. Yea, of a dungeon.
Blanuel. Why, how knew you that?   95
Rowley. Why, Berger told us.
Blanuel. Berger? Who told you of it?
Berger. One that I heard, by the Lord.
Blanuel. Oh, excellent, you are still playing the wag!

Enter LEMOT *and* MOREN[, *and the* BOY].

Lemot. Good morrow, gentlemen all. Good morrow, good   100
   Monsieur Rowley.
Rowley. At your service.
Lemot. [*To Moren*] I pray, my lord, look what a pretty falling
   band he hath. 'Tis pretty fantastical as I have seen made,

---

99.1 SD. *and the* BOY] *This ed.; not in Q.*   103 SD.] *This ed.; not in Q.*

86. *dungeon upon dungeon*] More than one possible pun might be intended
here. A dungeon could be any dark or confined room, not only a jail cell
(*OED n.*), so Verone may simply be saying that bawd and pander were
transported from one dungeon (the brothel) to another. But Blanuel was
taken 'learning tricks'; therefore he had 'done [a] gin', i.e. a 'trick' (*OED
n.*[1]), and so ended up in a dungeon.

92. *delivery*] release from prison, the most common usage in this period.
Blanuel plays on this with his reference to delivering a baby in the next line.

99.1 SD. *and the* BOY] Having left the stage to see to Berger's pipe
(l. 79), which is never mentioned again, the Boy needs to re-enter at some
point before being sent off again at l. 109. It seems logical to have him show
Lemot and Moren in.

103–4. *falling band*] Rowley is wearing a flat neck-band or collar, which
was then replacing the ruff as the fashionable choice for both men's and

with good judgement, great show, and but little cost.   105
Moren. And so it is, I promise you. Who made it, I pray?
Rowley. I know not, i'faith, I bought it by chance.
Lemot. It is a very pretty one; make much of it.

Enter CATALIAN *sweating.*

Catalian. Boy, I prithee call for a coarse napkin.

[*Exit* BOY.]

Good morrow, gentlemen. I would you had been at the   110
tennis court; you should have seen me abeat Monsieur
Besha, and I gave him fifteen and all his faults.

---

105. little] *Shepherd*; tittle *Q.*   109.1 SD] *Holaday; not in Q.*   112. Besha]
This ed.; Besan *Q.*

---

women's apparel. In *The Malcontent*, Maquerelle informs Bianca and Emilia:
'And do ye hear, you must wear falling bands, you must come into the falling
fashion; there is such a deal a' pinning these ruffs, when the fine clean fall
is worth all' (5.5.17–20). Such falling bands were often highly ornamental,
as we see in *The Fair Maid of the Exchange*, where Phillis, the 'fair maid',
tells two gentlemen that at her shop, one 'may have choice / Of lawns,
or cambrics, ruffs well wrought, shirts, / Fine falling bands of the Italian
cut-work' (p. 44).

108.1 SD. sweating] It was something of a badge of honour to arrive at
an ordinary all sweat-stained from a game of tennis. *The Gull's Hornbook*
advises, 'rather than your tongue should not be heard in the room but that
you should sit like an ass with your finger in your mouth and speak nothing,
discourse how often this lady hath sent her coach for you and how often you
have sweat in the tennis-court with that great lord' (p. 94). But having to
keep extra shirts at the tennis court, and to pay for their cleaning, could be
bothersome: the Bawd of *Northward Ho* complains of lending 'gentlemen
holland shirts, and they sweat 'em out at tennis, and no restitution, and no
restitution' (4.3.80–2).

109. napkin] most commonly, a table-napkin, but here a small towel
(*OED n.* 1b). While impersonating Scoto of Mantua, Volpone describes his
cure for an upset stomach, which involves 'applying only a warm napkin to
the place, after the unction, and fricace' (2.2.94–5). The word was also
interchangeable with 'handkerchief', as in *Othello*, 'I will in Cassio's lodging
lose this napkin' (3.3.321).

111. abeat] an archaic form of 'beat' (*OED v.*), also found in *The True
Tragedy of Richard III*, 'slept the garrison that should abeat them back?' (sig.
H2r).

112. Besha] *Q* has 'Besan', which could easily be a misreading of 'Besha'.
Catalian and Labesha left Dowsecer's house together at the end of Scene 7,
so it seems likely that Labesha was the opponent.

gave…faults] Elizabethan tennis bore little resemblance to today's game,

Lemot. Thou didst more for him than ever God will do for
thee.

Catalian. Jaques, I prithee fill me a cup of canary, three parts   115
water.

Lemot. You shall have all water, an if it please you.

Enter Maid [JAQUENA]

Jaquena. Who called for a coarse napkin?

Catalian. Marry, I, sweetheart. Do you take the pains to bring
it yourself? Have at you, by my host's leave.   120

Jaquena. Away, sir, fie, for shame!

Catalian. Hark you, my host, you must marry this young
wench. You do her mighty wrong else.

Verone. Oh, sir, you are a merry man.   [*Exit.*]

Enter FOYES *and* LABESHA.

Foyes. Good morrow, gentlemen. You see I am as good as   125
my word.

117.1 SD. JAQUENA] *This ed.; not in Q.*   124 SD.] *This ed.; not in Q.*

but it was scored exactly as it is now: fifteen, thirty, forty, deuce, advantage,
game. Florio's English–Italian phrase book, *Second Fruits*, has an account of
a match where the score progresses from 'I have fifteen' to 'fifteen for
fifteen…I am thirty…you have forty then…and I a deuce then…I have
the advantage' and finally 'I have won the first game' (pp. 25, 27). *OED* cites
this line as the earliest instance of 'fault' meaning 'a stroke in which the
server fails to make the ball fall within the prescribed limits'. For one to
'give' an opponent a certain number of faults or points to even the odds was
common, especially as bets were often placed on the outcome (see Noel and
Clark, pp. 319–20).

115. *canary*] newly fashionable sweet wine from the Canary Islands,
probably the first mention of it on the English stage. *OED*'s earliest citation is from 2 *Henry IV*, first performed in 1598 or 1599, with Mistress
Quickly telling Doll Tearsheet, 'I'faith, you have drunk too much canaries'
(2.4.260),

120. *Have at you*] an expression usually associated with fencing, similar
to *en garde*.

124 SD. Exit] Verone takes no further part in the scene until he announces
that dinner is ready at l. 348, so it is logical to have him exit here.

Moren. You are, sir, and I am very glad of it.

Lemot. You are welcome, Monsieur Foyes. [*To Labesha*] But
you are not, no, not you.

Labesha. No? Welcome that gentleman. 'Tis no matter for   130
me.

Lemot. How, sir? No matter for you? By this rush, I am angry
with you. As if all our loves protested unto you were dis-
sembled. No matter for you?

Labesha. Nay, sweet Lemot, be not angry. I did but jest, as I   135
am a gentleman.

Lemot. Yea, but there's a difference of jesting; you wrong all
our affections in so doing.

Labesha. Faith and troth, I did not, and I hope, sirs, you take
it not so.   140

All. 'No matter for me'! 'Twas very unkindly said, I must
needs say so.

Labesha. You see how they love me?

Foyes. I do, sir, and I am very glad of it.

Labesha. And I hope, Lemot, you are not angry with me still.   145

Lemot. No, faith, I am not so very a fool to be angry with one
that cares not for me.

Labesha. Do not I care for you? Nay, then.

Catalian. What, dost thou cry?

Labesha. Nay, I do not cry, but my stomach waters to think   150
that you should take it so heavily. If I do not wish that I
were cut into three pieces, and that these pieces were

---

128 SD.] *Holaday; not in Q.*   132. for] *Parrott*; to *Q, Holaday.*

128–34.] This seems an extremely weak joke to be playing on Labesha.
Lemot makes a point of being unfriendly to him, but then scolds him for
saying that he does not care, and demands he retract the statement. Labesha,
all too eager to please, apologises. Perhaps some other meaning can be
inferred from these lines, but it is anything but apparent.

132. *matter for*] *Q* reads 'matter to', but since Labesha has said 'matter
for', which Lemot repeats twice subsequently (ll. 134, 161), Parrott's emendation is probably correct.

rush] straw used to cover a floor, hence a thing of no value. Here it is
used as a mild oath.

150. *stomach*] Citing this passage, *OED* notes that 'stomach' (*n.* 6a) may
be 'used (like "heart", "bosom", "breast") to designate the inward seat of
passion, emotion, secret thoughts, affections, or feelings'.

turned into three black puddings, and that these three
black puddings were turned into three of the fairest ladies
in the land for your sake, I would I were hanged. What   155
a devil can you have more than my poor heart?

Catalian. Well, hark you, Lemot, in good faith you are to
blame to put him to this unkindness. I prithee, be friends
with him.

Lemot. Well, I am content to put up this unkindness for this   160
once; but while you live, take heed of 'no matter for me'.

Labesha. Why, is it such a heinous word?

Lemot. Oh, the heinousest word in the world.

Labesha. Well, I'll never speak it more, as I am a
gentleman.   165

Lemot. No, I pray do not.

Foyes. [*To Moren*] My lord, will your lordship go to cards?

Moren. Yea, with you, Monsieur Foyes.

Rowley. Lemot, will you play?

Lemot. Pardon, good Monsieur Rowley. If I had any disposi-   170
tion to gaming, your company should draw me before
any man's here.

Foyes. Labesha, what, will you play?

Labesha. Play? Yea, with all my heart! I pray, lend me
threepence.   175

        [*Moren, Foyes, and Labesha play cards.*]

Rowley. I'll play no more.

Catalian. Why, have you won or lost?

Rowley. Faith, I have lost two or three crowns.

Catalian. Well, to him again! I'll be your half.

Lemot. [*Speaking privately with Catalian*] Sirrah Catalian,   180
while they are playing at cards, thou and I will have some
excellent sport. [*Indicating Rowley*] Sirrah, dost thou
know that same gentleman there?

---

167 SD.] *This ed.; not in Q.*   175.1 SD.] *This ed.; not in Q.*   180 SD. *Speaking
privately with Catalian*] *This ed.; Aside Parrott; not in Q.*   182 SD.] *Holaday;
not in Q.*

---

154. *black puddings*] a kind of sausage made of blood and suet, sometimes
with the addition of flour or meal (*OED*).

162. *word*] phrase, saying (*OED n.* 10a).

179. *be your half*] put up half the stakes, an offer Baptista makes, to his
regret, in *The Taming of the Shrew* (5.2.78).

Catalian. No, i'faith, what is he?

Lemot. A very fine gull and a neat reveller, one that's heir to   185
a great living. Yet his father keeps him so short that his
shirts will scant cover the bottom of his belly, for all his
gay outside, but the linings be very foul and sweaty, yea,
and perhaps lousy, with despising the vain shifts of the
world.   190

Catalian. But he hath gotten good store of money now,
methinks.

Lemot. Yea, and I wonder of it. Some ancient servingman of
his father's, that hath gotten forty shillings in fifty years
upon his great good husbandry, he swearing monstrous   195
oaths to pay him again, and besides to do him a good
turn – when God shall hear his prayer for his father – hath
lent it him, I warrant you. But howsoever, we must speak
him fair.

Catalian. Oh, what else!   200

Lemot. [*To Rowley*] God save, sweet Monsieur Rowley, what,
lose or win, lose or win?

Rowley. Faith, sir, save myself and lose my money.
          [*Lemot and Catalian speak privately again.*]

---

201 SD.] *This ed.; not in Q.*   203.1 SD.] *This ed.; not in Q.*

185. *neat*] In this context, 'finely dressed' (*OED n.* 2a) is the most likely
meaning.

189. *shifts*] Lemot is punning on 'shifts' as both 'shirts' and 'devices'
(Parrott).

198–9. *speak him fair*] flatter him.

203.] Lemot's comment on Rowley's response rests on his having quoted
a well known proverb, but nothing in Tilley, Dent, or Erasmus's *Adages*
corresponds to the wording. One possibility is that, in ruefully accepting his
losses as unimportant, Rowley is paraphrasing (and quite closely) Mark,
8.36, 'For what shall it profit a man, if he win all the world, and lose his
own soul?' In general terms, Rowley adopts the attitude Staines recommends
to his newly rich master Bubble in John Cooke's splendid *Greene's Tu
Quoque, or the City Gallant*: 'If you be at an ordinary, and chance to lose
your money at play, you must not fret and fume, tear cards, and fling away
dice, as your ignorant gamester or country-gentleman does, but you must
put on a calm temperate action, with a kind of careless smile, in contempt
of Fortune, as not being able with all her engines to batter down one piece
of your estate, that your means may be thought invincible; never tell your
money, nor what you have won, nor what you have lost: if a question be
made, your answer must be, what I have lost, I have lost, what I have won,
I have won' (ll. 762–72).

Lemot. There's a proverb hit dead in the neck like a coney.
  Why hark thee, Catalian, I could have told thee before   205
  what he would have said.
Catalian. I do not think so.
Lemot. No? Thou seest here's a fine plump of gallants, such
  as think their wits singular and their selves rarely accom-
  plished; yet to show thee how brittle their wits be, I will   210
  speak to them severally, and I will tell thee before what
  they shall answer me.
Catalian. That's excellent; let's see that, i'faith.
Lemot. Whatsoever I say to Monsieur Rowley, he shall say,
  'O sir, you may see an ill weed grows apace.'   215
Catalian. Come, let's see.
Lemot. [*To Rowley*] Now, Monsieur Rowley, methinks you
  are exceedingly grown since your coming to Paris.
Rowley. O sir, you may see an ill weed grows apace.
                              [*They speak privately again.*]
Catalian. This is excellent. Forward, sir, I pray.   220
Lemot. Whatsoe'er I say to Labesha, he shall answer me,
  'Black will bear no other hue.' [*Indicating Foyes*] And that

---

217 SD.] *This ed.; not in Q.*   219.1 SD.] *This ed.; not in Q*   222 SD.] *This
ed.; not in Q.*

---

204. *dead...coney*] In (or on) the neck usually refers to one thing following immediately upon another, as Hotspur says of Henry IV, 'In short time
after, he depos'd the King, / Soon after that depriv'd him of his life / And
in the neck of that task'd the whole state' (4.3.90–2). In this instance, Lemot
probably refers to the hunting of coneys (hares, or rabbits) by hounds, who
would take their prey 'dead in the neck', just as Rowley has taken hold of a
proverb.
  208. *plump*] group, company (*OED n.*[1] 1a).
  209. *singular*] See 3.10–11 n.
  209–10. *accomplished*] distinguished, of many accomplishments (cf. l. 2 n.).
  215. *ill weed grows apace*] a very common proverb (Dent W238), one that
Richard III enjoyed repeating to his nephew, York: '"Ay", quoth my nuncle
Gloucester, / "Small herbs have grace; great weeds do grow apace"'
(2.4.12–13).
  222. *Black will bear no other hue*] a saying going at least as far back as
Pliny, who writes 'black fleeces will not take dye of any colour' (3: 135). It
is common in Elizabethan drama, including Aaron's proud defence of his
son in *Titus Andronicus*, 'Coal-black is better than another hue / In that it
scorns to bear another hue' (4.2.99–100).

same old Justice, as greedy of a stale proverb, he shall
come in the neck of that and say, 'Black is a pearl in a
woman's eye.'   225

Catalian. Yea, much, i'faith.

Lemot. Look thee, here he comes hither. [*Aloud*] Labesha,
Catalian and I have been talking of thy complexion, and
I say that all the fair ladies in France would have been in
love with thee, but that thou art so black.   230

Labesha. O sir, black will bear no other hue.

Foyes. O sir, black is a pearl in a woman's eye.

Lemot. You say true, sir, you say true, sir. [*Aside*] Sirrah
Catalian, whatsoe'er I say to Berger that is so busy at
cards, he shall answer me, "Sblood, I do not mean to die   235
as long as I can see one alive.'

Catalian. [*Aside to Lemot*] Come, let us see you.

Lemot. [*Aloud*] Why, Berger, I thought thou hadst been dead.
I have not heard thee chide all this while.

Berger. 'Sblood, I do not mean to die, as long as I can see   240
one alive.

Catalian. [*Aside to Lemot, indicating Moren*] Why, but hark
you, Lemot. I hope you cannot make this lord answer so
roundly.

Lemot. [*Aside to Catalian*] Oh, as right as any of them all, and   245
he shall answer me with an old Latin proverb, that is,
usus promptos facit.

Catalian. [*Aside to Lemot*] Once more, let's see.

---

227. here he comes] *Shepherd*; here comes *Q.* SD.] *This ed.; not in
Q.* 233 SD.] *Parrott; not in Q.* 237 SD. *Aside to Lemot*] *This ed.; Aside
Parrott; not in Q.* 238 SD.] *This ed.; not in Q.* 242 SD. *Aside to Lemot,
indicating Moren*] *This ed.; Aside Parrott; not in Q.* 245 SD. *Aside to
Catalian*] *This ed.*; Aside *Parrott; not in Q.* 247, 252 promptos] *Parrott;
promptus Q; promptum Holaday.* 248 SD. *Aside to Lemot*] *This ed.; Aside
Parrott; not in Q.*

---

224. *in the neck of that*] See l. 204 n. above.

224–5. *Black...eye*] Dent (M79) gives a number of examples, nearly all
specific to skin colour. In Heywood's *Second Part of the Iron Age*, Sinon
compares himself to Vulcan, whose skin was blackened from his work at the
gods' forge. Still, he says, Venus 'wedded with that smith, / And bedded too,
a black complexion / Is always precious in a woman's eye' (p. 364).

235–6. *I do not...one alive*] possibly a variant on 'let the longer liver take
all' (Dent L395).

247. *usus promptos facit*] practice makes perfect (Dent, U24).

Lemot. [*To Moren*] My lord, your lordship could not play at
　　this game very lately, and now methinks you are grown　　250
　　exceeding perfect.
Moren. O sir, you may see, *usus promptos facit.*

Enter JAQUES.

Jaques. Monsieur Lemot, here is a gentleman and two gentle-
　　women do desire to speak with you.
Lemot. What, are they come? Jaques, convey them into the　　255
　　inward parlour by the inward room, and there is a brace
　　of crowns for thy labour. But let nobody know of their
　　being here.
Jaques. I warrant you, sir.　　　　　　　　　　[*Exit* JAQUES.]
Lemot. See where they come! Welcome, my good lord and　　260
　　ladies, I'll come to you presently. [*Aside*] So, now the
　　sport begins! I shall start the disguised King plaguily; nay
　　I shall put the lady that loves me in a monstrous fright
　　when her husband comes and finds her here.

[*Enter* BOY.]

Boy. [*To Lemot*] *The* gentleman and the two gentlewomen　　265
　　desires your company.
Lemot. I'll come to them presently.
The Boy speaks in Foyes his ear.

---

249 SD.] *This ed.; not in* Q.　259 SD.] *Parrott; not in* Q.　261 SD.] *Holaday
(at beginning of speech); not in* Q.　264.1 SD. *Enter* BOY] *Parrott; not in* Q.
265 SD.] *Holaday; not in* Q.　266. desires] Q, *Holaday;* desire *Shepherd.*
267.1 SD.] *Right margin,* Q.

---

256. brace] pair (*OED n.* 15), most famously spoken by the Duke in
Romeo and Juliet, 'And I for winking at your discords too / Have lost a brace
of kinsmen' (5.3.293–4).
　260–1. See...presently] Lemot is probably speaking to the (unseen) new
arrivals through the stage door.
　262. start] startle (*OED v.* 15a), as the King to a nervous Parolles in *All's
Well,* 'every feather starts you' (5.3.232).
　plaguily] in a plaguey manner, perniciously, annoyingly (*OED adv.*); as in
A Chaste Maid in Cheapside, 'the knave bites plaguily' (1.1.109).
　266. desires] Shepherd (2nd ed.) and Parrott emend to 'desire', apparently because Jaques says 'desire your company' at l. 296, but the Boy and
Jaques need not speak the same way, and either form is correct in Elizabethan usage.

Foyes. Gentlemen, I'll go speak with one, and come to you
    presently.   [*Exit* FOYES.]

Lemot. [*To Moren*] My lord, I would speak a word with your   270
    lordship, if it were not for interrupting your game.

Moren. No, I have done, Lemot.

Lemot. My lord, there must a couple of ladies dine with us
    today.

Moren. Ladies? God's my life, I must be gone!   275

Lemot. Why, hark you, my lord, I knew not of their coming,
    I protest to your lordship. And would you have me turn
    such fair ladies as these are away?

Moren. Yea, but hark you, Lemot, did not you hear me swear
    to my wife that I would not tarry if there were any   280
    women? I wonder you would suffer any to come there.

Lemot. Why, you swore but by a kiss, and kisses are no holy
    things, you know that.

Moren. Why, but hark you, Lemot, indeed I would be very
    loath to do anything that, if my wife should know it,   285
    should displease her.

Lemot. Nay, then you are too obsequious. Hark you, let me
    entreat you, and I'll tell you in secret: you shall have no
    worse company then the King's.

Moren. Why, will the King be there?   290

Lemot. Yea, though disguised.

Moren. Who are the ladies?

Lemot. The flowers of Paris, I can tell you: fair countess
    Florilla and the lady Martia.

Enter JAQUES.

---

269 SD.] *This ed.; not in Q.*   270 SD.] *This ed.; not in Q.*

    268. *with one*] with someone. We may assume that Lemot has told the
Boy to say something to Foyes in order to draw him away, since Foyes must
not see Martia at Verone's, when she is supposed to be fasting together with
Florilla.

    273–4. *there...dine*] two ladies (i.e. Martia and Florilla) are to dine with
us today.

    281. *suffer*] allow.

    come there] Perhaps this should be 'come here', since Moren is talking
about Verone's, but, as the dinner is to be served in another room, 'there'
might be intended.

    282. *by a kiss*] as happened at 7.246.

Jaques. Monsieur Lemot, the gentleman and the two gentle-   295
    women desire your company.

Lemot. I'll come to them straight. But Jaques, come hither, I
    prithee. [*Aside to Jaques*] Go to Labesha, and tell him that
    the countess Florilla and the lady Martia be here at thy
    master's house, and if it come in question hereafter, deny   300
    that thou told him any such thing.

Jaques. What, is this all? 'Sblood, I'll deny it, and forswear it
    too.

Lemot. [*To Moren*] My lord, I'll go and see the room be neat
    and fine, and come to you presently.   305

Moren. Yea, but hark you, Lemot, I prithee take such order
    that they be not knowing of any women in the house.

Lemot. Oh, how should they? [*Aside*] Now to his wife go,
    i'faith!

                                                             Exit.

Jaques. Hark you, Monsieur Labesha, I pray let me speak a   310
    word with you.

Labesha. With all my heart. I pray look to my stake; there's
    three pence under the candlestick.

Jaques. I pray, sir, do you know the countess Florilla and the
    lady Martia?   315

Labesha. Do I know the lady Martia? I knew her before she
    was born; why do you ask me?

---

298 SD.] *This ed.; not in Q.*   304 SD.] *This ed.; not in Q.*   307. knowing]
This ed.; knowne *Q.*   308 should they? Now] *subst. Shepherd;* shuld they
now *Q.*   SD.] *Parrott; not in Q.*   308–9 go, i'faith!] *This ed.;* go yfaith! *Q;*
go I, faith *Parrott;* go I yfaith *Holaday.*   314 sir] *Parrott;* see *Q.*

---

295. *the gentleman*] the King, who is 'disguised' (l. 291).

301. *thou told*] 'Thou toldst' is more common, but this form also appears
in texts of the period.

306–7.] a very difficult line. It is hard to make sense of Q's 'that they be
not knowne of any women in the house', as it unclear who 'they' are. Assuming that Moren means the other gallants, I emend 'knowne' to 'knowing',
in the sense of 'aware' (*OED ppl. a.* 5; cf. 1.33 n.). Moren asks that the others
be kept unaware of the ladies' presence, lest one of them tell his wife. Lemot
has already promised Florilla that she will be in a 'private room' (6.120).

312–13.] most likely said to one of the other card players.

316–17. *before she was born*] presumably a variant of 'when she was a
gleam in her father's eye', or similar. This contradicts the impression we get
in Scene 3, where Labesha and Martia appear to be meeting for the first
time, but he may simply be boasting.

Jaques. Why, they are both here at my master's house.
Labesha. What, is mistress Martia at an ordinary?
Jaques. Yea, that she is.   320
Labesha. By skies and stones, I'll go and tell her father!

                                                            Exit.

            Enter LEMOT *and the* COUNTESS[, *above*].

Countess. What, you are out of breath, methinks, Monsieur
    Lemot?
Lemot. It is no matter, madam. It is spent in your service, that
    bear your age with your honesty better than an hundred   325
    of these nice gallants; and indeed it is a shame for your
    husband, that contrary to his oath made to you before
    dinner, he should be now at the ordinary with that light
    huswife Martia, which I could not choose but come and
    tell you. For indeed it is a shame that your motherly care   330
    should be so slightly regarded.
Countess. Out on thee, strumpet, and accursed and miserable
    dame!
Lemot. Well, there they are, nothing else. [*Aside*] Now to her
    husband go I.   *Exit.*   335
Countess. 'Nothing else', quoth you? Can there be more?
    Oh, wicked man! Would he play false
    That would so simply vow and swear his faith,
    And would not let me be displeased a minute,
    But he would sigh and weep till I were pleased?   340

321.2 SD. *above*] *This ed.; not in* Q. *No scene division in this ed. or* Q; Scene
9 *Parrott*; Sc. ix *Greg*; III.ii *Holaday.*   334 SD.] *Parrott; not in* Q.

321. *tell her father*] We may assume that he will also inform Labervele
about Florilla's presence, as Lemot intends (ll. 298–300).
    321.1 SD.] Parrott's opinion, that this sequence was played on the tiring
house gallery 'while the other actors remained seated on the main stage' (p.
693), is most persuasive. Previous editors start a new scene here (and at
l. 346); the convention of this edition is that scene breaks occur only when
all actors exit the stage (see, pp. xi–xii).
    322. *out of breath*] something of a meta-theatrical joke, as Lemot would
have just raced up the backstage stairs.
    325. *bear your age*] As he did with his 'passing from your loveliness'
comment at 5.56, Lemot enjoys reminding the Countess of her advancing
years.
    328–9. *light huswife*] See 4.228 n., 8.30 n.

I have a knife within that's razor sharp.
And I will lay an iron in the fire,
Making it burning hot to mark the strumpet.
But 'twill be cold, too, ere I can come thither.
Do something, wretched woman! Stays thou here?   345

Exit.

Enter LEMOT[, *below.*]

Lemot. [*To Moren*] My lord, the room is neat and fine. Will't
please you go in?

[*Enter* VERONE.]

Verone. Gentlemen, your dinner is ready.
All. And we are ready for it!
Lemot. Jaques, shut the doors; let nobody come in.   350

Exeunt omnes.

SCENE 9

Enter LABERVELE, FOYES, LABESHA,
and the COUNTESS.

Labervele. Where be these puritans, these murderers?
          Let me come in here!
Foyes.   Where is the strumpet?

345.2 SD. *below*] *This ed.; not in Q. No scene division in this ed. or Q;*
Scene 10 *Parrott*; Sc. x *Greg*; IV.1 *Holaday.*   346 SD.] *Parrott; not in Q.*
347.1 SD.] *Parrott; not in Q.*   349 SH.] *Q, Holaday; Le Shepherd; Labes.*
Parrott.

Scene 9] *This ed.*; Scene XI *Parrott*; Sc. xi *Greg*; IV.i *Holaday; not in Q.*

345.2 SD.] The Countess's ten lines afford sufficient time for Lemot to
exit the gallery and re-enter on the main stage.
    347.1 SD.] Q has no entry direction for the innkeeper, but one is obvi-
ously needed.
    348.] Rowley, Berger, Blanuel, and Catalian will partake of Verone's fare
in one room; in another room will be the King, the ladies, and a very nervous
Moren.
    Scene 9] The action takes place in the street, near Verone's ordinary.
    1.] Labervele says 'thieves, puritans, murderers' at 4.246; in both cases it
seems an illogical burst of emotion.
    2. *Let me come in here*] Most likely Labervele and the others are demand-
ing entry at whichever stage door represents Verone's.

Countess. Where is this harlot? Let us come in here!
Labervele. What shall we do? The streets do wonder at us,
   And we do make our shame known to the world.   5
   Let us go and complain us to the King.
Foyes. Come, Labesha, will you go?
Labesha. No, no, I scorn to go; no king shall hear my plaint.
   I will in silent live a man forlorn,
   Mad and melancholy as a cat,   10
   And never more wear hatband on my hat.
                    [*Exit* LABESHA, *then the others.*]

                Enter MOREN *and* MARTIA.

---

9. silent] *Q*; silence *Shepherd.*   11.1 SD. *Exit* LABESHA, *then the others*] *This ed.; Exeunt Parrott; not in Q.*

---

   6. *complain us*] 'Complain' was often used reflexively at this time, cf. Ragan in *The History of King Leir*, 'He first begins for to complain himself, / When as himself is in the greatest fault' (sig. E1r), and Lucrece's 'To all the host of heaven I complain me' (*Lucr.*, l. 598).
   9. *silent*] Shepherd (2nd ed.) and subsequent editors emend *Q*'s 'silent' to 'silence', but adjectives are often used as nouns in Elizabethan texts (Abbott, p. 20). The conjurer Bolingbrook of 2 *Henry VI* appeals to 'Deep night, dark night, the silent of the night' (1.4.16).
   10. *melancholy as a cat*] Being 'cold' and solitary animals, cats were thought of as melancholic. Motto the Barber in Lyly's *Midas* is 'melancholy as a cat' (5.2.106), and Falstaff is as 'melancholy as a gib cat' (1*H*4, 1.2.73–4); see Paster, pp. 142–5.
   11. *hatband*] The hatband was another key fashion statement for the Elizabethan gallant. Stubbes complains of hats 'sometimes with one kind of band, sometimes with another, now black, now white, now russet, now red, now green, now yellow: now this, now that, never content with one colour or fashion, two months to an end' (p. 90). Instructions in *The Gull's Hornbook* on 'how a gallant should behave himself in Paul's Walks' include 'Suck this humour up especially: put off to none unless his hatband be of a newer fashion than yours and three degrees quainter' (p. 90). It is fitting, then, that, if Labesha is determined to adopt the dishevelled appearance of the love-struck melancholic, he make a point of dispensing with his hatband, just as the similarly affected Frank Golding does in *The Fair Maid of the Exchange*: 'therefore, hatband avaunt! ruff, regard yourself! garters, adieu! shoestrings—so and so!' (p. 22).
   11.2 SD. Enter MOREN *and* MARTIA] We may assume Moren and Martia are leaving Verone's, and enter from the stage door to which Labervele and the others were demanding entry. The rapid exits and entrances, with characters just missing one another, would have had the effect we associate with a Feydeau farce.

Moren. What dost thou mean? Thou must not hang on me.
Martia. O good lord Moren, have me home with you;
　　You may excuse all to my father for me.

Enter LEMOT.

Lemot. O my lord, be not so rude to leave her now.　　　15
Moren. Alas, man, an if my wife should see it, I were undone.
　　　　　　　[*Exeunt* MOREN *and* MARTIA.]

Enter the KING[, ROWLEY *and* BLANUEL].

King. Pursue them, sirs, and taking Martia from him,
　　Convey her presently to Verone's house.
　　　[*Exit the* KING *at one door,* ROWLEY *and* BLANUEL
　　　　　　　　　　　　　　　　　at another.]

Enter [FLORILLA] *the puritan to* LEMOT.

---

16 SH.] *subst.　Parrott;　Lord　Q.　*16.1　SD.] *Parrott;　not　in　Q.*
16.2 SD. ROWLEY *and* BLANUEL] *This ed.; and another Q.*　18. Verone's]
This ed.; Valeres *Q.*　18.1–2 SD. *Exit the* KING *at one door,* ROWLEY *and*
BLANUEL *at another*] *This ed.; Exeunt King and another Parrott; not in Q.*
18.3 SD. *Enter* FLORILLA *the*] *Parrott; Enter the (below l. 19) Q.*

16.2 SD. ROWLEY and BLANUEL] *Q* reads *Enter the King and another,*
but 'pursue them sirs' requires at least two men accompanying him. Since
Catalian and Berger are still with Verone at the start of Scene 10, I assume
that the King enlists Rowley and Blanuel to rescue Martia. Her next appearance is with the King at 13.21, so her 'capture' and return to the King's care
occur off stage.

　　18. *Verone's house*] As noted above (see 8.10 n.), *Q* has 'Valeres' here,
and again at 13.78. Given that the second instance is, beyond doubt, a misreading of 'Verones', it is more likely that the compositor would have made
the same mistake twice, rather than Chapman introducing a second innkeeper—indeed, it makes more sense for the King to ask the lords to 'convey'
Martia back to Verone's. We next see the King and Martia moments after
the Queen, Countess Moren, and Foyes arrive at 'the house' (13.1) where
Lemot has told them they are. That this house is indeed Verone's is shown
by the subsequent entrances in Scene 13 (ll. 67.1 SD, 87.2 SD) of Jaques,
Verone, and Florilla, who would have no way of knowing where the others
are if not outside Verone's ordinary, and then by the transfer of the action,
without any break, to an interior 'hall' for the lottery (13.143).

　　18.3 SD. Enter…to LEMOT] below l. 19 in *Q.* Stage directions, often
written in the margins of dramatic manuscripts, are easily misplaced by the
compositor.

Florilla. What villain was it that hath uttered this?

Lemot. Why, 'twas even I. I thank you for your gentle terms: 20
you give me 'villain' at the first. I wonder where's this
old doter? What, doth he think we fear him?

Florilla. O monstrous man! What, wouldst thou have him
take us?

Lemot. Would I, quoth you? Yea, by my troth, would I. I   25
know he is but gone to call the constable or to raise the
streets.

Florilla. What means the man, trow? Is he mad?

Lemot. No, no, I know what I do, I do it of purpose. I long
to see him come and rail at you, to call you harlot and   30
to spurn you, too. Oh, you'll love me a great deal the
better. And yet let him come, and if he touch but one
thread of you, I'll make that thread his poison.

Florilla. I know not what to say.

Lemot. Speak, do you love me?   35

Florilla. Yea, surely do I.

Lemot. Why then, have not I reason, that love you so dearly
as I do, to make you hateful in his sight, that I might
more freely enjoy you?

Florilla. Why, let us be gone, my kind Lemot, and not be   40
wondered at in the open streets.

Lemot. I'll go with you through fire, through death, through
hell.
Come, give me your own hand, my own dear heart,
This hand that I adore and reverence,
And loathe to have it touch an old man's bosom.   45
Oh, let me sweetly kiss it.   *He bites.*

---

19 SH.]*subst. Parrott; not in Q.*

---

22. *old doter*] an apt description of Labervele. Citations in *OED* show
that 'doter' and 'dotard' were interchangeable; each could be used in the
distinct sense of 'lover', or in the sense of a silly person, particularly an
old one. Clearly, the latter is intended here, as it is in Chapman's *Gentleman Usher*, with Bassiolo's 'A plague of all old doters, I disdain them'
(4.4.169).

26–7. *raise the streets*] arouse the citiizens with a 'hue and cry', the usual
means of apprehending felons in this era.

28. *trow?*] trow you, do you suppose? (cf. 4.113 n.).

Florilla. Out on thee, wretch! He hath bit me to the bone! O
  barbarous cannibal! Now I perceive thou wilt make me
  a mocking stock to all the world.

Lemot. Come, come, leave your passions. They cannot move   50
  me. My father and my mother died both in a day, and I
  rung me a peal for them, and they were no sooner brought
  to the church and laid in their graves but I fetched me
  two or three fine capers aloft and took my leave of them,
  as men do of their mistresses at the ending of a galliard.   55
  Beso las manos.

Florilla. O brutish nature, how accurst was I ever to endure
  the sound of this damned voice?

Lemot. Well, an you do not like my humour, I can be but
  sorry for it. I bit you for good will, and if you accept it,   60
  so; if no, go.

Florilla. Villain, thou didst it in contempt of me.

Lemot. Well, an you take it so, so be it. Hark you, madam,
  your wisest course is even to become puritan again, put
  off this vain attire, and say, 'I have despised all, thanks   65

---

56. *Beso las manos*] Parrott; *Besilus manus* Q *(uncorrected); Besilos manus* Q
(corrected), Besilas manos Shepherd *(see Yamada, p. 133).*

---

49. *mocking stock*] a variant of 'laughing stock', very common in the fifteenth and sixteenth centuries (*OED*). In Lodge's *Wounds of Civil War*, the
captured general Carbo challenges Scilla, 'let thy murderers hale me hence,
/ For Carbo rather likes to die by sword / Than live to be a mocking stock
to thee' (5.1.70–2).

53. *fetched*] performed (*OED v.* 9a), usually referring to wild or energetic
movements. In *The Merchant of Venice*, Lorenzo describes the calming effect
of music on a 'race of youthful and unhandled colts, / Fetching mad bounds,
bellowing and neighing loud' (5.1.72–3).

me] for or by myself, common in Elizabethan grammar (see Abbott, pp.
146–8).

54. *capers*] dancing leaps. Lemot could 'fetch' them; Sir Andrew
Aguecheek says he can 'cut' them (1.3.120).

55. *galliard*] a quick and lively dance in triple time (*OED n.*[1] 2).

56. Beso las manos] 'I kiss your hands', a Spanish greeting quite popular
amongst the English. In his *Ortho-Epia Gallica, or Fruits for the French* (1593),
John Eliot advises his readers, 'you must have a firm purpose and a resolution
to prosecute your studies, and not to do as many of our English do commonly,
who will begin one language today, and another tomorrow: then, after they
have learned a *Comm' portez vous?* in French, a *Come state?* in Italian, and *Beso
las manos* in Spanish, they think themselves brave men by and by, and such
fellows are worthy to be sent in embassage to the great Turk' (p. 3).

my God; good husband, I do love thee in the Lord'; and
he, good man, will think all this you have done was but
to show thou couldst govern the world and hide thee as
a rainbow doth a storm. My dainty wench, go, go! What,
shall the flattering words of a vain man make you forget   70
your duty to your husband? Away, repent, amend your
life! You have discredited your religion forever.

Florilla. Well, wretch, for this foul shame thou puttest on me,
The curse of all affection light on thee.   *Exit.*

Lemot. Go, Habakkuk, go! Why, this is excellent. I shall   75
shortly become a schoolmaster, to whom men will put
their wives to practise. Well, now will I go set the Queen
upon the King, and tell her where he is close with his
wench; and he that mends my humour, take the spurs,
sit fast. For by heaven, I'll yerk the horse you ride on.   80

          [Exit.]

---

73. wretch] *Shepherd;* wench *Q.* 75. Habakkuk] *This ed.,* Habbakuk
Parrott; Abacuck *Q, Shepherd, Holaday.* 80. yerk] *This ed.;* iurke *Q,*
Holaday; jerk *Shepherd.* 80.1 SD.] *Parrott; not in Q.*

71–2. *repent, amend your life*] *The Book of Common Prayer* reads, 'repent
you truly for your sins past, have a lively and steadfast faith in Christ our
Saviour. Amend your lives, and be in perfect charity with all men' (p. 258).
Lemot's allusion to scripture as a means of mocking Florilla's puritanism is
a nice touch.

74. *affection*] The context seems to require the rare definition of ill feeling,
or animosity (*OED n.* 7); perhaps 'affliction', a common biblical word, was
intended.

77–8. *now...upon the King*] Having just informed on Moren to his wife,
Lemot will brazenly do the same to the King, doubling the amusement to
follow.

79. *that mends my humour*] that would mend, i.e. change, my humour.

80. *yerk*] Lemot's metaphorical threat may be taken in two ways: first, he
will 'yerk', or 'whip' the horse; second, he will cause the horse to 'yerk', i.e.
'lash about with its hooves' and throw its rider, hence the warning to 'take
the spurs'. Before the battle of Alcazar in *Captain Thomas Stukeley*, King
Sebastian of Portugal tells Abdelmelec, the Moroccan king, 'We'll spur your
jennet, lusty African, / And with our pistols we'll prick her pampered sides /
Until with yerking she do break her girths' (22.26–8). His confidence was as
justified as that of the French at Agincourt, where, after the battle, Mountjoy
begs Henry V for leave to remove the dead from the field: 'their wounded
steeds / Fret fetlock-deep in gore, and with wild rage / Yerk out their armed
heels at their dead masters' (4.7.78–80).

SCENE 10

Enter my host [VERONE], CATALIAN, BERGER, JAQUES,
Maid [JAQUENA], *and* BOY.

Verone. Well, gentlemen, I am utterly undone without your
   good helps. It is reported that I received certain ladies or
   gentlewomen into my house. Now, here's my man, my
   maid, and my boy. – Now, if you saw any, speak boldly
   before these gentlemen.   5
Jaques. I saw none, sir.
Jaquena. Nor I, by my maidenhead.
Boy. Nor I, as I am a man.
Catalian. Well, my host, we'll go answer for your house at
   this time; but if at other times you have had wenches,   10
   and would not let us know it, we are the less beholding
   to you.

            Exeunt [JAQUES, JAQUENA, *and* BOY].

Berger. Peradventure the more beholding to him, but I lay my
   life Lemot hath devised some jest. He gave us the slip
   before dinner.   15
Catalian. Well, gentlemen, since we are so fitly met, I'll tell
   you an excellent subject for a fit of mirth, an if it be well
   handled.

Scene 10] *This ed.*; Scene XII *Parrott*; Sc. xii *Greg*; Iv.ii *Holaday; not in* Q.
0 SD. VERONE] *This ed.; not in* Q.   JAQUENA] *This ed.; not in* Q.   3. *Now*]
Shepherd; *No* Q.   12.1 SD. JAQUES, JAQUENA, *and* BOY] *This ed.; al, but
my host and the Gentleman* Q.

Scene 10] We return to Verone's ordinary.
   0 SD.] Blanuel is in Q's entry stage direction, but he neither speaks nor
participates in the scene. Although he could conceivably be present, though
mute, I omit him, to remain consistent with the previous decision to have
him and Rowley off in pursuit of Martia (see 9.16.2 SD n., Introduction pp.
34–5).
   2. *helps*] This plural form is often seen in texts of this period, e.g. King
John to the English lords in *The Troublesome Reign of John, King of England*,
'We craved once more your helps for to invest us / Into the right that envy
sought to wrack' (sig. G2r).
   7. *by my maidenhead*] a common expression, often spoken by those whose
maidenhead is a thing of the past, such as Juliet's Nurse: 'Now by my maidenhead at twelve year old, / I bade her come' (3.1.2–3).
   8. *as I am a man*] The Boy's reply, like Jaques's 'small bones' (see 8.39
n.), shows his opinion of the status of Jaquena's maidenhead.
   11. *beholding*] beholden, indebted (*OED a.* 1).

Berger. Why, what is it?

Catalian. Why, man, Labesha is grown marvellous malcon-   20
tent upon some amorous disposition of his mistress, and
you know he loves a mess of cream and a spice-cake with
his heart, and I am sure he hath not dined today, and he
hath taken on him the humour of the young lord Dowsecer, and we will set a mess of cream, a spice-cake, and a   25
spoon – as the armour, picture, and apparel was set in
the way of Dowsecer – which I doubt not but will work
a rare cure upon his melancholy.

Verone. Why, this is excellent! I'll go fetch the cream.

Catalian. And I the cake.   30

Berger. And I the spoon.

> *Exeunt* [VERONE, CATALIAN, *and* BERGER] *and*
> *come in again.*

Catalian. See where he comes, as like the lord Dowsecer as
may be. Now you shall hear him begin with some Latin
sentence that he hath remembered ever since he read his
accidence.   35

> [*They stand aside.*]

> *Enter* LABESHA.

Labesha. Felix quem faciunt aliena pericula cautum. O silly state
of things, for things they be that cause this silly state. And

---

31.1 SD. VERONE, CATALIAN, *and* BERGER] This ed.; not in *Q*.
36.1 SD.] *This ed.; not in* Q.

20–8.] This speech is all one sentence in *Q*, providing a good direction
to the actor. Catalian, who is essentially proposing what would today be
called an 'intervention', can show his eager anticipation of the fun to be had
by emphasising every 'and'.

21. *his mistress*] Martia, who has rejected him.

32–3. *as like…may be*] See Introduction, p. 30.

35. *accidence*] exercises in the 'accidents' (inflections) of Latin grammar
(*OED n.*). In *Merry Wives*, Mistress Page instructs Sir Hugh Evans to ask
her son William 'some questions in his accidence' (4.1.16).

36. *Felix…cautum*] Happy is he who learns from the perils of others
(Dent M612). This famous adage is found in Nigellus Wireker's twelfth-
century text *Speculum Mirror for Fools* or *The Book of Burnel the Ass* (Parrott).
In Richard Taverner's edition of the *Adages* of Erasmus (London, 1539),
we read 'He is happy, whom other men's perils maketh ware' (fol. 3r),
while Benjamin Franklin's *Poor Richard's Almanac* advises, '"Wise men",
as Poor Dick says, "learn by others' harms, fools scarcely by their own"'
(p. 559).

37. *things*] See 3.26 n., 5.95 n., 6.14 n.

what is a thing? A bauble, a toy that stands men in small
stead. (*He spies the cream.*) But what have we here? What
vanities have we here?   40
Verone. He is strongly tempted. The Lord strengthen him!
See what a vein he hath.
Labesha. O cruel Fortune, and dost thou spit thy spite at my
poor life? But O sour cream! What thinkest thou, that I
love thee still? No, no, fair and sweet is my mistress. If   45
thou haddest strawberries and sugar in thee – but it may
be thou art set with stale cake to choke me. Well, taste
it, and try it, spoonful by spoonful. Bitterer and bitterer
still! But O sour cream, wert thou an onion, since Fortune
set thee for me, I will eat thee, and I will devour thee in   50
spite of Fortune's spite.
          Choke I, or burst I, mistress, for thy sake,
          To end my life, eat I this cream and cake.
              [*He eats the cream and moves to the side of the stage.*]
Catalian. So he hath done. His melancholy is well eased,
I warrant you.   55
Verone. [*Aloud*] God's my life, gentlemen, who hath been at
this cream?
Labesha. Cream? Had you cream? Where is your cream? I'll
spend my penny at your cream!
Catalian. Why, did not you eat this cream?   60
Labesha. Talk not to me of cream, for such vain meat
I do despise as food. My stomach dies,
Drowned in the cream-bowls of my mistress' eyes.
                                                  [*He starts to leave.*]
Catalian. Nay, stay, Labesha.
Labesha.   No, not I, not I.   [Exit.]

53.1 SD.] *This ed.; not in Q.*   56 SD.] *This ed.; not in Q.*   63.1 SD.] *Holaday;
not in Q.*   64 SD.] *Parrott; not in Q.*

42. *vein*] disposition, humour (*OED n.* 14 b).

49. *wert thou*] even if you were.

59. *spend my penny*] urinate, or ejaculate. As *OED* notes, the modern
expression 'spend a penny' originated with the price of London's public
toilets in the 1940s, but early modern texts offer examples of bawdy puns
on 'spend', for emitting or allowing to flow out, and 'penny' for penis,
although this is the only text I have found to combine the two into one
expression. For detailed discussion of this vitally important topic, see
Edelman, 'Chapman's *An Humorous Day's Mirth*', *Explicator* 65 (2006): 2–4.

Verone. Oh, he is ashamed, i'faith. But I will tell thee how   65
    thou shalt make him mad indeed: say his mistress for love
    of him hath drowned herself.
Catalian. 'Sblood, that will make him hang himself.

                                 Exeunt omnes.

Scene 11

Enter the QUEEN, LEMOT, *and all the rest of the lords*
[LABERVELE, FOYES], *and the* COUNTESS,
Lemot's arm in a scarf.

Lemot. [*Aside*] Have at them, i'faith, with a lame counterfeit
    humour.
    [*Aloud*] Ache on, rude arm. I care not for thy pain;
    I got it nobly in the King's defence
    And in the guardiance of my fair Queen's right.
Queen. Oh, tell me, sweet Lemot, how fares the King,   5
    Or what my right was that thou didst defend?
Lemot. That you shall know when other things are told.
Labervele. Keep not the Queen too long without her longing.

Scene 11] *This ed.*; Scene XIII *Parrott*; Sc. xiii *Greg*; IV.iii *Holaday; not
in Q.*   0.1 SD. LABERVELE, FOYES] *This ed.; not in Q.*   1 SD.] *Parrott; not
in Q.*   2 SD.] *This ed.; not in Q.*   5 SH.] *Shepherd; Qu. Quee. Que. Queene
Q.*   6. my] *Parrott;* his *Q.*

66–7. *for love...drowned herself*] another parody of the ur-*Hamlet?*

Scene 11] The action returns to the street.
  0.2 SD. LABERVELE, FOYES] *Q* has *Enter the Queene, Lemot, and all the
rest of the lordes, and the Countesse: Lemots arme in a scarffe.* Labervele and
Foyes are the only two 'lords' who speak in the scene, and it is unlikely that
any of the others enters: Catalian and Berger have just followed Labesha out
of Verone's, Blanuel and Rowley are or have been occupied with Martia and
the King (see 9.16.2 SD n.), and Colinet takes no part in the action after
Scene 7 (see Introduction, p. 35).
  0.3 SD. scarf] sling (*OED n.*[1] 4).
  4. *guardiance*] guardianship (*OED*). In Chapman's *Iliad*, after the death
of Hector, Andromache cries over the danger now awaiting her son Astynax,
who once, when he cried, 'a careful nurse's arms / Took him to guardiance'
(22.435–6). Although the passage in the *Iliad* involves protecting an infant,
the primary meaning of 'guardian' is synonymous with 'guard' in a general
sense (*OED n.*).

Foyes. No, for I tell you it is a dangerous thing.

Countess. Little care cruel men how women long.   10

Lemot. What, would you have me then put poison in my
    breath,

    And burn the ears of my attentive queen?

Queen. Tell me whate'er it be. I'll bear it all.

Lemot. Bear with my rudeness, then, in telling it,

    For, alas, you see I can but act it with the left hand.   15

    This is my gesture now.

Queen.   'Tis well enough.

Lemot. Yea, well enough, you say. This recompense

    Have I for all my wounds. Then thus:

    The King, enamoured of another lady,

    Compares your face to hers and says that yours   20

    Is fat and flat, and that your nether lip

    Was passing big.

Queen.   Oh, wicked man!

    Doth he so suddenly condemn my beauty,

    That when he married me, he thought divine?

    Forever blasted be that strumpet's face,   25

    As all my hopes are blasted, that did change them!

Lemot. Nay, madam, though he said your face was fat,

    And flat, and so forth, yet he liked it best,

    And said a perfect beauty should be so.

Labervele. Oh, did he so? Why that was right even as it should   30
    be.

Foyes. You see now, madam, how much too hasty you were
    in your griefs?

Queen. If he did so esteem of me indeed, happy am I.

---

15. *with the left hand*] From the earliest times and across all cultures, to
do anything with the left hand was regarded as 'sinister' or 'gauche', the
Latin and French words for 'left' (see Wilson, pp. 62–76). This gloss kindly
supplied by your left-handed editor.

16. *gesture*] deportment, bearing (*OED n.* 1), as in *Henry V*, 'their gesture
sad, / Investing lank-lean cheeks and war-worn coats' (4.Prol.25–6).

25. *blasted*] balefully or perniciously blown upon, blighted (*OED ppl. a.*
1), as in the 'blasted heath' (1.3.77) where the three witches of *Macbeth*
reside.

30–1. *even as it should be*] proverbial (Dent S398.1).

Countess. So may your highness be, that hath so good a   35
    husband, but hell hath no plague to such an one as I.
Lemot. Indeed, madam, you have a bad husband. Truly, then
    did the King grow mightily in love with the other lady,
    And swore, no king could more enrichèd be
    Than to enjoy so fair a dame as she.   40
Queen. Oh, monstrous man and accursed, most miserable
    dame!
Lemot. But, says the King: 'I do enjoy as fair,
    And though I love her in all honoured sort,
    Yet I'll not wrong my wife, for all the world.'   45
Foyes. This proves his constancy as firm as brass.
Queen. It doth, it doth! Oh, pardon me, my lord,
    That I mistake thy royal meaning so.
Countess. In heaven your highness lives, but I in hell.
Lemot. But when he viewed her radiant eyes again,   50
    Blind was he strucken with her fervent beams;
    And now, good King, he gropes about in corners,
    Void of the cheerful light should guide us all.
Queen. Oh, dismal news! What, is my sovereign blind?
Lemot. Blind as a beetle madam, that awhile   55
    Hovering aloft, at last in cow-shards falls.

---

41 SH.] *Holaday; Cat. Q; Ca. Shepherd; Count. Parrott.*   44. her] *Shepherd; not in Q.*   56. cow-shards] *This ed.*; cowsheds *Q.*   falls] *Shepherd*; fall *Q.*

---

41 SH.] *Q*'s speech heading of *Cat.* is obviously wrong, but editors are divided as to whether the Countess (Parrott) or the Queen (Holaday) speaks the line. There is an argument for the Countess in that she says 'accursed and miserable dame' at 8.332–3, but I favour the Queen, since she must withdraw what she has just said in her next utterance.

46. *brass*] a proverbially hard metal (Dent B605.1); cf. Richard II's famous 'hollow crown' speech, 'As if this flesh which walls about our life / Were brass impregnable' (3.2.167–8), and Thorello in *Q* of *Every Man In*, 'I know thy faith to be as firm as brass' (3.1.86).

47. *my lord*] The Queen apostrophises her absent husband.

51. *strucken*] a common form of 'struck', as Oswald says to Lear, 'I'll not be strucken, my lord' (1.4.85). The choice here is obviously metrical.

fervent beams] eye-beams; see 6.72 n. and Introduction, pp. 19–20.

55–6. *Blind…falls*] a popular proverb (Dent B219, B221). Cow-shards ('cowsheds' in *Q*) are cow-dung (*OED n.*). In Dekker's *News From Hell* we are told, 'he that provides living for his child, and robs him of learning, turns him into a beetle, that flies from perfumes and sweet odours, to feed on a cow-shard' (2: 109).

Labervele. Could her eyes blind him?
Lemot. Eyes or what it was I know not,
 But blind I am sure he is, as any stone.
Queen. Come, bring me to my prince, my lord, that I may   60
 lead him. None alive but I may have the honour to direct
 his feet.
Lemot. How lead him, madam? Why, he can go as right as
 you, or any here, and is not blind of eyesight.
Queen. Of what, then?   65
Lemot. Of reason.
Queen. Why, thou saidst he wanted his cheerful light.
Lemot. Of reason still I meant, whose light, you know
 Should cheerfully guide a worthy king.
 For he doth love her, and hath forcèd her   70
 Into a private room, where now they are.
Queen. What mocking changes is there in thy words!
 Fond man, thou murderest me with these exclaims.
Lemot. Why, madam, 'tis your fault. You cut me off before
 my words be half done.   75
Queen. Forth, and unlade the poison of thy tongue.
Lemot. Another lord did love this curious lady,
 Who, hearing that the King had forcèd her
 As she was walking with another earl,
 Ran straightways mad for her, and with a friend   80
 Of his and two or three black ruffians more,
 Brake desperately upon the person of the King,
 Swearing to take from him, in traitorous fashion,
 The instrument of procreation.
 With them I fought awhile and got this wound,   85
 But being unable to resist so many,

---

59. *blind...stone*] proverbial (Dent S875.11).
67. *wanted*] lacked.
73. *Fond*] foolish (*OED a.* 2).
exclaims] exclamations, outcries, as Lady Anne to Richard III, 'thou hast made the happy earth thy hell, / Fill'd it with cursing cries and deep exclaims' (1.2.51–2).
76. *unlade*] discharge, unload, as one would a ship's cargo (*OED v.* 2).
77. *curious*] fine, beautiful (cf. 4.30 n.).
84. *procreation*] When Florilla speaks the word 'procreation' at 4.65, the verse requires the straightforward four syllables; here, as well as at l. 102, Lemot is encouraged to drag the word out, pro-cre-a-ti-on, to good comic effect.

Came straight to you to fetch you to his aid.

Labervele. Why raised you not the streets?

Lemot.   That I forbore,
Because I would not have the world to see
What a disgrace my liege was subject to,   90
Being with a woman in so mean a house.

Foyes. Whose daughter was it that he forced, I pray?

Lemot. Your daughter, sir.

Labervele. Whose son was it that ran so mad for her?

Lemot. Your son, my lord.

Labervele.   O gods and fiends forbid!   95

Countess. I pray, sir, from whom did he take the lady?

Lemot. From your good lord.

Countess. O Lord, I beseech thee, no!

Lemot. 'Tis all too true. Come, follow the Queen and I where
I shall lead you.   100

Queen. Oh, wretched queen! What would they take from him?

Lemot. The instrument of procreation.

                                        [*Exeunt omnes.*]

SCENE 12

Enter MOREN.

Moren. Now was there ever man so much accursed, that
when his mind misgave him such a man was hapless, to
keep him company? Yet who would keep him company

---

94. it] *Shepherd; not in Q.*   102.1 SD.] *Parrott; not in Q.*

Scene 12] *This ed.*; Scene XIV *Parrott*; Sc. xiv *Greg*; V.i. *Holaday; not in Q.*

99. *Queen and I*] 'I', rather than 'me', was common in constructions of this type (see Abbott, pp. 140–1).

Scene 12] The locale is a street, but otherwise unspecific. Although the previous sequence also takes place on a street, I start a new scene here as the stage would most probably be cleared before Moren enters.

2. *misgave*] gave him cause to doubt (*OED v.*), another form of having 'misgivings'; cf. Othello's 'Fetch me the handkerchief. My mind misgives' (3.4.89).

such...hapless] The 'hapless' man to whom Moren refers is Lemot, as he reveals at l. 4.

but I? O vile Lemot, my wife and I are bound to curse
thee while we live, but chiefly I. Well, seek her or seek   5
her not, find her or find her not, I were as good see how
hell opens, as look upon her.

> *Enter* CATALIAN *and* BERGER, *behind him.*

CATALIA*n.* [*Aside*] We have him, i'faith. Stop thou him there,
and I will meet him here.

> [*They go to separate doors.*]

Moren. Well, I will venture once to seek her.   10

> [*About to exit.*]

Berger. God's lord, my lord, come you this way? Why, your
wife runs ranging like as if she were mad, swearing to slit
your nose if she can catch you.   *Exit* [BERGER].

Moren. [*Going to the other door*] What shall I do at the sight
of her and hern?   15

Catalian. God's precious, my lord, come you this way? Your
wife comes ranging with a troop of dames, like Bacchus'
drunken froes, just as you go. Shift for yourself, my lord.

Moren. Stay, good Catalian!

Catalian. No, not I, my lord.   *Exit* [CATALIAN].   20

> *Enter* JAQUES.

---

8 SD.] *Parrott; not in Q or Holaday.*   8. have him, i'faith] *Shepherd*;
have yfaith *Q.*   9.1 SD.] *This ed.; not in Q.*   10.1 SD.] *This ed.; not in
Q.*   13 SD. *Exit* BERGER] *This ed.; Exit Q.*   14 SD.] *This ed.; not in Q.*
18. froes] *Parrott*; foes *Q.*   20 SD. *Exit* CATALIAN] *This ed.; Exit Q.*

9.1 SD.] My suggested staging, with Catalian and Berger going to
separate doors to warn Moren as he is about to exit, would work especially
well on the broad apron-type stage of the Rose.

15. hern] *OED* notes that this form of 'hers' is associated with southern
and midland dialects; Chapman was from Hertfordshire.

18. froes] female followers of Bacchus. 'Froe' can simply mean 'Dutch-
woman', from the Dutch *vrouw* (Hoy, 2: 232), but, as Parrott (p. 694)
observes, Golding's translation of Ovid's *Metamorphoses* has Medea murder-
ing Pelias 'with scattered hair about hir ears like one of Bacchus' froes'
(7.337), and also records the death of 'the Thracian poet' Orpheus at the
hands of a 'flock of Bacchus' froes' (11.1, 21). Chapman uses the latter
episode in *Monsieur D'Olive*, where Vandome says of St Anne, 'The ladies
of this land would tear him piecemeal / As did the drunken froes the Thracian harper / To marry but a limb, a look of him' (2.1.178–80); cf. Parrott,
p. 785.

Moren. How now, Jaques, what's the news?

Jaques. None but good, my lord.

Moren. Why, hast not seen my wife run round about the
streets?

Jaques. Not I, my lord. I come to you from my master, who   25
would pray you to speak to Lemot, that Lemot might
speak to the King, that my master's lottery for his jewels
may go forward. He hath made the rarest device that ever
you heard. We have Fortune in it, and she our maid
plays, and I and my fellow carry two torches, and our boy   30
goes before and speaks a speech. 'Tis very fine, i'faith,
sir.

Moren. Sirrah, in this thou mayest highly pleasure me. Let
me have thy place to bear a torch, that I may look on my
wife and she not see me, for if I come into her sight   35
abruptly, I were better be hanged.

Jaques. Oh, sir, you shall, or anything that I can do. I'll send
for your wife, too.

Moren. I prithee, do.

                                        Exeunt both.

---

27. *that*] so that (see Abbott, p. 193).

my master's lottery] In concluding the play with the lottery at Verone's,
Chapman borrows elements from both the public and private forms of the
event, which were well established in English life by the time Elizabeth's
reign was drawing to a close. The earliest recorded English state lottery was
announced in 1566, although lack of enthusiasm from the public delayed the
draw until 1569. Private lotteries go back at least to Roman times, as an
after-dinner pastime wherein each guest would receive a gift—this tradition
eventually became a form of court entertainment in Tudor England. In 1601,
Queen Elizabeth paid a visit to the estate of Sir Thomas Egerton, Keeper of
the Great Seal, at Harefield. Sir John Davies was engaged to write an elaborate entertainment of songs, speeches, and posies, in which gifts were dis-
tributed to the Queen and all other ladies present (see Ashton, pp. 1–27;
Davies, *An Entertainment at Harefield*, in *Poems*, pp. 207–14).

29. *Fortune*] Dame Fortune, by tradition the drawer of lots.

30. *my fellow*] Jaques's fellow servant (see 8.0 SD n.)

33. *pleasure me*] please me (*OED v.* 2).

34–5. *bear a torch…not see me*] The torchbearers at the lottery are to be
masked.

Scene 13

Enter the QUEEN, *and all that were in before* [COUNTESS MOREN,
LEMOT, LABERVELE, *and* FOYES].

Lemot. This is the house,
　　Where the mad lord did vow to do the deed.
　　Draw all your swords, courageous gentlemen.
　　I'll bring you there where you shall honour win;
　　But I can tell you, you must break your shin.　　　　　5
Countess. Who will not break his neck to save his king?
　　Set forward, Lemot.
Lemot. Yea, much good can I do with a wounded arm. I'll go
　　and call more help.
Queen. Others shall go. Nay, we will raise the streets.　　　10
　　Better dishonour than destroy the King.
Lemot. [*Aside*] 'Sblood, I know not how to excuse my villainy.
　　I would fain be gone.

　　　　Enter DOWSECER *and his friend* [LAVEL].

Dowsecer. I'll geld the adulterous goat and take from him
　　The instrument that plays him such sweet music.　　　15
Lemot. [*Aside*] Oh, rare! This makes my fiction true. Now
　　I'll stay.
Queen. Arrest these faithless traitorous gentlemen!
Dowsecer. What is the reason that you call us traitors?
Lemot. Nay, why do you attempt such violence

Scene 13] *This ed.*; Sc. xv *Greg*; V.ii *Holaday; not in Q or Parrott.*
0 SD. COUNTESS MOREN, LEMOT, LABERVELE, *and* FOYES] *This ed.; not
in* Q. 6 SH.] *subst. Parrott.*; Ca. *Q*; Cat. *Holaday.* 12 SD.] *Parrott; not in*
Q. 13.1 SD. LAVEL] *Parrott; not in Q or Holaday.* 16 SH.] *subst. Parrott*;
La. *Q*. SD. Aside] *Parrott; not in Q.* 19 SH.] *subst. Shepherd*; La. *Q.*

　　Scene 13] The first two lines show that the scene begins at the entrance
to Verone's ordinary; at l. 143, the action moves indoors without any
break.
　　5. *break your shin*] proverbial for annoyance (Dent S342.1); cf. Lorenzo
Junior in *Q* of *Every Man In*, 'Why, it is able to break the shins of any old
man's patience in the world' (1.2.58–9), and Moth in *Love's Labour's Lost*,
'Here's a Costard broken in a shin' (3.1.70).
　　6 SH. Countess] *Q*'s speech heading of *Ca.* is probably a misprint for
Co. (Countess). Her urging the men to break their necks if necessary is a
good comic touch.

Against the person of the King?   20

Dowsecer. Against the King? Why, this is strange to me!

Enter the KING *and* MARTIA.

King. How now, my masters? What, weapons drawn? Come
   you to murder me?

Queen. How fares my lord?

King. How fare I? Well. [*Aside to Lemot*] But you, i'faith, shall   25
   get me speak for you another time. [*To all, indicating
   Lemot*] He got me here to woo a curious lady, and she
   tempts him! Say what I can, offer what state I will in your
   behalf, Lemot, she will not yield.

Lemot. I'faith, my liege, what a hard heart hath she. [*Aside to*   30
   King] Well, hark you, I am content your wit shall save
   your honesty for this once.

King. [*Aside to Lemot*] Peace, a plague on you, peace! [*To the
   Queen*] But wherefore asked you how I did?

Queen. Because I feared that you were hurt, my lord.   35

King. Hurt? How, I pray?

Lemot. Why hurt, madam? [*Aside*] I am well again.

Queen. Do you ask? Why, he told me Dowsecer and this his
   friend threatened to take away –

---

25   SD.] *subst. Parrott; not in* Q.   26–7   SD.] *This   ed.;
not in* Q;   28. offer] *Parrott; over* Q.   30–1 SD.] *subst. Parrott; not in*
Q.   33 SD.] *subst. Parrott; not in* Q.   33–4 SD.] *Holaday; not in* Q.
37 SD.] *Parrott; not in* Q.

---

21. *strange to me*] This would indicate that Dowsecer believes the 'adulterous goat' (l. 14) is Moren, not the King. We have heard nothing of
Dowsecer since the end of Scene 7; how he learned of Martia's whereabouts
and the 'danger' she is in is left to the imagination.

21.1 SD.] The King and Martia would enter from whichever door represents the entrance to Verone's.

25–6. *But…another time*] The King promises to help Lemot with a lie
some time in the future if Lemot plays along here.

28. *tempts*] used here in the sense of 'teases' or 'plays with'.

28–9. *in your behalf*] This and similar expressions, with the preposition
'in', are as common in this period as those using 'on'.

37. *I am well again*] Holaday suggests that Lemot removes the scarf at
this point.

King. To take away? What should they take away?   40
Lemot. Name it, madam.
Queen. Nay, I pray, name it you.
Lemot. Why then, thus it was, my liege: I told her Dowsecer
  and this his friend threatened to take away, an if they
  could, the instrument of procreation. And what was that,   45
  now, but Martia? Being a fair woman, is not she the
  instrument of procreation, as all women are?
Queen. O wicked man!
Lemot. Go to, go to, you are one of those fiddles too, i'faith.
King. [*To the Queen*] Well, pardon my minion, that hath
  frayed you thus.   50
  'Twas but to make you merry in the end.
Queen. I joy it ends so well, my gracious lord.
Foyes. But say, my gracious lord, is no harm done
  Between my loving daughter and your grace?
King. No, of my honour and my soul, Foyes.   55
Dowsecer. The fire of love which she hath kindled in me,
  Being greater than my heat of vanity,
  Hath quite expelled –
King. Come, Dowsecer, receive with your lost wits your love,
  thought lost. [*To Labervele and Foyes*] I know you'll yield,   60
  my lord, and you, her father.
Both. Most joyfully, my lord.
King. And for her part, I know her disposition well enough.
Lemot. [*To Dowsecer*] What, will you have her?

---

49 SD.] *This ed.; not in Q.*   60. thought] *Holaday*; though *Q.*   SD.] *This
ed.; not in Q.*   64 SD.] *This ed.; not in Q.*

---

49. *fiddles*] (musical) instruments of procreation.
50. *frayed*] frightened (*OED v.*¹).
56–8.] Parrott's surmise that some text is missing here is probably
correct; Dowsecer appears to be answering a question no one has asked. If
the omitted lines relate to Dowsecer's loss of melancholy and his new-
found love for Martia, which the context, including the King's next line,
seems to require, then the admission that his melancholy was only vanity is
admirable. Dowsecer is the one character to go 'out of his humour', and it
is noteworthy that Lemot had nothing to do with it (see Introduction,
pp. 33–4).

Dowsecer. Yea, marry, will I.   65
Lemot. [*Aside, about to exit*] I'll go and tell Labesha
    presently.

Enter JAQUES *and my host*
[VERONE].

Jaques. [*Aside to Lemot*] Monsieur Lemot, I pray let me speak
    with you. I come to you from the Lord Moren, who
    would desire you to speak to the King for my master's   70
    lottery, and he hath my place to bear a torch, for bare-
    faced he dares not look upon his wife for his life.
Lemot. [*Aside to Jaques*] Oh, excellent! I'll further thy master's
    lottery an it be but for this jest only. [*To the King*] Hark
    you, my liege. Here's the poor man hath been at great   75
    charges for the preparation of a lottery, and he hath made
    the rarest device, that I know you will take great pleasure
    in it. I pray, let him present it before you at Verone's
    house.
King. With all my heart! Can you be ready so soon?   80
Verone. Presently, an if it like your grace.
King. But hark you, Lemot, how shall we do for every man's
    posy?
Lemot. Will you all trust me with the making of them?
All. With all our hearts.   85

---

66 SD.] *This ed.; not in Q.*   67.2 SD. VERONE] *This ed.; not in Q.*
68 SD.] *This ed.; not in Q.*   73 SD.] *This ed.; not in Q.*   74 SD. *This ed.;
not in Q.*   78. Verone's] *Shepherd*; Valeres *Q.*

---

78. *Verone's*] *Q*'s 'Valeres' is obviously a mistake (see 8.10 n.,
9.18 n.).
82–3. *every man's posy*] For state lotteries, individual or group entrants
would write posies, rather than their names, on the tickets to be entered.
Some of the better ones from 1569 are: 'We put in one lot, poor maidens
we be ten / We pray God send us a good lot, that all we may say, amen', 'I
would be content with a hundred pound / In my purse it would give a sound',
and from one desperate man, 'God send a good lot for my children and me,
/ Which have had twenty by one wife truly'. Unfortunately, he drew only
the minimum prize of 2s 3d (Ashton, pp. 18–19).

Lemot. Why, then, I'll go to make the posies, [*Aside*] and
  bring Labesha to the lottery presently.
     [*Exeunt* LEMOT, VERONE, *and* JAQUES.]

    Enter FLORILLA, *like a puritan.*

Florilla. Surely the world is full of vanity.
  A woman must take heed she do not hear
  A lewd man speak; for every woman cannot,   90
  When she is tempted, when the wicked fiend
  Gets her into his snares, escape like me.
  For grace's measure is not so filled up
  Nor so pressed down in everyone as me,
  But yet, I promise you, a little more.   95
  Well, I'll go seek my head, who shall take me in
  The gates of his kind arms, untouched of any.
King. What, madam, are you so pure now?
Florilla. Yea, would not you be pure?
King.   No, puritan.
Florilla. You must be then a devil, I can tell you. 100
Labervele. Oh, wife, where hast thou been?
Florilla. Where did I tell you I would be, I pray?
Labervele. In thy close walk, thou saidst.
Florilla.   And was I not?
Labervele. Truly, I know not! I neither looked nor knocked,
  for Labesha told me that you and fair Martia were at 105
  Verone's ordinary.
King. Labesha? My lord, you are a wise man to believe a fool.

---

86 SD.] *This ed.; not in Q.* 87.1 SD. *Exeunt* LEMOT, VERONE, *and*
JAQUES] *conj. Yamada; Exit Parrott; not in Q (see Yamada, p. 123).*

---

 86 SD. Aside] Lemot is telling us of his plan to include Labesha in the
festivities.
 87.1 SD.] No exit is indicated in *Q*, but Lemot must leave some time
before re-entering with Labesha at l. 118, and it makes sense for Verone and
Jaques to exit at this point, in order to prepare for the lottery (see Yamada,
p. 123).
 88–97.] The text is unclear as to when the others become aware of
Florilla's arrival. I believe she would deliver the speech directly to the audience, and that the King's 'What, madam' is in response to her appearance,
rather than what he hears.
 93. *grace's measure*] 'But unto every one of us is given grace, according
to the measure of the gift of Christ' (Ephesians, 4.7)
 107.] another allusion to the proverb (see 8.19–20 n.).

Florilla. [*To Labervele*] Well, my good head, for my part I
     forgive you.
   But surely you do much offend to be
   Suspicious. Where there is no trust, there is no love,   110
   And where there is no love 'twixt man and wife
   There's no good dealing, surely. For as men
   Should ever love their wives, so should they ever trust
       them;
   For what love is there where there is no trust?
King. She tells you true, my lord.   115
Labervele. She doth, my liege, and, dear wife, pardon this,
     And I will never be suspicious more.
Florilla. Why, I say, I do.

               Enter LEMOT, *leading* LABESHA *in a halter.*

Lemot. Look you, my liege, I have done simple service
     amongst you. Here is one had hanged himself for love,   120
     thinking his mistress had done so for him. Well, see, your
     mistress lives.
Labesha. And doth my mistress live?
King. She doth, O noble knight, but not your mistress now.
Labesha. [*Drawing his sword*] 'Sblood, but she shall for me, or 125
     for nobody else.
Lemot. How now! What, a traitor? Draw upon the King?
Labesha. Yea, or upon any woman here, in a good cause.
King. Well, sweet Besha, let her marry Dowsecer. I'll get thee
     a wife worth fifteen of her. Wilt thou have one that cares   130
     not for thee?
Labesha. Not I, by the Lord. I scorn her. I'll have her better
     if I can get her.
King. Why, that's well said.
                        [*Lemot and Florilla speak privately.*]

---

108 SD.] *This ed.; not in Q.*   125 SD. *Drawing his sword] This ed.; Drawing
Parrott; not in Q.*   134.1 SD.] *This ed.; not in Q.*

118.1 SD. Enter LEMOT] As the scene will soon shift to Verone's for the
lottery, how Lemot is supposed to have had time to write the posies, as
promised moments ago, is anything but clear—another example of the fluid-
ity of off-stage time in plays of this period.
   halter] noose.

Lemot. What, madam, are you turned puritan again?   135
Florilla. When was I other, pray?
Lemot. Marry, I'll tell you when: when you went to the ordi-
    nary, and when you made false signs to your husband,
    which I could tell him all.
Florilla. Cursed be he that maketh debate 'twixt man and   140
    wife.
Lemot. O rare scripturian! You have sealed up my lips. [*To*
    all] A hall! A hall! The pageant of the buttery!

> *Enter two with torches [and wearing masks], the one of*
> *them* MOREN, *then* [CATALIAN,] *my host* [VERONE] *and*
> [*the* BOY] *his son, then his maid* [JAQUENA,] *dressed like*
> *Queen Fortune, with two pots in her hands.*

King. [*Indicating Boy*] What is he?
Lemot. This is Verone's son, my liege.   145

142–3 SD.] *This ed.; not in Q.*   143.1–3 SD *and wearing masks*] *This ed.; not in Q.* CATALIAN,] *This ed.; not in Q.* ˙VERONE] *This ed.; not in Q.* *the* BOY] *This ed.; not in Q.* JAQUENA] *This ed.; not in Q.*   144 SD.] *This ed.; not in Q.*

135–42.] This exchange between Lemot and Florilla is probably private in that Labervele must not hear what Lemot says about Florilla's previous conduct, information he promises not to reveal.

140–1.] seemingly an allusion to Matthew, 19.6, 'Let not man therefore put asunder that which God hath coupled together.'

142. *scripturian*] possibly Chapman's nonce word for an expert on scripture. *OED* offers no earlier citation.

143. *A hall*] With Lemot's announcement, the scene changes to the interior of Verone's.

buttery] originally a store-room for liquor, which is kept in 'butts', later extended to provisions in a general sense (*OED n.* 1).

143.2 SD. CATALIAN] Yamada (p. 124) proposes Catalian for the second (masked) torchbearer, but Jaques, who has been replaced by Moren, has said that 'I and my fellow', i.e. Verone's other servant, will carry the torches (12.27).

143.4 SD. two pots] Presumably one pot holds the lots (the slips of paper with the posies written on them), the other has the prizes. Verone's lottery must be something of a low-budget affair—as anyone who has watched daytime television knows, Fortune should always have her wheel with her. The wheel of fortune was also absent, however, at the Harefield *Entertainment*: there a 'Mariner' conducted the proceedings. He entered 'with a box under his arm, containing all the several things following, supposed to come from the carrack' (Davies, p. 207).

King. What shall he do?

Catalian. Speak some speech that his father hath made for
    him.

Queen. Why, is he good at speeches?

Catalian. Oh, he is rare at speeches.   150

Boy. [*Reciting*] Fair ladies most tender
         And nobles most slender,
         And gentles whose wits be scarce –

King. My host, why do you call us 'nobles most slender'?

Verone. An it shall please your grace, to be slender is to be   155
    proper, and therefore where my boy says 'nobles most
    slender', it is as much to say, 'fine and proper nobles'.

Lemot. Yea, but why do you call us 'gentles whose wits be
    scarce'?

Verone. To be scarce is to be rare, and therefore, whereas he   160
    says 'gentles whose wits be scarce', is as much as to say,
    'gentles whose wits be rare'.

Lemot. [*To the Boy*] Well, forwards, truchman.

Boy. [*Reciting*] Fair ladies most tender
         And nobles most slender,   165
         And gentles whose wits be scarce,
         Queen Fortune doth come
         With her trump and her drum,
         As it may appear by my verse.

Labesha. [*To Verone*] Come hither. Are you a schoolmaster?   170
    Where was Fortune queen, of what country or kingdom?

---

151 SD.] *This ed.; not in Q.*   158. be] *This ed.*; are *Q.*   163. SD.] *This ed.;
not in Q.*   truchman] *conj. Deighton*; trunchman *Q.*   164 SD.] *This ed.; not
in Q.*   169. verse] *Parrott*; voice *Q, Holaday.*   170 SD.] *This ed.; not
in Q.*

155–6. *to be slender…proper*] Verone is correct. According to *OED*,
'slender', as well as meaning 'slim', often implies 'gracefulness of form'. His
excuses for what he has written are clever.

163. *truchman*] interpreter (*OED n.*), like Crites in *Cynthia's Revels*, 'Soft,
sir, I am truchman, and do flourish before this monsieur' (5.4.10–11).

168. *trump*] trumpet (*OED n.*[1]), very common in this era.

169. *verse*] Parrott's substitution of 'verse' for *Q*'s 'voice' is reasonable,
in that it rhymes slightly better with 'scarce'—indeed, it rhymes perfectly in
some regional accents of English. The same change is made at l. 189.

Verone. Why, sir, Fortune was queen over all the world.

Labesha. That's a lie; there's none that ever conquered all the
     world but Master Alisander, I am sure of that.

Lemot. O rare Monsieur Labesha! Who would have thought   175
     he could have found so rare a fault in the speech?

Verone. [*To the King*] I'll alter it, if it please your grace.

King. No, 'tis very well.

Boy. Father, I must begin again. They interrupt me so.

Verone. [*To the King*] I beseech your grace, give the boy leave   180
     to begin again.

King. With all my heart. 'Tis so good we cannot hear it too
     oft.

Boy. Fair ladies most tender
          And nobles most slender,   185
          And gentles whose wits are scarce,
          Queen Fortune doth come
          With her fife and her drum,
          As it doth appear by my verse.

          Here is Fortune good,   190
          Not ill, by the rood,

---

177 SD.] *This ed.; not in Q.*   180 SD] *This ed.; not in Q.*   189. verse] *Parrott*;
voice *Q, Holaday.*   191. Not] *Parrott*; but *Q.*

---

174. *Alisander*] Like Nathaniel in the parade of the nine Worthies that
concludes *Love's Labour's Lost*, who announces, 'My scutcheon plain declares
that I am Alisander' (5.2.564), Labesha seems to confuse the historical Alexander the Great with the hero of the late-medieval romance, *King Alisaunder.*

179. *Father*] This is the first time the Boy calls Verone 'Father'.

182–3. *cannot…oft*] proverbial (Dent T130). In his 1567 translation of
the *Enchiridion*, or *Manual* of Epictetus, James Sanford gives the stoic philosopher's advice on the manners one should adopt in conversation, including 'as the proverb is, *Bis & ter quod pulchrum est repetendum*: it is, that which
is goodly ought twice or thrice to be said or repeated' (sig. F6v–F7r).

188. *fife*] The fife was a 'trump' the first time the Boy spoke the verse
(l. 168). This could be just carelessness on Chapman's part, but one is
reluctant to emend the line, in that the Boy needs to start again after being
interrupted, an indication that he is reciting from (imperfect) memory rather
than reading.

191. *Not ill*] *Q* reads 'but ill', which is hard to make sense of, and Parrott's
emendation is appropriate. Even if intended as verse, the initial letter of the
line would have been in lower case in the manuscript, so the two words
would look similar.

by the rood] by Christ's cross, as when Hamlet replies to Gertrude's 'Have
you forgot me?', with 'No, by the rood, not so' (3.4.14).

And this naught but good shall do you, sir,
Dealing the lots
Out of our pots.
And so good Fortune to you, sir!   195

Lemot. [*To the King, indicating Moren*] Look you, my liege,
 how he that carries the torch trembles extremely.
King. I warrant 'tis with care to carry his torch well.
Lemot. Nay, there is something else in the wind. Why, my
 host, what means thy man Jaques to tremble so?   200
Verone. [*To Moren*] Hold still, thou knave! What, art thou
 afraid to look upon the goodly presence of a king? Hold
 up, for shame!
Lemot. [*Aside*] Alas, poor man, he thinks 'tis Jaques, his man.
 Poor lord, how much is he bound to suffer for his wife.   205
King. Hark you, mine host, what goodly person is that? Is it
 Fortune herself?
Verone. I'll tell your majesty in secret who it is. [*Aside to King*]
 It is my maid, Jaquena.
King. I promise you, she becomes her state rarely.   210
Lemot. Well, my liege, you were all content that I should
 make your posies. Well, here they be. Everyone, give
 Master Verone his five crowns.
King. [*Handing some coins to Verone*] There's mine and the
 Queen's.   215

---

192. sir] *Parrott; not in Q.*   196 SD.] *This ed.; not in Q.*   201 SD.] *This
ed.; not in Q.*   204 SD.] *Parrott; not in Q.*   208 SD.] *This ed.; not in
Q.*   214 SD.] *This ed.; not in Q.*

---

195. *sir*] Q lacks this word, but the metre and rhyme seem to require it.
196–7.] Lemot, ever the mischief-maker, has no intention of keeping
Moren's secret, and rather wickedly calls attention to the trembling
torchbearer.
199. *in the wind*] proverbial for 'going on', or 'amiss' (Tilley S628).
204–5.] The 'he' of the first sentence is Verone; the 'he' and 'his' of
second sentence refer to Count Moren.
205. *for*] on account of.
213. *five crowns*] A crown being worth 5s, tickets for this lottery are
much more expensive then those for the public lottery of 1569, priced
at 10s.

Labervele. There's ours!

Dowsecer. And there is mine and Martia's.

Lemot. Come Labesha, thy money.

Labesha. You must lend me some, for my boy is run away
    with my purse.   220

Lemot. Thy boy? I never knew any that thou hadst.

Labesha. Had not I a boy three or four years ago and he ran
    away?

Lemot. And never since he went, thou hadst not a penny? But
    stand by, I'll excuse you. But sirrah Catalian, thou shalt   225
    stand on one side and read the prizes, and I will stand
    on the other and read the posies.

Catalian. Content, Lemot.

Lemot. [*To Jaquena*] *Come* on, Queen Fortune, tell every man
    his posy. [*Jaquena draws a lot and hands it to Lemot.*] This   230
    is orderly, the King and Queen are first.

King. Come let us see what goodly posies you have given us.

Lemot. This is your majesty's: 'At the fairest, so it be not
    Martia.'

King. A plague upon you! You are still playing the villain with   235
    me?

Lemot. This is the Queen's: 'Obey the Queen' – an she speaks
    it to her husband, or to Fortune, which she will.

Catalian. A prize! Your majesty's is the sum of four shillings
    in gold.   240

King. Why, how can that be? There is no such coin.

Verone. [*Handing gold coins to the King*] Here is the worth of
    it, if it please your grace.

---

216 SH.] *subst. Parrott; Labesh. Q.* 229 SD.] *This ed.; not in Q.* 230
SD.] *This ed.; not in Q.* 235. villain] *Shepherd;* villaines *Q.* 242
SD. *Handing gold coins to the King*] *This ed.; Offering gold Holaday; not in Q.*

---

226. *read the prizes*] Catalian's job will be to give the description of each
prize as it is awarded.

233. *This is your majesty's*] Protocol requires that the lottery be fixed so
that the King's lot is the first to be drawn. At the Harefield lottery, the first
lot, drawn by the Queen, awarded her a set of (presumably bejewelled)
fortune's wheels: 'Fortune must now no more in triumph ride; / The wheels
are yours that did his chariot guide' (Davies, p. 208).

Queen. Well, what's for me?
Catalian. A heart of gold.   245
Queen. A goodly jewel!
                    [*Jaquena hands another lot to Lemot.*]
Lemot. Count Labervele and Florilla.
Labervele. What's my posy, sir, I pray?
Lemot. Marry, this, my lord:
        'Of all Fortune's friends, that hath joy in this life,   250
        He is most happy that puts a sure trust in his wife.'
Labervele. A very good one, sir, I thank you for it.
Florilla. What's mine, I pray?
Lemot. Marry, this, madam:
        'Good Fortune, be thou my good fortune-bringer,   255
        And make me amends for my poor bitten finger.'
Labervele. Who bit your finger, wife?
Florilla. Nobody. 'Tis a vain posy.
Catalian. Blank for my lord Labervele; for his wife a prize: a
        pair of holy beads with a crucifix.   260
Florilla. O bomination idol! I'll none of them!

246.1 SD.] *This ed.; not in Q.*   258. a vain] *Parrott;* vain *Q.*   259. prize] *This
ed.;* posie *Q.*

255–6.] Lemot's drawing attention to Florilla's bitten finger is delightful.
True to character, she just denies it.
    259. *Blank*] a lottery ticket that does not gain a prize (*OED n.* 4), hence
the expression, 'draw a blank'. The organisers of the 1569 lottery made a
point of advertising that it was 'a very rich lottery general, without any
blanks', but the minimum prize of 2s for a 10s ticket was not much better.
In the Harefield *Entertainment*, six of the thirty-nine draws were blank, one
of them drawn by Lady Digby. It said, 'You fain would have, but what you
cannot tell / If fortune gives you nothing, she doth well' (Davies, p. 213).
    prize] No previous editor has remarked on this, but *Q*'s 'posie' cannot be
correct. Lemot has just spoken Florilla's posy; Catalian is announcing her
prize. The two words would look similar on the manuscript.
    260. *holy beads with a crucifix*] Lemot, quite literally, now adds insult to
the (finger) injury. The prizes are Verone's jewels, so either they included a
jewelled crucifix that Lemot decided Florilla must have, or Lemot found one
on his own and inserted it. The posies all relate in some way to the humours
of the characters, and while Lemot has also fixed the prizes, seemingly this
is the only one directed at its recipient's humour.
    261. *bomination*] abominable (*OED a.*), as in *Sir John Oldcastle*, 'here's
such a bomination company of boys' (19.64–5).

King. Keep them thyself, Verone; she will not have them.
Lemot. Dowsecer and Martia: I have fitted your lordship for
   a posy.
Dowsecer. Why, what is it?   265
Lemot. Ante omnia una.
Martia. And what is mine, sir?
Lemot. A serious one, I warrant you: 'Change for the better.'
Martia. That's not amiss.
Catalian. A prize: Dowsecer hath a caduceus, or Mercury's   270
   rod of gold, set with hyacinths and emeralds.
Dowsecer. What is for Martia?
Catalian. Martia hath the two serpents' heads, set with
   diamonds.
Lemot. What my host Verone?   275
King. What? Is he in for his own jewels?

---

270. prize] *Q (reset sig. H1r)*; price *Q (original sig. H1r); see Intro., p. 39.*
caduceus] *Parrott*; cats eyes *Q.*

266. Ante omnia una] Before all things, one.

268. *Change for the better*] a cryptic posy. As there is no real reason to exhort Martia to change her behaviour, Lemot might be alluding to the welcome change in her life that comes with marrying Dowsecer, a reference to the proverbial 'seldom comes the better' (Dent B332).

270. *caduceus*] Parrott's emendation for *Q*'s 'cats eyes' must be correct. Originally, the emblem of Asklepios, god of medicine, was a single serpent coiled around a staff. Later it devolved into the caduceus, the wand of Hermes (Mercury) entwined with two serpents (Arikha, pp. 17–18). Henslowe includes one in his inventory, taken 13 March 1598, of the Admiral's Men's properties (Henslowe, p. 320).

271. *hyacinths*] Most would think of flowers today, but here in the original meaning of precious stones. In *The Alchemist*, Sir Epicure Mammon dreams of dining off 'Dishes of agate, set in gold, and studded / With emeralds, sapphires, hyacinths, and rubies' (2.2.73–4). An excellent choice for Dowsecer, to ward off any return to his former humour: in his *Treatise of Melancholy*, Timothy Bright advises that 'melancholic persons' can be helped through judicious choice of jewellery – 'no kind of seemly ornament would be omitted which might entice the sense to delight, and allure the enclosed spirits to solace themselves'. Amongst the precious stones 'said to have virtue against vain fears and baseness of courage', the hyacinth is 'a great cheerer of the heart, and procurer of favour' (p. 264).

273. *serpents' heads*] evidently the serpents on Dowsecer's caduceus. Martia and Dowsecer seem to receive a joint prize.

275. *What*] what is for.

Lemot. Oh, what else, my liege? 'Tis our bounty, and his posy
     is:
          'To tell you the truth in words plain and mild,
          Verone loves his maid, and she is great with child.'   280
King. What, Queen Fortune with child? Shall we have young
     Fortunes, my host?
Verone. I am abused, an if it please your majesty.
Jaquena. I'll play no more.
Lemot. No, faith, you need not now. You have played your   285
     belly full already.
Verone. Stand still, good Jaquena. They do but jest.
Jaquena. Yea, but I like no such jesting.
Lemot. Come, great Queen Fortune, let see your posies. [*She
     hands him the Countess's posy.*] What, madam? Alas, your   290
     ladyship is one of the last.
Countess. What is my posy, sir, I pray?
Lemot. Marry, madam, your posy is made in manner and
     form of an echo, as if you were seeking your husband,
     and Fortune should be the echo and this you say: 'Where   295
     is my husband hid so long unmasked?' 'Masked?' says
     the echo. 'But in what place, sweet Fortune? Let me
     hear.' 'Here', says the echo.
King. There you lie, Echo, for if he were here, we must needs
     see him.   300
Lemot. Indeed, sweet King. There, methinks the echo must
     needs lie. If he were here, we must needs see him. 'Tis
     one of them that carries the torches. No that cannot be,
     neither.

                    [*Enter* JAQUES.]

289–90 SD.] *This ed.; not in Q.*   304.1 SD.] *This ed.; not in Q.*

---

294. *echo*] It is appropriate that Countess Moren's posy should employ
an echo, since the original echo was created by another jealous wife, the
goddess Juno. As Ovid tells the story in his *Metamorphoses*, the 'talkative'
Echo was a nymph who would distract Juno while Jove dallied with other
nymphs on the mountainside. When Juno discovered the deception, she
punished Echo by restricting her power of speech to repeating what others
have said. Echo's other misfortune was to fall in love with Narcissus; she
pined away, yet 'in the woods she hides and hills around / For all to hear,
alive, but just a sound' (3.360, 400–1).

And yet, by the mass, here's Jaques! Why, my host, did   305
not you tell me that Jaques should be a torchbearer? Who
is this? [*Unmasking Moren*] God's my life, my lord!

Moren. An you be gentlemen, let me go!

Countess. Nay, come your way, you may be well enough
ashamed to show your face, that is a perjured wretch. Did   310
not you swear, if there were any wenches at the ordinary,
you would straight come home?

King. Why, who told you, madam, there were any there?

Countess. He that will stand to it: Lemot, my liege.

Lemot. Who, I stand to it? Alas, I told you in kindness and   315
good will, because I would not have you company long
from your husband.

Moren. Why, lo you, bird, how much you are deceived.

Countess. Why, wherefore were you afraid to be seen?

Moren. Who, I afraid? Alas, I bore a torch to grace this hon-   320
ourable presence, for nothing else, sweet bird.

King. Thanks, good Moren. – See, lady, with what wrong
You have pursued your most enamoured lord.
But come, now all are friends. Now is this day
Spent with unhurtful motives of delight,   325
And overjoys more my senses at the night.
And now for Dowsecer: if all will follow my device,
His beauteous love and he shall married be.
And here I solemnly invite you all
Home to my court, where with feasts we will crown   330
This mirthful day, and vow it to renown.

                                        [Exeunt.]
                    FINIS.

---

307 SD. *Unmasking Moren*] *Parrott; Revealing Moren Holaday.*   325. unhurt-
ful] *Q (reset sig. H2r)*; an hurtfull *Q (original sig. H2r)*; *see Intro., p. 39.*
331.1 SD. *Exeunt*] *This ed.; not in Q.*

---

314. *stand to*] maintain, or abide by, a statement (*stand OED v.* 70 d).
'Stand by' is more common today.

316. *company*] keep company (*OED v.* 3).

318. *lo you*] behold, as the Gentlewoman tells the Doctor when the sleep-
walking Lady Macbeth approaches, 'Lo you, here she comes' (5.1.19)

326.] The approaching night fills my senses with extreme joy; an uncom-
mon use of 'overjoy' (*OED v.* 2) in this transitive sense.

Appendix
Dowsecer's Defence of Cosmetics (7.141–51)

From the biblical Jezebel to Carl Sandburg's 'painted women under the gas lamps luring the farm boys', the use of cosmetics has always been the subject of moral and satirical attack. The early modern period was no exception: Stubbes carries on for several pages about the 'colouring of women's faces in England',[1] while Marston, in *The Scourge of Villainy*, speaks of a woman

> ...so vizarded,
> So steep'd in lemon's-juice, so surfled[2]
> I cannot see her face.
>> (Satire 7, 166–8)

In Jonson's *The Devil Is an Ass*, Wittipol, disguised as a Spanish lady, tells Lady Tailbush what 'her' countrywomen use:

> They have
> Water of gourds, of radish, the white beans,
> Flowers of glass, of thistles, rosemarine,
> Raw honey, mustard-seed, and bread dough-baked,
> The crumbs o' bread, goats milk, and whites of eggs,
> Camphor, and lily roots, the fat of swans,
> Marrow of veal, white pigeons, and pine-kernels,
> The seeds of nettles, purslane, and hare's gall.
> Lemons, thin skinned...
>> (4.4.18–24)

proceeding to such exotic ingredients as 'turpentine of Abezzo' and '*Grasso di serpe*' (snake fat), all to make an 'admirable varnish for the face' (4.4.31, 34, 36).

Surprisingly, and delightfully, Dowsecer does not follow suit: the lady's portrait 'inspires...a witty and paradoxical defence of the use of cosmetics'.[3] If all women painted themselves, he says, 'twere safer dealing with them'; indeed, it might encourage them to match their good looks with good deeds. Clarence, in Chapman's *Sir Giles Goosecap*, holds similar sentiments:

For outward fairness bears the divine form,
And moves beholders to the act of love,
And that which moves to love is to be wish'd,
And each thing simply to be wish'd is good.
So I conclude mere painting of the face
A lawful and commendable grace.

(4.3.67–72)

Dowsecer and Clarence have an ally in John Donne, whose second *Paradox* is entitled *That Women ought to Paint Themselves.* Donne argues,

> Who forbids his beloved to gird in her waist, to mend by shooing her uneven lameness, to burnish her teeth, or to perfume her breath? Yet that the face be more precisely regarded it concerns more...The stars, the sun, the sky, whom thou admirest, alas have no colour, but are fair because they seem colour'd; If this seeming will not satisfy thee in her, thou hast good assurance of her colour, when thou seest her lay it on. If her face be painted upon a board or a wall, thou wilt love it, and the board and the wall. Canst thou loathe it then, when it smiles, speaks, and kisses, because it is painted? Is not the earth's face in the most pleasing season new painted? Are we not more delighted with seeing fruits, and birds, and beasts painted, than with the naturals?[4]

Donne even provides scriptural justification. In a sermon preached upon *Psalms, 51.7, Purge thou me with hyssop and I shall be clean: Wash thou me, and I shall be whiter than snow,* he states that the Jewish women of the Old Testament, 'whom the kings were to take for their wives, and not for mistresses (which is but a later name for concubines) had a certain and a long time to be prepared by those aromatical unctions, and liniments for beauty'. Indeed, when Abraham and his wife Sarah went into Egypt, Abraham was afraid 'that every man who saw her would fall in love with her. Sarah was then above threescore, and when King Abimilech did fall in love with her and take her from Abraham, she was fourscore and ten.'[5]

As to the secret of Sarah's remarkable beauty at the age of ninety, Donne believes, 'they do not assign this preservation of her complexion, and habitude, to any other thing than the use of those unctions and liniments which were ordinary to that nation'.[6]

NOTES

1 Stubbes, pp. 107–10.
2 To 'surfle' is to paint or wash the face with a cosmetic (*OED v* 2). Originally, the term referred to embroidery.
3 Charlotte Spivack, *George Chapman*, New York, 1967, p. 65.
4 Donne, *Paradoxes and Problems*, ed. Helen Peters, Oxford, 1980, pp. 2–3.
5 Donne, *Sermons*, ed. George R. Potter and Evelyn M. Simpson, 10 vols, Berkeley, 1953–62, 5: 302.
6 Donne, *Sermons*, 5: 302.

Index to the Introduction and Annotations